Dame Edna Everage

AND

the Rise of Western Civilisation

Dame Edna Everage

AND

the Rise of Western Civilisation

BACKSTAGE WITH BARRY HUMPHRIES

BY

JOHN LAHR

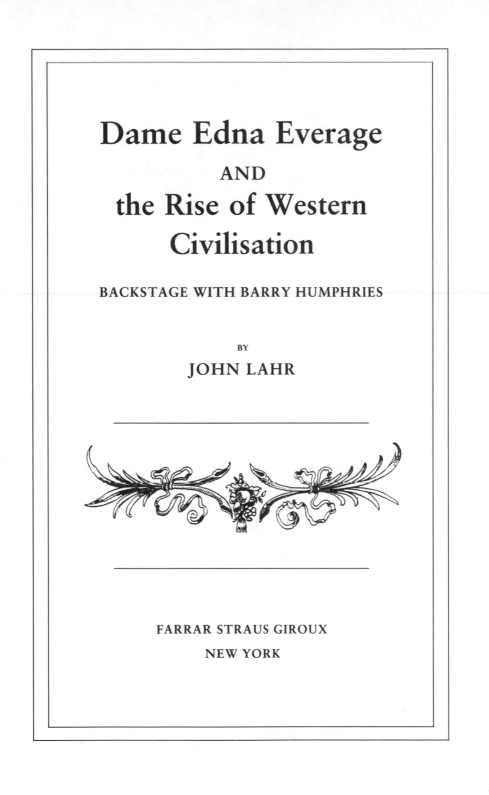

FARRAR STRAUS GIROUX

NEW YORK

Portions of this book have appeared
in a different form in *The New Yorker*

LIBRARY OF CONGRESS CATALOGING-IN-PUBLICATION DATA
Lahr, John.
Dame Edna Everage and the rise of Western civilization:
backstage with Barry Humphries / John Lahr.
p.   cm.
1. Humphries, Barry.   2. Comic, The.   I. Title.
PN3018.H85L34   1992   792'.7028'092   dc20   [B]   92-2261 CIP

To

Connie, Chris, Margo, and Sylvia

and

In memory of

Dick Hummler

(1943–90)

Contents

Illustrations

Preface

When you are raised, as I was, in the household of a famous clown, certain privileges accrue. You get to carry Buster Keaton's ukulele to the railway station. You get to pick up Groucho from the hotel. Your godfather is Eddy Foy Junior of the vaudeville act The Seven Little Foys who, when his wife said she was leaving him, nailed all her clothes to the floor. You come to terms with the grief behind the zaniness of this mutant breed so articulately defended by Thomas Mann in *The Confessions of Felix Krull* as 'exceptions, side-splitting world-renouncing monks of unreason, cavorting hybrids, part human and part insane art'. You also learn to recognise the genuine article and to honour its rare appearance in the life of a community.

Barry Humphries is among us, and he is the goods. 'The art of the comedian is perishable,' said Humphries in a recent interview. 'Not only is it gone by the time you get home and pay the babysitter, but you're thinking, "What was it we were laughing at? What did Edna say? Did you get a gladdy? Oh, I did but it's dead, you sat on it." Or "I left it in the back seat of the car and now it's shrivelled up" . . . that's all we've got to remember.'

This book is meant to stop time and to chronicle a moment in the prime of a great clown's life.

J.L.
July 1991

1

Dame Edna's Royal Box

'One day Caprice arises . . .'

Jules Barbey D'Aurevilly

March 8th, 1989. It's 3 pm, but the marquee above the Theatre Royal, Drury Lane, the oldest and most venerable of London theatres, is already switched on. Passers-by as far away as Covent Garden can pick out the sign's blinking red neon message: DAME EDNA'S SECOND COMING – SHE'S BACK BECAUSE SHE CARES.

In Britain's rich and vicious 1980s 'caring' was high concept that became high parody. Margaret Thatcher, only recently caricatured on the cover of the *Spectator* as a Dame Edna look-alike complete with pink diamenté harlequin glasses, assured the nation that the Tories cared. 'Labour Cares' was the theme of the Opposition. And, always up to the minute, Dame Edna was repeating her 1987–8 revue *Back with a Vengeance!* and raking in approximately £160,000 a week from selling out the 2,245 seats, all because she also cared. 'I mean that in a very caring, nurturing way,' Dame Edna was fond of saying after delivering a particularly low blow. The manoeuvre was in keeping with the vindictive style of the times. In her previous season at the Drury Lane (1982), Dame Edna cloaked her celebrated aggression in the joke of the show's title: *An Evening's Intercourse with the widely liked Barry Humphries.* But by the late 1980s revenge on liberalism was such a blatant part of the English political climate that malice – Dame Edna's comic stock in trade – could be uninhibitedly flaunted. And Dame Edna was nothing if not uninhibited and illiberal.

Dame Edna had announced herself to the critics and the newspapers weeks before the opening of her 1989 show in her own inimitable style: 'My gynaecologist, my numerologist,

1

my biorhythmologist, my T'ai Chi instructor, my primal scream therapist, and my aromatherapist all tell me that I will be at the height of my powers as a woman from March 9, 1989, for a strictly limited season.' The press release, featuring a Russian constructivist logo of a clenched fist full of gladioli, added, 'It's not so much a show, more a private audience. And since I'm writing my autobiography this could just be one of the last chances you have of seeing me before my millennium comeback. DO YOURSELVES A FAVOUR – see the Turn of the Century *before* the turn of the century.'

This was not a conventional press release, but then Dame Edna is not a conventional star. Dame Edna is, in fact, a theatrical phenomenon: the only solo act to play (and fill) the Theatre Royal, Drury Lane since it opened for business in 1663 with Beaumont and Fletcher's *The Humorous Lieutenant*. The *Observer* named Dame Edna as 'one of the idols of the 80s', and the public keeps faith with her. The 1987 *Back with a Vengeance!*, which ran for nine months and played to a 100 per cent capacity, had the third highest advance in the history of the West End, only exceeded by *Phantom of the Opera* and *Chess*. For the thirty-one shows in Dame Edna's 1989 season, the box office was showing £600,000 in advance sales the day before opening. Television has won her an even wider popularity and a new theatre-going audience. A seventh of the British Isles, or about eight million three hundred thousand people, representing 48.7 per cent of the network share, tuned in to *The Dame Edna Experience* at prime pub time, 10.30 on a Saturday night, to watch Dame Edna, the supremo of narcissists, treat the celebrity guests on her TV talk show like audio-visual aids.

But Dame Edna's influence on the imagination of British culture is best registered by how she has been incorporated into some of the most cherished of English institutions. Dame Edna has opened the Harrods sale, turned on the Regent Street Christmas lights, played a cameo on the long-running radio soap opera *The Archers*, and twice been a radio guest on that surest barometer of British success, *Desert Island Discs*. Dame Edna has sung in the Royal Albert Hall, where 10,000 people in two nights heard her cantata, 'The Song of Australia'. A street has been named after her in Moonee Ponds, the suburb of Melbourne from which she hails. She is one of four Australians whose waxwork effigies are on display at Madame Tussauds. The College of Heraldry has unofficially drawn up Dame Edna's coat of arms, which bears the motto 'I share and I care' with the heraldic symbols of a gladiolus, a funnel web spider, a blow fly and the Sydney Opera House. 'Dame Edna has been notionally advanced to GBE,' reported *The Times*, 'so that she qualifies for armorial supporters. They are a shark and a possum, both wearing butterfly glasses.'

Dame Edna has also blitzed the commercial world. Between 1981 and 1989 her billing, always monumental, has undergone a subtle shift from 'housewife-superstar' to 'megastar'. She is now, like the celebrities of whom she is a parody, a multi-national corporation of one, who franchises every last particle of her persona that the public will buy. And it will buy a lot. Dame Edna is the spokesperson for an airline and an electrical appliance company. Her piercing singing voice, sounding like an Outback Jerry Colonna, is on tape cassette doing both disco versions of rock 'n' roll standards and her own golden oldies like 'Niceness', 'The Night We Burnt My Mother's Things' and 'Every Mother Wants a Boy Like Elton'.

The Dame Edna Social Calendar 1989 includes some of the important days in her life and the legendary people who share it ('February 24: Start reading one of Patrick White's novels; April 1: Madge Allsop's Birthday; June 1: Norm and Edna's Wedding; August 16: Day I conceived Kenny; October 4: St Edna's Day; October 20: Charles and Di's anniversary; October 28: World Prostate Day'). Dame Edna's outline – the 'natural wisteria' bouffant, the toothy grin, the glasses – has become as memorable and marketable to the English community as Groucho's to the American. There are mugs ('A Dame Edna Everage Beverage'), badges ('I'm into Edna') and even 'Hello, Possum' spectacles. These yellow plastic replicas of Dame Edna's 'face furniture', complete with a star cluster sweeping up and over the rims, cram the joke shop window across the street from the Drury Lane,

3

while a behemoth green neon version flickers on the billboard above the theatre entrance.

Dame Edna's presence is an invitation to play; and the paying customers know it from the minute they enter the theatre lobby. In one of Dame Edna's 1970s shows the lobby was festooned with Christmas decorations three months early to put her public in an infantile mood; in another the box-office personnel were daubed with blood to give the punters an extra Dame Edna *frisson*. Dame Edna doesn't just appear on stage; she's invisibly working on her audience the minute they come near her theatre. Placards like LOW BROW ENTERTAINMENT AT LAST — HURRY LAST YEARS!!, and THOSE WANTING BRAILLE PROGRAMMES TRY SEEING THE MANAGER, and MINORITIES WELCOME UP TO A POINT are some of Dame Edna's most piquant pre-show attempts to whip up the heady festival atmosphere in which she specialises. 'This show is ozone friendly,' says the sign beside the Drury Lane box-office window, where there is a queue even at the unfashionable mid-afternoon hour. Another sign reads:

If this show is probably full, Dame Edna recommends —
THE WOMAN IN BLACK
FORBIDDEN BROADWAY
SINGLE SPIES
THE SNEEZE
For excellent seats, mention my name.

Dame Edna's name is synonymous with surprise, and even with shock. As her sobriquet 'housewife/superstar' implies, she is a celebration of contradictions: hilarious and malign, polite and lewd, generous and envious; high and low comic. But the most sensational of all Dame Edna's contradictions is, of course, that *she* is a *he*.

Dame Edna is the creation of Barry Humphries. Or, as the letterhead of his yellow stationery would have it, 'Barry Humphries is a division of the Barry Humphries Group.' This is true. Dame Edna has taken on a visibility and a reality for the public that vie with, even subsume, Humphries' own public persona. A star

4

is an impresario of himself; but Humphries is the impresario of his selves. The small print at the bottom of his stationery says, 'The recipient is advised to preserve this memorandum as it could well become a very extremely valuable collector's item.' This also is true. The fifty-seven-year-old Humphries is a prodigious comic talent. His co-presence in Edna – a character so real to the public that her autobiography, *My Gorgeous Life*, is being sold by his English publisher Macmillan on its non-fiction list – incarnates the essence of the grotesque: the sense that things that should be kept apart are fused together. This style, which Baudelaire called 'the absolute comic', also creates in an audience a paroxysm, a swoon, 'something profound, primitive, axiomatic, which is much closer to innocent life and absolute joy'.

I know the feeling. At Dame Edna's 1981 show, I was blind-sided by one of Dame Edna's startling observations and fell off my seat laughing. I can't account for the next two minutes of the show. I was on the floor.

Afterwards, I determined to write about Humphries from the wings. I still have notes from our first backstage meeting when I sat with him between acts, talking and watching this strapping, urbane Australian man of letters transform himself into Dame Edna, whom he has been impersonating sporadically since 1955.

'There's something of the clown, something rather ritualised in the character,' said Humphries, putting on his 'lippie'. 'It's a clown in the form of an Australian housewife. It also belongs to a rather long pantomime and music hall tradition. It belongs a bit to the pantomime dame tradition though it doesn't exploit the pantomime dame, which is generally a rather sturdy man. The joke of the pantomime dame is the tension between the female of the clothes and the stocky footballer's legs and boots. The drag queen is the other extreme, really a man who is mocking a woman and at the same time trying to titillate the audience. Edna is somewhere in between, closer really to character acting, a man playing a woman and making points about life.'

In the intervening eight years Humphries has become more famous (the marquee announces 'the almost legendary Barry Humphries') and Dame Edna's frivolity more majestic. But as I walk through the safety doors on to the vast eighty-foot-square Drury Lane stage where the technical run-through is noisily in progress, neither the actor nor his creation is to be found. Backstage feels drab and mundane. But the props, scattered like so many jigsaw pieces on a gargantuan table, promise something bright and extraordinary. An Australian flag stretching the width of the proscenium is being battened down to be flown up in the labyrinth of catwalks and ropes. The cherry picker, a crane with a basket which will lift Edna fifty feet above the stalls to sing her finale straight into the eyes of her balcony fans, whom she collectively refers to as 'the paupers', is shunted off into the shadows. The basket itself, which usually hoists more earnest citizens like telephone repairmen or firemen, has been turned into a kind of surrealist sculpture: its sides are now a dress of white organza and its base is disguised with a red, white, and blue crinoline and a pair of Dame Edna's red size 9 high heels. Edna's magic wand, an electrified plastic gladiolus into which a microphone has been rigged, rests on the side of the basket. I make my way toward the steps that lead from the stage into the auditorium, tripping in the gloom on a loose piece of linoleum and bumping into a wooden column that forms part of the backdrop to Dame Edna's non-celebrity talk show. The column has a stuffed koala already in place at the top of it. No space in the theatre is without its little touch of Humphries' surprise.

The lighting board has been set up in the centre of row J. Behind it, slumped in conversation on the greenish gold seats, are two men. The trim one in the V-neck with the full head of hair and the clipboard turns out to be Humphries' producer/manager Dennis Smith, a no-nonsense Australian whom Humphries employed from 1982 to 1989. The other man in tie and jacket, hunched patiently over a crossword puzzle, is Ian Davidson, a comedy writer whom I recognised from my 1981 visit to Drury Lane. Davidson's name comes up in the credits of almost all Humphries' comic activities since the late 1960s, when he directed some of Edna's sketches for *The Late Show*, the BBC's unsuccessful attempt to catch the receding wave of satire before it washed out.

A modest, quiet man who began as an actor and even performed with Alan Arkin and Barbara Harris in America at the improvisational Second City in the mid-1960s, Davidson is one of three men billed as providing 'additional acceptable jokes'. 'Periodically Barry says, "These topical lines are getting a bit tired. Better have a think about them," ' explains Davidson, pulling away his *Evening Standard* to reveal a pad on which he's jotted a few droll notions for his friend. 'Then we have a phone call about them. But Barry brings around other people as well. It's not a sort of solo position I have, although quite often I do get things in. One of the shows I virtually co-wrote was *Housewife/Superstar* [1976]. I always work with Barry when he does television. And I help with bits on the other stage shows. It's mainly making a show which was developed in Australia into a show for London.' Humphries' quickness and his memory make him a particular joy for a comedy writer to serve. 'It's Rolls-Royce work,' says Davidson. 'Sometimes Barry can play things a little close to the chest. You feel a bit left out. But I don't make too much of a fuss. I go with it because the moments of joy are so good.'

Davidson was whispering comic ideas to Humphries even when I interviewed him in the middle of his 1981 Drury Lane season. 'I like to hear what the public are saying at the interval,' he told me while Edna was slipping into the tennis outfit she was wearing for that show. 'I stumbled upon a quarrel between a couple. She was accusing the man of sighing. He'd obviously bought the tickets. She was drunk and took exception to the show. "You were sighing," "I never sigh." "Don't be so combatative." She put an extra syllable in. I told Barry. He thought it was funny; and that night Edna said: "Oh Norm. I used to take Norm to the theatre, but he didn't enjoy it. And when I said, 'You've been sighing,' he'd say, 'Don't be so combatative.' " Barry's got this sort of total recall. He just threw it in during a little lull. I went back after the show and Barry said: "Two people have had an unforgettable night." '

A BBC-TV crew appears in the Royal Box to the left of the stage and begins setting up its equipment. Smith checks his watch. 'She's late.'

'She's probably on the phone,' says Davidson, jotting something down on his piece of paper.

7

'Got anything?'

'Something for Les,' Davidson says, meaning another Humphries character in the show, Sir Les Patterson, the well-hung Australian cultural attaché and the author of *The Traveller's Tool* as well as the star of *Les Patterson Saves the World* (1989), Humphries' latest venture into feature films. Sir Les, with his 'enormous encumbancy', has his own special way of opening Dame Edna's revue, and Davidson has come up with an idea in keeping with the full moral authority of the character. 'Catch-69,' he says. 'If you do this thing, you're wrong. If you do that thing, you're wrong. It's a Catch-69 situation. That's a Les possible. If you get a funny idea, it could be used for Les, or for Edna. Or it could end up a notice in the foyer.'

Davidson is also trying to work up gags on the recently opened film *Scandal* about the Profumo affair in the early 1960s and about Senator John Tower. 'He's a topical. The papers are full of his battle to be America's Secretary of Defense. "As busy as John Tower." That's a possibility. Obviously Les would claim to know John Tower, both hard drinkers. One trick Barry plays is always saying, "Oh, John Tower? Now who is that?" And you have to explain. And then you realise half-way through the explanation he knew quite well who John Tower was, possibly better than you did. But he's just playing for a little time whilst his mind is working. So by the time you say something, he's got something to come back with.'

'Tonight's big prize . . .' says Dennis Smith, testing part of the movable feast of Dame Edna's topical material, a player like everyone else backstage at the game of seducing Humphries' imagination with a funny idea.

'What is tonight's big prize?' asks Davidson mournfully. 'I dunno.'

'Tonight's big prize. It's the intimate examination by a top medical woman.'

'Oh yeah. It's a voucher,' he glances over at me. 'Redeemable in Cleveland.'

The show's publicist, Lynne Kirwin, looks out into the auditorium from the corner of the stage. 'Edna's just coming,' she says as if the falsetto voice somewhere up and to the left of the lights being tested in the Royal Box could leave any doubt.

Davidson says, 'We always talk about Edna as though she exists. "Edna could say this", not "you" could say this. As a character she is separate from him.'

Dame Edna stands against the balustrade of the Royal Box while the TV crew press lights, microphones and recording machines up under her double chin. In high heels and hairdo, Edna is surprisingly large, around six feet four inches, with wide shoulders and very well-shaped legs: a kind of amazon of outrageousness. Her dress, a garish sunburst of colours, is matched by lensless glasses scalloped today with what look like variegated coffee beans. She stares out at the theatre along the Dress Circle, in front of which are the names, emblazoned in gold leaf, of the literary and theatrical giants who have made the theatre's legend: BYRON, DRYDEN, GARRICK, SHERIDAN, KEAN. 'Dennis?' Dame Edna pipes in the high-pitched voice which is her calling card. 'Wouldn't it be nice if Edna's name was added to those in front of the Dress Circle?' Dennis smiles and makes a note.

Dame Edna hitches up her panty-hose, and turns back to the task at hand which is to talk to the presenter, Cathy McGowan, herself a media star in the 1960s when she hosted the popular music show *Ready Steady Go*. The interview starts, and Dame Edna, an expert at media manipulation, goes to work. The character is in the voice; and its command never wavers. The mouth may twitch in mock anxiety at a probing question, the timbre may lower in cod intimacy, but the swagger in Edna's falsetto is resolutely consistent. 'There's very little danger of going out of character,' Humphries told me in 1981, 'unless I lose the falsetto. I have once given a couple of baritone performances. You could see the audience's jaws drop. You have to win them back. You have to play Edna very hard with the eyes.' No need for eyeballing on this pre-opening interview; Dame Edna is in her element and taking energy from the laughter of the TV crew.

'I feel I know you, Cathy . . . I do. That fresh little face has looked at me in black and white and colour. And your natural colouring is gorgeous . . . It is. And what a survivor you are, aren't you? As fresh and lovely as you were in those old Swinging Sixties days. You were a famous television star then and I was just an ordinary Melbourne housewife. And look at me now . . . ha, ha! The young adore me. I can't analyse it. I don't analyse these things. But I struck a note with young people. There are a lot of Ednaboppers and Wannabeednas. Kiddies copy me slavishly, Cathy . . . as they did you in the old days. Remember the whole of London was filled with little Cathy lookalikes, wasn't it? Remember?'

'No,' says Cathy, a little nonplussed to find the ball suddenly back in her court.

'I do.'

'Can I ask you about the outfits you wear? Your clothes. I don't really recognise the designer, Dame Edna.'

'No,' says Dame Edna, her voice slipping into its confidential mode. 'I don't think designers should be too recognisable. That means an extreme of style and you can only wear it about once and it goes out of fashion. I like to wear something a bit like Her Majesty, the Queen – a close personal friend.' She turns to the camera: '. . . Hello! . . .' then back to Cathy: 'She's just watching. She just rang me to tell me that . . . Actually she faxed me. I've got a little fax in my purse. I'm one of the very few people with an in-purse fax.'

'What did she say in the fax?'

'I'm not allowed to say. Our friendship would be at an end. But it was intimate. I can tell you that.'

'Would you consider plastic surgery, Dame Edna?'

'No. I've thought about my little chins. People have said they're a nice part of me, and they're very much me. I'm not a classical-looking woman, am I, let's face it . . . But I am one of the world's great beauties. It's funny . . . I never thought of myself as one of the world's great beauties. But people tell me so often that I'm beginning to believe it. And I'm a very nice-looking person. This is not vanity, is it? It doesn't seem like it. It's just a healthy self-esteem. I've thought of having this bit', Dame Edna touches the wattles under her chin, 'Hoovered out, you know . . . What they do is make a little hole in your chin . . . and they suck out a kind of horrible sausage of fat. I don't like the idea of that, do you?'

'Dame Edna, thank you so much for inviting me to the Royal Box.'

'That's all right. This is the Royal Box. Where members of the royal family and very selected friends of mine come and watch my beautiful shows. And there's a lovely ante-room off it where they can have "sambies". Beautiful sandwiches. "Sambies" is an Australian word for sandwiches. An old aboriginal word. (It's not a very difficult language) . . .'

Even after the camera is lifted off its tripod and the lights are packed away, Dame Edna is still in the Royal Box holding forth. In character, Humphries exudes what Charlie Chaplin, mourning its absence in his own music hall performance, called 'that come hither thing'. Dame Edna enjoys the exhilaration of the liberty she takes. Her pleasure is infectious. She's regaling the assembled about her special Australian ointment for stretch marks. 'Ever seen a kangaroo with stretch marks? It contains an extract of a kangaroo's spleen . . . It does. You don't use too much of it. Princess Diana actually uses it. She said she was starting to develop a pouch. So follow the instructions.'

Dame Edna seems extraordinarily actual. Whether watching her on TV or face to face, an audience soon loses the sense that this is a man-as-woman and accepts her as real. (So real, in fact, that Edna is impersonated at drag parties.) This sense of actuality is due, in part, to the rich coherence of her story, which Humphries has built up in public over the years; and also to his own performance, which is relaxed and vivid within the parameters of her monstrous character. But identity is a story at once claimed by the individual and conferred by the group. Dame Edna compels belief. The public wills her to be real. And, like Tinker Bell, she *is* if you believe in her. (She won't reply to questions addressed to 'Barry'.) By maintaining Edna's persona, Humphries also keeps the people around him playing his game. For both performer and public it's an exercise in improvisation, but in this battle of wits the public is unarmed. Dame Edna turns

11

everyone into a sounding board and catalyst for her proliferating wit. The experience is eerie and elating. Life is turned into theatre; and theatre into life.

Dame Edna walks slowly down the back stairs toward the stage. She's a little ungainly on her pins, like a footballer in studs on the concrete walkway from locker room to field. 'I'm feeling just a bit sorry for John Tower, aren't you?' Dame Edna says to me. 'I mean, if you're going to put your finger on the nuclear button, you might as well be drunk.' Dame Edna looks for a reaction, gets it, and then, with handbag in the crook of her arm, ambles out on to the Drury Lane stage, which is illuminated now only by a rehearsal light. The stage is empty except for the drum kit of the three-piece band which accompanies the show.

This is the first time since 1981 that Dame Edna's been on the Drury Lane stage, and she's all too aware of its theatre history. 'Guess what, possums?' boasted her press release. 'I've just hired the most famous theatre on the planet.' David Garrick, Mrs Siddons, John Kemble, Sir Henry Irving, Edmund Kean, Joseph Grimaldi have all worked the stage she's testing. The boxes loom high and close above her. The space itself is expectant. Seats, lights, boxes, aisles, all point toward centre stage where Dame Edna moves around getting a feel of the Drury Lane's size and its atmosphere. Dame Edna has a heavy-hipped, awkward, almost royal gait. She does not mince, her step has a thrust to it. A great performer on an empty stage is always poignant, like a footballer checking the pitch, summoning up the courage to get the job done with glory. 'I like to acquaint myself with the empty auditorium,' Humphries told me in 1981. 'I make strange sounds, rather like whales or dolphins do. I do a bit of vocal bouncing.' Tonight, Dame Edna just comes down to the front of the stage and starts confiding to no one in particular: 'All you do is stand on the stage and talk to the people as though you were just talking on the phone. Just have a chat . . . People make such a fuss about it. I hate shows, don't you, where you go and they're not talking to you, they're talking to each other. It's very rude . . .'

12

From the shadows of the stalls Davidson answers back. Dame Edna reacts.

'. . . Extremely rude. Pretending the audience isn't there . . . Imagine if you rang someone up and they were talking to someone else all the time?'

Dame Edna does some more vocal bouncing and then looks down toward the lighting board where Dennis Smith is standing. 'How's the box office?'

'People were lining up until three thirty.'

'We should bring them coffee,' says Dame Edna, strolling over in my direction in the wings.

'Who are the people in the news, Ian? Winnie Mandela. Has she been in the news? What's that film Dustin's done?'

'*Rainman*,' I shout, caught up like everyone else in getting Dame Edna ready for the challenge of opening night.

'*Rainwoman*,' says Dame Edna, sharpish. 'I was offered the part.'

Davidson lobs something up about Roy Orbison's death.

'Little Roy,' says Dame Edna, 'one of the nicest albinos I ever knew.'

Dame Edna paces the stage in silence and then looks out toward the producer, who's moved down to the front row. 'What time are we starting the tech?' Dame Edna asks.

'Seven thirty.'

'Perhaps I should have a nibble now. Come into the dressing room.' Dame Edna starts off the stage, where she's met by Dennis Smith. As Dame Edna passes me in the wings, she says to her producer, 'Look at this mysterious figure.'

As the technical rehearsal begins, the BBC newsreader John Humphreys comes up on a screen that has dropped down in front of the Drury Lane proscenium. He is at his news desk. His papers are neatly placed in front of him. His grave and measured voice, which over the years has brokered many a world calamity to the citizens of Britain, is broadcasting the latest jolt to the national psyche. 'Sad news I'm afraid,' he says, putting down the phone at his elbow which keeps the BBC newsreaders in instant touch with their correspondents on breaking stories. 'We've just had confirmed reports that one of Australia's most famous men has died. Mr Norman Everage, husband of world famous actress, Dame Edna Everage, passed away peacefully in London just about an hour ago. Norman Everage was a shy, modest man. He distinguished himself as a soldier in the Second World War and married Edna May Beazley in the nineteen forties. They had three children: Bruce, Valmai, and Ken. However, soon after Mrs Everage, as she then was, made the first of her highly successful public appearances, her husband developed a urological disorder for which he's been undergoing treatment for a quarter of a century . . .'

Norman Everage never made an appearance in one of Dame Edna's shows, but Dame Edna has turned his prostate into legend. 'Norm's prostate has been hanging over my head for years,' she's confided on stage and in her autobiography, as the rolling joke of her browbeaten mate and their family changed with the times and with the rise of Edna's star. In *An Evening's Intercourse with the widely liked Barry Humphries* (1982), Dame Edna told how Norm had to have his hands strapped to the side of the hospital bed and was learning to knit with his mouth. 'He's into oral socks,' she explained.

Now another BBC reporter, Sue Cook, is pictured outside 'the world's first prostate transplant unit' interviewing doctors, nurses, and Dame Edna herself. The effect of seeing the representatives of the real world incorporated into Dame Edna's fantasy is unnerving. But it's a confusion Humphries relishes. For Dame Edna's autobiography Humphries has chosen an epigraph from Benedetto Croce: 'All history is fiction, just as all fiction is history.'

And Dame Edna makes a fiasco of history. Looking at a picture of Dame Edna amidst the royals in his dressing room, Humphries said, 'That's a joke in itself.' And so it is. Dame Edna's mere presence at public occasions and amidst public figures calls the reality of society into question. She is frivolity incarnate and therefore irony in action. In the early days Edna sometimes had to thrust herself into the paths of the famous, like Australian

Prime Minister Sir Robert Menzies for whom she waited with photographer until he appeared outside the Savoy Hotel. 'I'm one of your electors,' she said, as he snubbed her. 'You're doing a fine job.' But as the programme celebrates in snapshot, the famous now flock to Dame Edna. She is shown variously meeting and greeting a gallimaufry of the celebrated: the Queen Mother, Princess Diana, Joan Baez, Bob Geldof, Zsa Zsa Gabor, Larry Hagman, Charlton Heston, Joan Rivers, Jeffrey Archer, Mary Whitehouse.

This is not the first time Edna has been photographed with Mary Whitehouse, Britain's self-proclaimed moral guardian whose righteousness Dame Edna both voices and lampoons. 'There was a wonderful encounter between Mary Whitehouse and Edna in Melbourne,' Humphries told me in 1981. 'She was out there giving lectures on morality, and I asked her to the show. She didn't see the show; but she came and was photographed with Edna. She addressed Edna as Edna and embraced her in a sisterly manner saying how people had said they looked alike. Very funny photographs. A bit like Genghis Khan and Adolf Hitler falling into each other's arms.'

Dame Edna dethrones the seriousness of authority, but at the same time exploits that authority to make her fantasy into legend. Humphries broke new ground again in 1980 with *An Audience with Dame Edna Everage*, in which the studio audience with whom Dame Edna interacts are among the most famous people in the land. History is fable agreed upon; and the sight of these powerful figures being teased by Dame Edna confirms both their place in history and hers. The BBC news programme rings a new change from one of Humphries' oldest games. Over the years Dame Edna has staged herself against the monuments of fame, the monuments of architecture (Marx's tomb, Notre Dame cathedral, the Houses of Parliament) and now, with BBC reporters covering Norm's death, the monuments of official reality. When Dame Edna is involved, all values, even the habitual gravity and objectivity of the BBC, are turned upside down.

Ian Davidson slides into the seat beside me, back from dinner at Orso's, where he and Humphries have been looking over his page of ideas. He's just in time to see himself on screen as the head of Dame Edna Everage's prostate transplant unit sombrely tell the camera, 'Now, in a very real sense, his prostate belongs to prosterity.' It's a good joke; and the laugh reminds Davidson that Humphries has had to educate the public to his brand of humour. 'The title of the first revue I saw him in, *Just a Show* (1968), puzzled people at the time. Now it makes them laugh. He's sort of taught people his vocabulary.'

' "Seminal", "mould-breaking", "spooky", "sharing", "*per se*", "pivotal". You can't hear those words without somewhere hearing Edna.'

'There's a notice outside this theatre which says THIS IS A NICE SHOW,' Davidson says. 'Once upon a time that would have merely bemused people, now it tickles them.' Even the macabre beginning of Dame Edna's act, which raises the issue of death only to banish it, is part of the wicked liberation Humphries has in mind for his audience. 'He likes pushing it,' says Davidson. 'He likes heightening the atmosphere.' At a National Press Club talk in Australia in 1978 Humphries explained, 'I always find that an audience laughs much louder if they're extremely anxious and therefore I think at the beginning of my new show [*Housewife/Superstar*] I'll remind them of all the terrible things that could be happening at home – was the kitchen window really firmly locked? What kind of cigarettes was the babysitter smoking? How many friends is she at present entertaining? That should put them in a very receptive mood.'

Davidson recalls the blood-stained nurses posted around the auditorium in *Housewife/Superstar*: 'He wanted to infantilise the audience, upset it, and at the same time have the audience entrust itself to his care. At one point Barry said we ought to try and make the theatre smell like a school. I loved the idea of getting the theatre audience slightly worried. In *An Evening's Intercourse with the widely liked Barry Humphries* you could hear over the loudspeaker a taxi radio message that the star wasn't going to arrive.'

The first stage-managed moment of anxiety in the current show comes at the end of the BBC broadcast. The BBC newsreader looks out at the audience and says, 'We have confirmation that

Dame Edna has cancelled all stage performances. No money will be refunded. And that's the news tonight.'

The screen flies up. The musicians are soon in place ready for Humphries to start running through his material. Victy, the pianist, has a pad beside her to jot down any tasty one-liners that Humphries might improvise and want to put into the act. Humphries strolls out on stage wearing the headmike that fits under Edna's wig. He's in blue jeans, white socks, and sandals, an altogether unlikely Edna. Humphries speeds through the prose portions of his act in double time: 'And so and so and so and so and so and so . . . I feel a song coming on!' In a V-neck and Edna's voice, Humphries launches into the boffo opening, a hymn to frivolity's refusal to suffer.

'A minute ago
I was locked in my room
My life seemed pointless and hollow,
Where before it was warm
With the presence of Norm
And I thought "Where he's gone I must follow."
I looked at the Valium, I considered the stove,
I weighed up the stern moral issues,
But the strength inside me grew
When I was almost through
My last box of Kleenex tissues.
So I hope you'll all applaud my great achievement
I am here tonight in spite of my bereavement . . .'

When Dame Edna sings about the triumph of fame over grief, her big-heartedness always admits the spirit of revenge, an impulse which is never far from the aggressive wellsprings of great comedy. It's a game that Humphries, too, has been known to play with his public. 'In Melbourne I used to like sitting in a little Greek restaurant called Café Florentino at about eight ten in the evening and see old Melbourne Grammar boys, contemporaries perhaps of our Prime Minister [and himself], hurrying with their wives down the stairs in order to attend one of my performances which I had

17

absolutely no intention of starting for another three-quarters of an hour,' he told the National Press Club in 1978. 'The advantage of course of being a solo performer is that they can never start without you – and I think that is probably one of the few advantages except it keeps me off the streets and fills my evenings entertainingly.'

Humphries stops the song to adjust the arrangement with the band: 'Be nice if we could add a note there. A little Kurt Weillish note. "And now you know/I'm too much of a pro/To let *yooooooou* down ..."' Davidson says, 'One time when I was in his dressing room, Harriet, the stage manager, came around: "We're five minutes late! We're five minutes late!" He said, "Is the house full?" "Of course, it's full," she said. "Every seat's full." And Barry said, "This is a bit different from the Fortune Theatre, Ian [where *Just a Show* was staged]. We used to have to wait till the audience arrived." I said: "Don't revenge yourself for what happened then on these people here tonight." That absolutely started him off. With all the clamour going on around him, he told this story: when he was at school at Melbourne Grammar there was this particular bully who made his life a misery. Years later when he was at Melbourne University, he'd seen the guy out in the middle of the lawn reading a book. He was working at the university theatre then and he went back to get a bag of size, the white powder they use for covering flats. He crept up behind the guy, called his name, dumped the lot on him and ran for his life because he was a big, powerful, vengeful figure. I was sitting there thinking now what's this story got to do with anything? Barry went on about how he ran for his life, but then he looked back at this outraged white figure and realised it wasn't the bully. He said he still had the same feeling of satisfaction at having revenged himself. So it didn't matter if it was a different audience tonight. It was still a good feeling.'

After the song, Humphries comes down into the stalls and sits talking with us while the crew gets the next set in place. He is a more reserved presence than the ebullient Dame Edna. Edna's voice is tight and sharp; but Humphries' voice is breathy and light. Where Edna is garish, Humphries is suave. Where she is direct and downright rude, he is oblique and well mannered. Edna is unaware of what she projects, which empowers the public to laugh at her; Humphries is knowing, and his knowingness keeps those around him at a distance and on the defensive. His smile is tired tonight, but the furrowed laugh lines around his mouth and his high fleshy cheekbones give his face a dramatic – even youthful – definition. The eyes, when they focus on you, are bright and warm and convey a very definite sense of authority.

Dame Edna's biases are there for the world to see, but Humphries is much harder to fathom. As you would expect of a comedian who treads so gracefully between insight and outrage, Humphries is a man of intelligence and taste. Dame Edna says the first thing that pops into her airhead, but Humphries listens. He is reflective, choosing his words carefully and well. Humphries has talked of the feeling of 'allegiance' to the 'fellowship of music hall artistes', but his articulacy separates him from the old-timers whose glorious tradition he is almost single-handedly carrying into the twenty-first century. Buster Keaton had two days of official schooling; Charlie Chaplin learned a new word a day; Bert Lahr built up his vocabulary by doing crossword puzzles. But Humphries, whose act combines lowbrow antics with a highbrow aesthetic, is both well educated and well read, as the range of images and references in his conversation displays. The talk shifts to whether Dame Edna's name is going to be added to the theatrical luminaries writ large on the façade of the Dress Circle.

'Certainly,' says Humphries. 'I mean, Byron's dramatic works . . .'

'Very limited, aren't they?' says Davidson.

'Very limited. He doesn't really belong with Garrick or Sheridan, does he?' says Humphries, turning to me. 'Has Ian told you about some of the signs we're going to put up outside?'

'I was hoping you'd have "Ednatollah says".' A few weeks before, after a meeting at the Groucho Club with Humphries to discuss writing about him, the subject of Salman Rushdie came up. Rushdie had only recently gone to ground after the

Ayatollah Khomeini's order of execution for *The Satanic Verses*. 'Has Edna had her say?' I asked, as Humphries and I walked along Old Compton Street. 'Edna hasn't expressed an opinion,' he said. But soon Humphries was playing with the idea. 'The Ednatollah,' he suddenly announced, 'the Ednatollah says, "See my show or die."' He thought again. 'See my show, or I'll kill you.' Now, Humphries was remembering the incident. 'Ednatollah,' he smiles, weighing the comic notion.

'Is it *the* Ednatollah?' said Davidson.

'The Ednatollah.' Humphries sounds the phrase out and starts to laugh. He turns to his producer a few rows away. 'Dennis, I'm afraid there's one more for the sign writers,' he says, his voice cracking into a high-pitched register which is the signal that he's genuinely amused. 'The Ednatollah says . . .'

'Is this going to create a bomb disturbance outside the theatre?'

'You think I'd suggest anything that would cause a bomb threat?'

'Yes,' says Dennis Smith and turns his mind to the placard. 'No, I don't think so.'

'You serious?' says Humphries.

'Your huge Iranian audience will take offence,' says Smith, walking away, unruffled by the other reference to Rushdie that Dame Edna has already worked into her finale. Sings Dame Edna, 'What makes me quite so self-effacing/Like Salman Rushdie/I am almost a recluse . . .'

The stuntmen are having trouble wiring themselves up for Humphries' most outrageous effect: the spectacle of paupers plummeting from a box seat. So Humphries, who hates still life, turns back to me and begins our scheduled conversation a day early. 'My German Expressionist touch,' he says of the stunt. 'I was in the film society at university, and I deliberately disinterred a lot of German Expressionist films. I liked the kind of spooky, rather frightening effects that some of these actors produced in the movies. I very much liked the sense of melodrama and – what are they – the *frissons*. I like to produce this in the theatre, and I like to combine it with comedy. I don't know why I liked shocking people. I think it just gave me a sense of identity. I guess it gave me a sense of power too, because I felt rather powerless and swamped by, well, the dullness of Melbourne. Although I'm very fond of it, Melbourne is a transcendentally dull city. It's subsequently been *taught* by another of my characters, the Melbourne ghost Sandy Stone, that this is its appeal. I've learnt through my own characters. Dullness is Sandy Stone's element as fire is the element of the salamander. And it's not so bad, after all. But I was rather puritanical in those early days, and moralistic. Anxious to *show* people. Edna was conceived as a character to remind Australians of their bigotry and all the things that I found offensive. She was a rebuke. She was a silly, bigoted, ignorant, self-satisfied Melbourne housewife. They're still around. They're still there. Now they just wear a different uniform. They drive Volvos and occasionally swear. No one before me in Australia had looked at the suburbs and said here is the stuff of comedy. It's only when Edna took on a life of her own, when she was invested *with a life*, that she turned the tables on me in a way.'

Eddy, the stuntman, yells down that they're ready, so Humphries hoists himself up and goes back on stage to work through 'The Gladdy Song' which is the segue out of his *coup de théâtre*. 'Now let's try and throw a few gladdies up to the paupers,' Humphries says in an uninflected Edna voice, not lingering to act the words. 'I don't think I can. But I will . . . uh . . . uh . . . uh . . .' Humphries mimes the backhanded flip with which for a quarter of a century he's been heaving the Australian national flower at the audience. The drummer does a rimshot as each imaginary gladdy lands in the audience.

'What about me, Dame Edna?' waves the stuntwoman sitting on the balcony railing.

'Where do you do that?' Humphries asks her.

'Off the front.'

'Wait until I've succeeded in getting a gladdy up there and then the audience applauds.'

'Barry,' says Dennis Smith, 'at the Strand, you only had two boxes to reach. So you went one . . . two . . .'

21

'Well, I'm going to try and reach it. If I get there, the audience will applaud. When we get the applause, wait till it's nearly dark so we see you. OK, let's go over the cue.'

'What about me, Dame Edna?'

'Oh, I don't think I can. Uh . . . uh . . .'

'AAAAAAAH!!' The woman tips out and over the balcony, dragging the man with her. They dangle above the empty stalls like rock climbers rappelling a cliff.

'Can you see them?' says Humphries, as the woman swings on wires and halter concealed by her dress. 'Will enough people see that?'

'Everybody and his dog will see that,' says Dennis Smith.

Anxiety assuaged, Humphries continues running the lines as the stuntwoman is hauled back into the box.

'You all right? What a miracle there was a rope ladder up there, paups. Heaven be praised. Heaven be praised. Oh, dear. You all right, budgies?'

'We love you, Dame Edna.'

Humphries stops. 'Maybe you should say, "Yes, Dame Edna, we love you. Yes, we're OK and we love you."'

'Yes, Dame Edna, we love you.'

'Oh, you move me when you say that, lemming. Wouldn't it be ghastly if that happened every night?'

Even in rehearsal, the lines get a laugh from the crew. 'On the first night at the Strand', says Davidson, 'they dropped out of the top box like that. Someone from the stalls – an intrepid man – ran up on the box below and climbed out on the ledge to help the woman. Thereafter, they had to have someone standing in the corridor to stop anyone trying to make a brave rescue. The man was terribly brave. The box wasn't as high as this, but it was still damned high. I can't imagine any other comedian who would have such a stunt take place in an auditorium – have such amazing, riveting attention taken away from you in that way. It all rebounds to Edna's benefit in the end, but even so . . .'

'Comedians jealously guard their time on stage,' Dennis Smith cuts in. 'What an unselfish, caring, sharing person Edna is.'

'She pretty soon gets it back from those people dangling over the balcony.'

'When she says: "Aren't we lucky that doesn't happen every night?" everybody roars with laughter,' says Smith. 'Barry's always wanted something like that to happen. We've never been in a position to do it. The minute we got into a theatre where people could fall from a great height he did it. It's a helluva thing. It scares the shit out of people.'

'Edna's already done her stuff about "plummeting paupers". So the image of falling is ready in the audience's mind,' smiles Davidson. ' "A downpour of the disadvantaged." On opening night at the Strand I was sitting next to a frail little old lady. I'm afraid I had to warn her.'

In true pantomine tradition Humphries always gets his audience to sing along, although the meanings of the words are not always what they fondly think. The 'Gladdy Song' is scrolled down on the stage. 'It seems a bit high. I doubt if the Upper Circle can read it. Can it be dropped a bit lower?' Humphries asks his producer.

'Not by tomorrow,' calls Smith, wandering in the back of the stalls.

'In future performances, if there is a song to sing, I rather like the words coming along on a strip. I'll be very surprised if they can read that in the Circle, frankly. Can they?'

'It's not exactly small writing,' says Smith, who gives lessons to the stage management on how to parry his star's worries. 'Up! . . . Up! . . .'

Humphries picks up the cue. 'Up . . . Up . . . Up . . . and over. All right.' The band strikes up, and Humphries is singing to the tune of 'Bicycle Built for Two':

'Gladdies, gladdies, yellow and pink and blue
We could wave them happily all night through.
They're Australia's favourite emblem
And it's raunchy when we tremble 'em
So thrust like mad, get off on a glad,
And let all of your dreams come true . . . Good-night possums!!!'

Humphries breaks off. 'Applause. Applause. Any chance of any glitter dropping? Petals? Balloons?'

'Do you mean for tomorrow night or on a permanent basis?' says Smith.

The smoke machine starts working, and the cherry picker moves downstage. 'I see. That's good,' Humphries says. 'Tell me, have you got nice colour on that? Are there flashing lights? Great blasts of colour?' He goes over to the stagehand driving the crane. 'When I start moving, you start bringing me up. Can't I first move downstage as though I'm walking down and then rise? Don't forget I need the illuminated gladdy. This looks good 'cause you don't see the mechanism.'

Humphries, whose first ambition was to be a painter, thinks visually; and his shows make extraordinary stage pictures. In the past he has tried to shoot gladioli into the balcony with a cannon, kicked a giant Malteser back and forth between stage and stalls, fielded people's shoes from the stalls with a butterfly net, pulled a rip cord on his dress that turned it into a Union Jack. But in having Dame Edna rise fifty feet above his audience at the finale of *Back with a Vengeance!*, Humphries has outdone himself. 'It's a parody of the Assumption as though painted by Murillo or perhaps a late Venetian master,' he says.

Humphries locks himself in the basket of the crane and begins to work through 'Shyness', Edna's last song. As instructed, the cherry picker moves him slowly downstage and then thrusts him out and up over the stalls. Just the sight of Humphries suspended in air makes those of us in the audience laugh. The machine judders. Humphries grasps the rails. 'There's terrible lurches down there,' he says, the word 'lurches' reverbs in the sound system. 'Hello, paupers!' says Humphries in Edna's brightest falsetto. 'I feel like Edna Poppins up here. I do. I hope I don't do anything involuntary. Be it on your heads, if I do.' The machine judders again. 'My God!' says Humphries, who for once lets his fear show. 'It's metal fatigue that worries me.'

As Humphries smooths out the stage picture so that it will seem effortless on opening night, Davidson says, 'I couldn't imagine theatrical effects on this sort of scale. All these tricks. Like using huge Maltesers. I could only say yes when he thought of it; but it passed my imaginings what was going to happen with those balls. It's his command on stage. I always recall the moment that I was in a box at *Housewife/Superstar*. Barry was playing on two levels. He was pretending that Edna was suddenly bereft of words. He'd engineer some member of the audience to say something that apparently caught Edna short. Edna would turn upstage as if laughing at her own powerlessness in front of this clever member of the audience. And the audience would hoot with delight that Edna had been finally topped. At the same time, you knew quite well that what she'd say next was going to top the whole bloody thing. He could play it beautifully. Even though the audience were perfectly in tune with Edna, he could still kid them. He was kidding them and at the same time he was winking at *me* in the box. And I thought, Jesus Christ, this man can do it all! He was contriving to be invisible, to make his winking invisible as well. The audience never noticed. The skill of the man on stage. He was so much in command. I was horrified when he winked at me. I thought, Barry, don't blow it. It didn't matter – they never noticed. And the idea of having the people falling from the box or rising up above the audience on a crane. That's extraordinary to be able to carry that off. I mean, have someone fall out of a bloody box when you're on stage. The vast majority of comedians would say: Not on your life. I won't have anything to do with it, not while I'm on stage. It'll kill the atmosphere stone dead. How he manages to recover, I just don't know. Edna sweeps on through and has the audience high as a kite by the finale.'

Even without costume and disguise, Humphries in Edna's voice whips up the tired crew and scattered audience as the band builds to the song's climax:

'So . . . now . . . gooooood-bye
I got my act together and my head held high
So high
I'm a merry widow with a roving eye
Yet I get so terribly shy

When the time finally comes for me to say
Was it good for you too, possums . . .?!'

Down below all of us shout 'Yes!'

'And gooooood-bye . . . good-night. Darlings.'

The smoke stops. Humphries is lowered down. The band plays the show's samba reprise with Humphries twisting in Dame Edna's eccentric dance and blowing a Rio carnival whistle. And then, almost as abruptly as it started, the technical is over, and Humphries has left the stage.

'Who's for north London?' Humphries says. Davidson and I join him. He's in a long zebra-striped mohair overcoat. His black fedora is pulled down at a raffish angle over his face. Humphries lugs two plastic bags full of stuff as he exits wearily out of the backstage door and on to Drury Lane. He stands under the portico facing the Fortune Theatre across the street, the scene of earlier, more punishing theatrical memories.

We walk toward Covent Garden looking for a taxi which, like the man's purse Humphries carries, somehow he can never seem to find. But finally a taxi appears, and Humphries slumps exhausted into it. He props his black and white wing-tipped shoes up on the jump seat. The cab rolls north toward Hampstead. Davidson glances mournfully out the window.

'I'd like to write tomorrow,' Davidson says.

'That's OK. I think we're in pretty good shape. That's why we tried out in Blackpool and Bournemouth. Les was a little ropey, but he's OK.'

'Catch-69 worked.'

Humphries nods and falls silent. Then: 'You know when I rewrote the lyrics to "Shyness" I forgot "bashful". Hard to rhyme. But I got it. "I met Dolly Parton in Nashville/But I didn't sing 'cause I'm bashful . . ." '

Davidson smiles. 'Edna's *Rainwoman* worked.'

'Yes, but *Scandal* did nothing.'

Davidson agrees. 'You know, I read somewhere that Hoffman interviewed forty autistic people to do the part.'

'He's finally discovered that actors do research,' says Humphries.

'Hoffman's doing a Shakespeare for Peter Hall. *Richard the Third*, I think.'

'I wonder', says Humphries, 'if he's going to interview hunch-backs for it.'

2

Dame Edna Teeters on the Brink of Fashion

'Can you imagine a dandy addressing the common herd, except to make game of them?'

Charles Baudelaire, *Intimate Journals*

Dame Edna stands at the top of the circular staircase that leads to the Theatre Royal's Dress Circle bar. The day is bright and blowy with a shine that feels heaven-sent for her opening night. She pauses to adjust her lustrous frock. Downstairs another camera crew gets last-minute orders from the director, with Angela Rippon, another famous female media face, waiting to share perky confidences with her. Dame Edna is relaxed and eager. Her blue eyes are wide with fun.

'You're looking very nice this morning, Dame Edna.'

'This is my opal dress, John. It's inspired by Australia's gem – its national gem – the opal.'

Humphries, who has described himself as an 'Aussie *arriviste*', is also a dandy. He has detailed knowledge of nineteenth-century *fin de siècle* Europe and the aesthetes who made a romance of individualism. Over the years Humphries has affected the dandy's advertisements of impertinence and leisure: the monocle, the walking stick, the silk polka-dot cravat or bow tie, the long hair. In his Dimitri Major tailored suits and his Jermyn Street shirts, he cuts a fine, colourful figure. Humphries, the self-confessed *parvenu*, wants to be accepted into the mainstream of society; but Humphries the satirist wants out of it.

This contradiction coalesces in Dame Edna. Through her, Humphries allows the audience to share and to excuse his exhilaration at bad taste and his aristocratic pleasure in giving offence. Through Dame Edna he vents both the dandy's insolent superiority and his rebellion against the rigidities of the workaday world, using the solvent of wit to bend that world to him. 'Most personalities have been obliged to be rebels. Half their strength has been wasted in friction,' wrote Oscar Wilde, another dandy who, like Humphries, used joking as a form of 'non-friction' to smooth his way into the English mainstream. 'Such battles do not always intensify strength: they often exaggerate weakness.'

For both Wilde and Humphries, the dandy makes a subversive spectacle of perfect poise. Frivolity stage-manages this masterful show of equanimity by disguising anger with laughter. 'I keep my serious intentions very carefully and cunningly disguised,' said Humphries in 1974. 'I insist vociferously on my total flippancy and superficiality. I maintain to the death that I am merely filling my own evenings. And I think that as Australia becomes more and more regimented and humourless that [even] if it's the pose of the buffoon and dilettante, it's important that there be a few around.' The perfect personality, according to Wilde, was 'one who is not wounded, or maimed, or worried, or in danger'. In Dame Edna Humphries too has found a powerful way of dissimulating his anxieties and turning the public life around him into a kind of Superbia.

Dame Edna epitomises the power of a contemporary dandy's imagination to both revenge and enthral the world on its own terms. Dame Edna's magnificent existence gives Humphries a similar aura of mysterious prowess, while allowing him to pass in the vulgar world as a normal citizen. 'Every dandy *dares* but he dares with tact,' wrote Jules Barbey D'Aurevilly in his treatise on the subject. Dame Edna is a study in dramatic tact. Dame Edna negotiates for Humphries between his originality and his ambitiousness, his comic aggression and his good breeding, his narcissism and his decency. Dame Edna exudes a passionate gregariousness that allows Humphries, the aesthete, a proud and solitary self-consciousness. Dame Edna can revel in the vertigo of people's heads turning at the spectacle she makes of herself, while Humphries can remain properly sedate. Dame Edna can brag about the glitterati among whom she moves, a momentum

29

generated solely by her creator; and Humphries can exhibit a blasé disinterest about the whole embarrassing, tainted business of fame and fortune. Humphries has contrived to be a gentleman spectator at Dame Edna's famous career, a king among dandies who has found the perfect incognito. His public composure and bemusement at Edna's grandiosity satisfy the dandy's impulse to make a legend at once of his mystery, his exquisite originality, and his social finesse. It's she, not he; it's he, not she.

This agile shell game of personality works the dandy's trick of equating *seeming* with *being*. Dame Edna personifies the boldness of action, the sumptuous impertinence, the breathtaking self-absorption which Humphries has split off from himself but which still allows him, as D'Aurevilly has written of all dandies, 'to make rules that shall dominate the most aristocratic and most conservative sets'. Through Dame Edna, Humphries' progress in English and Australian society has been impressive. Prince Charles, an 'Ednabopper' of long standing, comes occasionally to Humphries' house in Hampstead for dinner.

Dame Edna descends the staircase waving to imaginary crowds and moving to imaginary music. The performing self is the perfected self, the self surrounded by light and glory, the self empowered and invulnerable. And Dame Edna embodies the fantasy. Neither she nor her creator are dreaming of mere approval on this opening night. They want something more daring and dangerous from the public: total capitulation. In this dry run Dame Edna has won the game before the first ball is pitched. Says Angela Rippon, totally in tune with Dame Edna's fantasy, 'That regal megastar, Dame Edna Everage. A great pleasure. A great entrance. To the manner born.'

Humphries' performing day begins with Dame Edna reinventing him and his past for British Airways' in-flight video: 'The show's about me, really. It's a vehicle for me. Of course my manager, Barry Humphries, appears in his various guises, but I'm the draw card. It's funny, isn't it? An ordinary housewife transported into this world of make-believe. The Theatre Royal, Angela, too.'

'Royal, of course, being the operative word because it's been

30

a place where many members of the royal family have come in their time.'

'They come to me. They're close personal friends. They adore you, they told me.'

'Oh, that's very nice.'

'They sent their love, as a matter of fact. I said I'd tell you.'

'You've actually had a member of the royal family in one of your shows, haven't you? Major Ronald Ferguson.'

'Oh yes. Major Ferguson. Well, he's an honorary royal . . . ha, ha! He's delightful. He's Fergie's father,' says Dame Edna, proud enough of the connection to reproduce a photo of the Major with her in the programme. 'He appeared on the stage at a charity night. He was criticised by a lot of yukkie downmarket press people. But it was a charity night to help people. There was nothing undignified. In fact, it's an honour to be on stage with me.'

'Oh, very much so,' says Angela, who was coaxed out from behind her BBC newsreader's desk to show her legs in a TV dance routine with the famous music hall team of Morecambe and Wise. 'You've had the opportunity of meeting many royals and, like them, you must be someone who is constantly under scrutiny. Do you feel that you're under similar pressure?'

'I do, Angela,' Dame Edna says, taking her arm. 'At the moment, you know, I'm having a nice intimate talk with you; and yet I feel there's a camera watching me the whole time. It's a spooky feeling.'

The camera stops, and they move to the next setup in the bar where tea has been placed on a table in front of the sofa where they'll sit.

'You don't have to promote my show continually, darling. We can talk about other things,' Dame Edna says to Rippon, who laughs heartily since Dame Edna is one long advertisement for herself.

'Do you go to America much?'

'No, I don't. I'm a bit . . . They haven't quite cottoned on to me. They will. After all, they speak English, but what are they? Puerto Rican Eskimos.'

31

'I worked there for a while,' says Angela, who left the BBC for a fling with the American media. 'You have to get used to the fact that they do speak a totally different language.'

'I have a feeling I'm going to be a sensation . . . if I'm alive to enjoy it.'

'Do you think that awful Barry Humphries is going to wear you out?' says Angela, one female professional to another.

'He's exhausting,' says Dame Edna.

'He's over-committed you, has he?'

Dame Edna, surprised by Angela Rippon's confident banter, gives a high-pitched guffaw and stops in her tracks. A leggy blonde appears from behind the lights. 'Sorry, Dame Edna,' says Lizzie Spender, Humphries' girlfriend and the actress-writer daughter of the poet Stephen Spender, as she yanks a loose thread off the opal dress. Dame Edna and Angela sit down on the plush red sofa. The camera rolls and both players in this game continue without missing a beat. Dame Edna regards the tea: 'Oh look, there's a cup of tea waiting for us. Yes, I am a caring person. And I cared so much I arranged this for you, Angela.'

'How very kind of you,' she says. 'We were talking just now about the royal family and the amazing exposure that they have. You handle that so well. Have they ever asked your advice on perhaps how they might cope with the pressures of the job?'

'Well, they have. That was one of the biggest compliments I've ever been paid, passengers. The phone rang. I remember vividly. It was about three o'clock in the morning. And it was a very famous member of the royal family. I can't divulge who she is. I'm sorry. Protocol forbids it . . .'

'Of course not.'

'. . . But she sits on a throne and wears a crown. And her name begins with "E". I can say . . . no . . . more. And she's Church of England. She said to me, "I'm thinking of going shopping in Harrods tomorrow." She said, "I'm going to be mobbed by people, but I want to be anonymous. What should I do?" I said, "Wear a simple headscarf with pictures of dogs with their tongues hanging out and horseshoes all over it." Simple, isn't it? To us it would seem so simple. With a funny old coat. She rang me the

next night. And she said, "Edna – may I call you Edna? . . ."
I said, "Of course." And she said, "It worked like a charm."
She said no one asked for her autograph. She passed unnoticed
in that beautiful shop. And that was a suggestion of mine. I like
to help people in that way. It's amazing what a headscarf can do,
mmmmn? It wouldn't work with me. I've tried it. Naturally, it
wouldn't disguise me because I'm, well, very, very well-known.'

'And you wouldn't want to disguise that beautiful head of
hair.'

'No, I wouldn't. And also frankly, I don't like being anonymous.
I've a very high profile, and I like it that way. Sorry. Call me old-
fashioned.'

'You've been coming to Britain for many years. In fact you first
came here as a tourist yourself.'

'I was on a boat at first, not even travelling on a plane. We had
a marvellous time. I was just an ordinary Melbourne housewife,
little dreaming that one day I'd be a megastar. We went to all the
places – Westminster Abbey, the Tower of London where those
old Beefeaters were. It was not . . . well, it was the early fifties.
The Beefeaters were a bit hungry. They looked as if they could do
with a little beef, those poor old Beefeaters. Actually they were
eating ravens at the Tower of London when I was there. It was
a big scandal. They were eating raven sandwiches. Poor little legs
sticking out . . .'

At this point, Dame Edna picks up her teacup, lifts it to her
lips, and in a moment of inspired capriciousness, refuses to lower
it. 'Would you like to give a message of welcome to Britain
to many of the people who are travelling today?' says Angela
Rippon, asking Edna for a moment of earnestness which it is
not within her power to produce. She looks over at Dame Edna,
whose nose is buried inside the cup from which she seems to
guzzle. For a split second, amidst the dead air and the sight
of Dame Edna lost to her cup, Rippon is confounded: 'Dame
Edna?'

'Oh. Yes,' she says, finally looking up. 'You're going to have
the experience of a lifetime. Sorry, I was drinking my tea then.
I wanted to see what the tea leaves said. I'm sorry, I'm a little

superstitious.' She extends the cup mischievously toward Angela Rippon: 'Can you see them there?'

'Yes.'

'What do you see there?' says Dame Edna, dropping the interviewer in it.

'Well,' she says. 'Good fortune and full houses at the Drury Lane.'

Dame Edna peers into the cup: 'I think I can. Bless you for mentioning my show. One of the things to see in London is my show. A limited season. But it's a hot ticket. There are lots of other things . . .'

Dame Edna is frisky today. While we wait for the gladioli to arrive so Dame Edna can throw them from the balcony on to a hastily assembled throng, she suddenly bolts into the grand red-carpeted foyer with Dennis Smith and Lizzie Spender scampering behind her. Dame Edna is putting her glasses on the bronze bust of Ivor Novello.

'That looks good,' says Lizzie Spender.

'What we should do is get a donation from those "Hello Possum" glasses and cover all the statues.'

'Get the company to give us about a dozen rejects. And somehow attach them around the back.'

'That can be done,' says Smith, who adds another note to a legal pad already surprisingly full for this hour. 'Steve rang up and suggested a photograph of Joan and Edna after the show.'

'Joan?'

'Joan Collins.'

'That upstart is going to come to my show?' says Dame Edna. 'Is Bungalow Bill coming?'

'No,' says Smith, of Collins' much publicised toy boy. 'Bungalow's stopped the extensions and the erecting.'

'In my last show, I'd pick up the phone and talk to Joan,' Dame Edna says to me. 'I'd say, "How's Bungalow Bill? Oh, he's planning an extension?"'

'A photograph might be appropriate.'

'I don't know about that,' says Dame Edna. 'She didn't pay for her ticket.'

34

'Sort of singing for her supper?'

Dame Edna smiles. 'I'll wear my Tony Newley T-shirt. "What Kind of Fool Am I?" ' Dame Edna's reflex betrays the ingrained first principle of Humphries' dandyism: always to expect the unexpected.

But the unexpected has to be seen to be believed. And to achieve the show of effortless aplomb, the dandy lavishes painstaking attention on every detail of his effect. This commitment of time and money to something so transitory as a brief glimpse of his extraordinariness gives the dandy, the prince of vanity, a sense of aristocratic, almost heroic, frivolity. Through Dame Edna, Humphries has turned his sense of refinement and well-judged audacity into a star turn. His eternal vigilance was apparent at the afternoon tech rehearsal as Humphries put Dame Edna and his other characters through their paces. ('Don't forget there are people up there in the upper circle,' he cajoled the *softig* four-girl chorus, collectively dubbed the 'Lesettes'. 'You've got to speak to them all. There's nothing like sitting in the upper circle and never being looked at.') Dame Edna is Humphries' public prank, an extension of a life-long appetite for putting himself at the centre of stage-managed happenings.

'We were at Ronnie Scott's one night,' recalls Ian Davidson. 'As we were getting up from the table and getting our coats, Barry went ahead. We finished up on the pavement and waved down a cab. As we drove along, the cab driver said, "Eh? Is that Mr Barry Humphries in the back?" Barry said yes. The cab driver said, "Can I say, Mr Humphries, how much I admire your art?" Barry said, "Oh, thank you very much." The cab driver said, "In fact, would you have a drink with me?" Barry said, "Yes, if you'd like." The cab driver reached down and picked up a tray with champagne and glasses! Barry'd been out, organised the cab, and got back in the time it took us to get our coats.'

When the smoke lifts from the last stage effect, Humphries has cleared off, padding his way back to the dressing room. A strange lassitude fills the theatre in the final hours before the opening. Humphries' dresser, Katie Harris, has turned a costume trunk into a table, a kind of altar of artifice on which many of the disembodied features of Humphries' characters are on view. The table holds Dame Edna's natural wisteria wig, her rings and diamanté bracelets, Sir Les's fluorescent-green socks and his brown-and-white platform shoes, whose soles are stamped 'Made from genuine dead kangaroo'. There is also a box of black-and-white publicity postcards of Humphries in bow tie, with one eye hidden under the brim of his fedora and the other eye glaring up at the viewer. 'I look like a minor surrealist painter in that,' says Humphries, who has befriended such major surrealists as Salvador Dali and Marcel Duchamp, as he gets into his terry-cloth robe. He takes the day's mail and sits down at his dressing table where his make-up and brushes have been laid out as meticulously as instruments in an operating theatre. Aerosols of hair spray and deodorant, pots of make-up, a polishing pen for Edna's nails, a bottle of Lea & Perrins Worcestershire Sauce (the finishing touch to Sir Les's ruffled tuxedo shirt) are ranged against the back mirror. At his right hand is a small palette for blending the make-up; at his left is Sir Les's snaggle-toothed denture. A white towel has been laid out in the centre of the dressing table on which are three sable brushes and two Hudson's Eumenthol jujubes. To the left of the make-up but no less important to Humphries' backstage ritual is the telephone. Beside it, Elia Kazan's *A Life* inscribed from me on this opening night: 'One legend of vindictive triumph deserves another.'

Humphries sits at his dressing table reading the day's mail, itself a fair barometer of his talent for astonishment. A lady from Blackpool writes to complain that she's been upset for two days over Dame Edna's mockery of bereavement. A single parent from Surrey giggles along in Edna's idiom ("gladdies", "possums", "nice"). Someone has cut out an ad for the show and scrawled across it: 'Take that shit off your face and do some work you lazy bugger.' And Doris from Bournemouth writes: 'Nine days ago you were kind enough to point out to me in front of 2,000 people the discrepancies in my bedroom decor. REMEMBER . . . you called it that "hell-hole in Bournemouth". I have to tell you, and I think you'll understand, Dear Dame Edna, that ever since I have been unable to sleep a *wink*. The mistakes of my former choices glare at me accusingly and will not be dismissed.' She wants £600 for redecorating her flat. 'Dearest darling Dame Edna, will you be my Fairy Godperson and grant my tiny little wish?'

Humphries himself is hardly ensconced in luxury. The dressing room consists of a small changing room and a large dingy waiting room with a sofa bed, two chairs, and a table, on which bottles of soft drinks and mineral water have been set out for opening night. Bouquets from well-wishers have been placed around the room, but nothing can renovate its drabness. There is not a picture on the wall, not a lick of new paint. The sense of colour, texture, fun, which so distinguishes Humphries' performances on stage, is entirely absent from the grey room as if all energy and imagination were being saved for front of house. But the barrenness and boredom that the dressing room exudes provide the climate that feeds the exasperation that Humphries turns into outrageousness.

'I'm always conscious of the desert inside Australia, of the vacuum,' he has said. 'Sunday afternoon in Melbourne, the exquisite boredom. The exhilarating depression. Neat houses. Somewhere down the street there's a Celica being cleaned; otherwise no sign of life. That appeals to me in a terrible way. But I feel too there's a decadence, amongst all the health and the prosperity.' Edna, Sandy, even garrulous Sir Les are, by Humphries' own admission, 'portraits of bores'; products of a subversive imagination which sees itself as 'sinking artesian wells into the suburban desert, drawing up composite portraits'. The notion pleases him. 'I'm in the boredom-alleviation business, aren't I? This art is meant to be an antidote to boredom,' he says, speaking as much for himself as his audience.

The telephone rings; and while Humphries eases into what sounds like a long conversation, I retreat to the waiting room and my book, J. K. Huysmans' *Against Nature*, which had such an influence on Humphries in his university days. 'I became a sort of fifties' Des Esseintes,' he told me, about the novel's aesthete hero. 'I was a kind of "Dez" Esseintes as it were.' So Humphries would introduce himself at parties. 'I used to feel slightly like him.

37

Like a Church of England version of old Dez.' Soon I am reading, '. . . then his soul was swept by tumultuous emotions: a longing to take vengeances for the boredom inflicted on him in the past, a craving to sully what memories he retained of his family . . .'

In *Who's Who in Australia* Humphries' entry includes this sentence: 'self-educated, attended Melbourne Grammar School'. The man who would become a dandy of delirium traces the origins of his rebellion to the oppressiveness of Melbourne Grammar School, the city's poshest private educational institution – the one that the upwardly mobile Humphries family chose for their first-born, and to which he was admitted in 1947 at the age of thirteen. Humphries was not happy with the choice and has spoken of the move from his friends at the nearby Camberwell Grammar School as 'a great bereavement'. The trauma has never been forgiven by Humphries or forgotten by Melbourne Grammar. As he later wrote:

> What a long waiting list to get in there!
> Unless your dad was an old boy or Vicar,
> Though donations of cash to the bishop
> Helped many to jump the queue quicker.
> But what a strange school to *bribe* yourself into –
> How odd that one had to form queues
> To get into a concentration camp
> Where so few of the inmates were Jews.

Over the years Humphries has been sensationally banned from the Old Melbournians' Association for the irreverent sculpture 'Old Fool's Tie': a bottle of beer with a Melbourne Grammar tie knotted around it. Humphries was eventually welcomed back, and made an equally sensational return to the fold at an Old Melbournians' night in his honour in 1971: he entered riding on a camel.

Dame Edna, a swaggering comic grotesque of philistinism and propriety, owes some of her paternity to Humphries' fierce disgust at the blinkered conformity of the school and its masters, whom he has called in print 'picturesque ignoramuses'. Humphries, whose bibliomania started by the age of nine, had already acquired 'a snobbishness about books'. Says Humphries, 'I was in fact very precocious in my reading before I was thirteen. I was familiar with the works of Picabia, with the writings of Salvador Dali, with most of the texts by the French nineteenth-century writers who had inspired the surrealists, with the Dadaists. I knew all about Cubism and was indeed painting in the Cubist style.' Already a talented painter in oils, Humphries had been introduced through the influence of one Camberwell art teacher, Ian Bow, to 'the exhilaration of eccentricity' and the ravishing thought of 'what a marvellous liberating thing it must be to be an artist, to be able to escape from the humdrum world of mathematics, compulsory sport, gymnasium, cold showers, boxing and all these terrible imperatives of a boys' school'. When Humphries was five and his mother had asked him what he wanted to be, he answered, 'A genius.' But Melbourne Grammar put no premium on originality. 'It's significant that very very few people of any artistic sensibility at all emerged from the school after the war,' he has said. 'But out of a kind of rebellion against the school system I developed certain techniques which have been very useful to me in my subsequent artistic life – certain forms of rebellion and anarchy, certain artistic methods.' The humiliation and frustration that Humphries felt at Melbourne Grammar was still apparent years later when he tried to write about 'the terror and bewilderment' of the first weeks at the school. He wrote in 1977, in an article entitled 'The Getting of Ignorance':

Aged masters slouched across the quadrangle in gowns so tattered and green with antiquity that they resembled the ragged creepers which descended from the bluestone walls of the school chapel. Prefects and probationers, the school's licensed bullies, preyed mercilessly upon the new boys, and anyone who had not been recently scalped by a barber and who was caught cap-less on the Toorak tram might expect a thrashing from some impetiginous youth but a few years his senior ... the boarders formed an elitist group of the kind even a socialist would grudgingly admire, uniformly dull of wit, loud-mouthed and ferociously conformist.

Humphries also hated the school uniform which draped his dreamy artistic persona in a navy-blue serge version of a 1930s business suit, turning him and the rest of the luckless internees of Melbourne Grammar into 'double-breasted, tie-pinned parodies of Ronald Colman or the Man from Prudential'. This later seemed to Humphries a self-fulfilling prophecy. 'Most of my contemporaries at school entered the World of Business, the logical destiny of bores.' The school's motto was 'Work and Pray'. But it was sports and the homogeneity of attitude that games instil to which the school seemed dedicated. Humphries was not, and never would be, a team player. 'I hated sports. I still do,' says Humphries, whose aversion to physical exercise earned him the nickname 'Granny' at Camberwell and 'Queenie' at Melbourne Grammar. 'Where was I to find an identification? Amongst a handful of people at school and in literature. It didn't take me long to realize that the people who taught English were barely literate and had just about waded through some of the set texts. I was already interested in other things. For example, at a school fête I bought a lot of the 1920–30 American editions of the novels and stories of Scott Fitzgerald who hadn't been reprinted then. In books about American small-town life like Sinclair Lewis' *Main Street* and Sherwood Anderson's *Winesburg, Ohio*, I got a strong echo of Melbourne. I became rather interested in the decade just before my own birth. It's a common phenomenon. I was interested in people like Ronald Firbank and the Sitwells.'

Humphries' sport was frequenting second-hand bookshops, especially one on Bourke Street whose owner, a Mrs Bird, called him 'Mr Humphries' and imbued him with an enthusiasm he still holds for the 'curdled late romantics' like Ann Radcliffe, Monk Lewis, Charles Robert Maturin, Byron, Mary Shelley. Even rummaging in the dusty shop among stacks of old volumes had maverick overtones to Humphries, because his parents insisted he have new books. 'Schoolboys generally didn't go into second-hand bookshops,' Humphries says. 'One was discouraged from "dirty books", that is to say books that other people had owned. It was a very hygienic society. Hygiene was a great god.'

As a child, Humphries dreamed of being a magician. 'The big

advantage of being a magician was that you could make people disappear.' But at Melbourne Grammar he discovered that if he couldn't make the school disappear, his laughter could keep the people in it at bay. Humphries found himself in the dandy's dilemma: at once dominated by and attempting to dominate convention. In this delicate situation wit was the acceptable face of insolence; and his school years were spent learning effrontery. 'We sat', he remembers about his small circle of friends, 'in a rebellious and probably rather irritating little group at the back of the class, drawing attention wherever possible, to areas of ignorance in the schoolmaster. These were considerable, I need hardly say.' He acted out what he calls his 'dandiacal rage' in caricature both of the teachers and of himself. 'I had always drawn, particularly caricatures,' he has said. 'I consider that my gift for caricature is closely related to the theatre work that I do now, because I am in a way a theatrical caricaturist, or cartoonist, in that I strive to reduce to the barest essential lines a complex subject for the edification and amusement of the public. I used to do caricatures of teachers on the blackboard. So when they entered the classroom they could see themselves up there on the board to the amusement of others. I found I had a gift for amusing my schoolmates which, in a way, protected me from bullies. If you could make them laugh, they wouldn't hit you.'

A renegade reputation requires courage; and Humphries, a church-going and well-bred young man, had to summon it up. 'It didn't come naturally to me,' he says. 'One had to impersonate a brazen person. One had to act as if one were courageous.' Astonishment was linked early in Humphries' mind with liberation and power. 'The ability to startle people, to go *against* the tide, gave me a sense of identity and allayed my fears about myself,' says Humphries. He was emboldened by the sure knowledge that 'I had absolutely no desire to be like *them*, whatever happened – *them* were these boys in school uniforms.' Humphries grew his hair long. 'By modern standards it wasn't long. But it was certainly long for the school, where they insisted, "Long hair is dirty hair." I later had that translated into Latin – *Crines Longi, Crines Foetidi* – and called it the motto of the school. There was such a

41

strong emotional feeling about long hair. It aroused such primitive revulsion and fear in people that I knew I was on the right track.' Humphries also refused to join the Cadets, a compulsory school activity that meant changing into military uniform and learning military drill. 'It was very hard,' he recalls. 'I'd been reading the memoirs of Siegfried Sassoon, and I learnt about conscientious objection. I was told the only way to get out of Cadets was for health reasons. Since I was not unhealthy, I told the headmaster I was a conscientious objector. It had a mesmerising effect on him. He was so startled by this explanation, which had never been put forward before, that I got off Cadets.'

Although he bucked the system, Humphries could not always beat it. He became a subject of scandal and concern when his ruse for avoiding school sports was uncovered. As he explained it, 'I had to have my name ticked off while I was dressed in my football attire. Then an accomplice would put my school uniform into a Gladstone bag. After my name had been ticked off, I would go to the school lavatories and hide in a cubicle. A few minutes later there would be a tap on the door, and the Gladstone bag would slide underneath it. I would change out of football attire into my school uniform, escape through the gates and on to a tram into town to the second-hand bookshops. I did the same for this friend, you see, on the night that he had to turn out, as it was called. This went on for over a year, until one day there was a tap on the door. It opened, and the head of school was standing there. He said, "The game's up, Humphries." I'll never forget those words, "The game's up, Humphries." I was caned. It sometimes pleases me to think that this schoolboy, only a couple of years older than me, who unmasked me so brutally and punished me so mercilessly, is now a traveller for a cheap brand of port. Dame Nature, as Edna would call it, has a way of settling some of these accounts.' The humiliation was compounded by the headmaster, who called Humphries into his study and said, 'I hope you're not turning pansy.' Says Humphries, 'I hadn't the *faintest* idea of what he meant, except that it was rather threatening. There was no way to formulate a reply to this.'

Then, as now, Humphries' way of dealing with his anger was

to perform a kind of psychic ju-jitsu – to 'throw people' by using the force of their attitude to defeat them. He exaggerated the implications of stupidity until it became laughable. Having been labelled effeminate and made to attend football matches in the name of school spirit, Humphries sent up both injustices by sitting with his back to the playing field and knitting.

In later years, still exacting comic revenge for old psychic wounds, he turned the memory of his humiliating encounter with the headmaster into a set piece of vindictive triumph, 'A Melancholy Memoir', a poem he recited at speech day at a New South Wales country public school:

One dread day I was called to his study
They said, Humphries, you're wanted by the Head
The chill memory lingers, he folded his fingers
'I hope you're not turning pansy?' he said.
I stared at the wall and I can't now recall
How the interview ended, or how
I struggled through school, boring philistine cruel
And became the ratbag you're looking at now.
But public schools and cold showers were no respecters
    of flowers
Whether pansies or gladdies or dahlias
And the thought has oft entertained me that the
    prefects who caned me
Have all ended up middle-aged failures.

Last year grown up and brave
I saw my Headmaster's grave
A plain tombstone he had, nothing fancy
And there in the grass, six feet up from his arse,
Grew a single, impenitent pansy.

At Melbourne Grammar Humphries was, as he said, 'becoming conscious of "The Enemy". He was the Philistine who plagued my favourite nineteenth-century aesthetes, now reincarnated as the captain of the school. There were several of them, of course, during my education, but prefects and captains merge, in my memory into one odious type: a bully with the face of a still-born stockbroker.' Humphries also had identified shock as a positive force in battling smug credulity. 'It seemed to me that the best art was art that shocked people, that jolted them into some kind of sense of outrage,' he said. His first public reflection on the subject was an essay on modern art for *The Melbournian* (May 1950) in which he considered public response to surrealism and cubism, only to find no generational parallels of temperament 'save in this one particular: their joint capacity for being "shocked and surprised" within their own set limits of "naughtiness"; but not beyond . . .' In the Humphries canon, the word *beyond* takes on a prophetic meaning all its own. For although comedians traditionally are the instinctive enemies of boundaries, no clown has ever set out in quite such a systematic public way as Humphries to test the contemporary limits of the acceptable.

The older generation of clowns to whom Humphries is a legitimate successor took their urgency from poverty; Humphries took his urgency from privilege. They wanted a way into the mainstream; Humphries wanted a way out of it. 'The word art never entered my head,' Chaplin said, speaking of the time in music hall, before it did. And Keaton was equally matter-of-fact: 'I never realised that I was doing anything but trying to make people laugh when I threw my custard pies and took my pratfalls.' The old guard were inspired by business, not art. Humphries was inspired by art, not business. Even at grammar school, he felt a special kinship to the German Dadaists and their subversive gestures of unreason. The Dadaists rejected a bourgeois world that made war; Humphries rejected a suburban world that made banality. The Dadaists were zanies of insubordination who touched in Humphries a yearning for permanent and playful revolt. 'I was instantly fired with admiration,' he says of his first exposure to them in William Gaunt's *March of the Moderns*. 'It seemed to me that, even though these stunts had occurred forty years before, they still produced a *frisson* that was the kind of artistic performance that I aspired to.'

Humphries wanted to create his own 'ferocious Dada jests'. He helped to form the Art Club and to start a Dadaist faction, which organised a sculpture exhibition at the school. But the forces of authority won the first round against Humphries' aspiring anarchy. The Dada sculptures were judged to be too subversive and were withdrawn. But Humphries' gift for provocation, so carefully held in check in his Melbourne Grammar days, was unleashed on the world when he took up his infamous residence at Melbourne University between 1951 and 1953.

'The only Australian who ever understood the Dada principle of *provocation*', wrote Robert Hughes in *The Art of Australia* (1966), 'was the actor Barry Humphries, who organised two Dada shows in Melbourne and (before leaving for England in the late 1950s) performed a number of gratuitous public acts whose ferocity and point might have pleased Tristan Tzara.' The Dada exhibitions and the pranks made a legend both of Humphries' desire to shine and of his sense of displacement. 'It was important to emancipate oneself from this suburban milieu because it was so seductive and oppressive. You thought it was inescapable. It was so disturbing,' says Humphries. 'I had absolutely no idea of what I would do in life. I remember a friend of mine had a printing press. I had a visiting card made with my name on it. He said, "We had better put occupation." I said, "Put 'Dilettante'." A very effective card to have. In fact, it didn't entertain me very much to be a dilettante. I became a specialist.'

The first Pan-Australian Dada Exhibition (1952) announced Humphries' expertise at creating a panic. Humphries was not only inventing himself, he was inventing his Australia, which he lists as his hobby in *Who's Who*. 'I had to incorporate into my new portrait of Australia, an irritant,' he says. 'Something which would annoy the spectator or listener to the point where he *had to* look or hear what I was saying. To affront and outrage them so they'd say, "But how? Why?" And then, perhaps, to stop for a second and actually tell lies about a place, to defame venerated figures and things.

'I had packages, for instance, printed up called PLATITOX (really just sawdust in packages). It was a "poison" to put in creeks and streams to kill the platypus which is a very much protected, loved, endearing indigenous Australian animal. In fact, if there was a chance of saving a platypus, at some risk to myself, I would probably attempt it. So why have an exhibit which offers a pesticide to destroy these animals? *Because* everything was in its place in Australia. On the package in small print it said it was also rather good for aboriginals. Aboriginals didn't exist; and in a way, one was led to believe that they lived a long way away and were dying out anyway, which was terribly sad but there it was . . . This was all part of the tyranny of niceness and order. I didn't want to *overthrow* order. I just instinctively wanted to give it a bit of a *jolt*, so that people could *see* it.'

POX VOBISCUM was the motto of the Dada Group. The public who strolled into the Men's Lounge of the Student Union and were surrounded by the sound of diabolical laughter counterpointed by a record rigged to repeat from *South Pacific* – 'And you will note there's a lump in my throat/I'm in love . . . I'm in love . . . I'm in love . . .' – soon got the splenetic message. Humphries had filled a pair of rubber Wellington boots full of custard and titled them 'Pus and Boots'. Under the title 'Her Majesty's Male', Elizabeth II was shown with five o'clock shadow. The punning titles of many of the works disabused art of its gravity and proclaimed Dada's faith in life as a joke: 'Yes, We Have No Cézannas', 'Roof of the Cistern Chapel', 'James Juice', 'Christopher Fried', 'Erasmus-Tazz', 'My Foetus Killing Me', 'Purée of Heart'. Humphries created a series of works that rotted and smelled to send up the notion of genteel art collecting. He produced 'Shoescape' from old shoes; 'Stinkscape' from lambs' eyes; 'Cake-scape' from cake pressed between glass to create a kind of Jackson Pollock abstraction. 'This endows them with the permanence of the Parthenon,' Humphries told a local newspaper in 1952, already enjoying the slap and tickle of publicity, 'plus undiminished protein value.' To another paper he explained, 'Here are the artistic media which best express the multi-faceted image of Australian life – cake, shoes and tomato sauce. From footwear, custard, and chutney, you can create the Old Masters of the future.'

'Dada', said Tzara, 'shows its truth in action.' Inevitably Humphries and the Dada Group were drawn toward performance.

Their Dada revue *Call Me Madman*! (1952) achieved scandal. The furore was not caused by the blanks being fired over the audience's head, nor the din of the orchestra playing combs, bottles, and gongs, nor the spectacle of Humphries dressed as a nun singing, 'I Wish I Could Shimmy Like My Sister Kate'. What made the front page of the *Melbourne Sun* was the finale, 'The Indian Famine'. A missionary sat across a table from his wife, played by Humphries with a dress over his suit. Between them was a table piled high with cauliflower, cake, and raw meat. 'It looked like a harvest festival,' Humphries recalls. The missionary read aloud statistics of a recent famine. As each horrific figure was announced, the 'wife' laughed and repeated, 'I don't care I've got plenty of food, lots of food. And they've got nothing.' Says Humphries, 'The point was crudely moral in order to dramatise public indifference to these kinds of catastrophes and to provoke respectable undergraduate audiences into some kind of irrational behaviour, some kind of demonstrative feeling.'

Humphries succeeded all too well. As the missionary's broadcast of statistics grew louder, so did the 'wife's' hysterical laughter. They started throwing food at each other; and some food found its way into the audience. The audience started hurling the food at the actors, who in turn threw it back at them. A food fight had begun. 'We had an audience of affluent Australian university students throwing perfectly good food about the auditorium,' explains Humphries, 'while statistics about the current famine were being broadcast over the amplifiers at them, an act therefore of total anarchy. The satirical intention is very apparent in all this. It, however, eluded the audience, who stormed the stage after my blood. I remember hiding in the broom cupboard under the stage.' The Dada Group was banned from ever again using the Student Union theatre.

Humphries also started making a spectacle of himself. He cultivated his legend. 'I was entertained by the idea of slightly fictionalising myself,' he says. Humphries' tailored suits, his still longer hair, his mauve ink (an affectation acquired from reading Ronald Firbank) broadcast the dandy's intention of inhabiting a world of his own. Humphries gathered around him a group of women he dubbed 'hoydens' and 'doxies', one of whom was Germaine Greer. 'He would dress them up as schoolgirls and passionately kiss them in the street,' reports the Australian critic Clive James in his essay 'Approximately in the Vicinity of Barry Humphries', 'until the police arrived, whereupon birth certificates would be produced.'

University life disappointed Humphries because 'everybody was wearing another uniform – an undergraduate uniform – suede shoes, knitted ties, all smoking pipes and drinking beer and doing "grown up" things. That seemed to me appalling too. They were already set on the inexorable path to middle age. So the Dada activities were very important in provoking them. What was almost the most offensive thing was their new-found liberalism. Their tolerance for foreigners. They were reading Hopkins and Eliot. I'd been there. I'd gone beyond all that. I wanted somehow to *scratch* the surface of this liberalism a bit.'

And so began a series of legendary pranks in which Humphries began to move from 'a visual vocabulary to a theatrical one'. The dandy prefers astonishing to pleasing; and terror, as Dame Edna has taught the world, is the ultimate astonishment. In one notorious escapade, Humphries had his accomplice, John Perry, dress as a blind man and take a seat in a non-smoking compartment of a Melbourne commuter train. Perry had dark glasses, his leg in a cast and was reading from a piano roll that looked as if it was braille. Humphries entered the compartment and began to smoke. He was dressed garishly and reading a foreign newspaper. Later, as he got up to exit, he unleashed a barrage of foreign-sounding gibberish, grabbing the 'braille' and tearing it, kicking at the 'blind man's' leg, throwing his spectacles to the floor and leaving. 'Commuters were invariably transfixed in horror,' Humphries says. 'No one ever pursued me. Mind you, I ran as fast as I could. People tried to comfort John Perry. He would always say, "Forgive him." It was also very funny to do, and very hard not to laugh. It's a bit hard to say what effect the stunt was meant to have, since it was meant to amuse us, a kind of outrageous public act.'

The pranks achieved something deeper than visibility for

Humphries. 'I'd found the release of eccentricity which I admired in so many other artists,' he says, seeing in eccentricity 'a means of surviving in a mysteriously oppressive society'. The pranks turned life 'into a mini-spectacle with me as the audience'. They also gave Humphries a 'theatrical thrill', which he explains as 'changing people's lives slightly by making them the witness to some rather remarkable and absolutely inexplicable thing that could not happen in real life'. In one Melbourne stunt, later repeated in London, Humphries buried a roast chicken and a split of champagne in the rubbish bin beside a local bus stop. Then, dressed as a tramp, he came along and started rooting in the rubbish while the bus queue looked on. Says Humphries, 'If they saw a tramp rummaging in a dustbin, people generally averted their eyes as from a kind of social horror. Someone eating garbage. Then suddenly the tramp seemed to be striking it lucky. This struck people as remarkable and somehow inexplicable because they couldn't explain it theatrically. They couldn't say, "Oh no, that's not really a tramp that's someone dressed up as a tramp since *why* would a person do a thing like that? There'd be no point to it." This was before television and *Candid Camera*. The fact is this was not addressed to an audience. The audience was me. It was just really to astonish people with an inexplicable happening.' But Humphries was also trying to inspire 'a chain reaction of irrational behaviour and to get the onlookers themselves to rummage in the garbage in the hope that they would also find similar treasures that had been vouchsafed this tramp'. Later, Humphries would get himself banned temporarily from Qantas flights for tipping a tin of Russian salad into a sick bag, loudly feigning illness, and then eating his 'vomit'. 'If an air hostess sees you,' he said, 'it can produce what I call the Chain Chunder. Five minutes later the pilot is throwing up.'

Humphries, who had dreamed of possessing a magician's omnipotence, had discovered the power of putting feelings into other people. It was a dangerous game, but one with which he experimented after he'd dropped his university studies (law, then liberal arts) and joined the repertory theatre on the Melbourne University campus in the mid-1950s. The actress Zoe Caldwell was part of the same repertory and got caught up in Humphries' masquerade. 'He used to do a very strange thing. He would pretend to be a spastic, a genuine spastic. People would pity him. It's still in Dame Edna – he pushes responses in people. He forces you to feel emotions,' she says. 'I was his "sister". That's what he cast me as. It wasn't my idea of a swell night out. We'd go to a restaurant and ask for tea. The waitress would bring the tea, and he'd take the milk and pour it on his head. The girl was trying to keep her patience. Then Barry would pour the sugar on the floor. He did the whole thing, never stopped. Watching people pity him and pity me, I knew what he was after. He wanted to see the reactions people had to disability. Barry forced you to look at the ugly and the monstrous. He was trying it out. The genesis of what he wants to trap – bogus emotion, denial, what we all do – was there. I think he wants to trap it and say, "Look, look what you do." And so he's outrageous. At parties he used to sing:

"Lasso that spasso
And beat him till he's sweatin'
Lasso that spasso
I'm a-hangin' on to this here cretin . . ."

'People used to say "How cruel," or "Oh, Barry!" That's the response he wanted. He was trying to provoke and entrap their sentimentality. I see this in Edna Everage, only now Barry makes people laugh. He didn't make people laugh too much at the time. He's wonderful as Edna because he's so free, as if he's found exactly what's right for him.'

The Dada antics, to which Dame Edna is heir, turned the deadening tranquillity of Humphries' Australia into an exciting playground. 'This insulated world was comfortable and nice and nothing was really allowed to ruffle the surface,' he says of Melbourne. 'No debt, no poverty, no contamination.' His Dada antics aspired to agitate the community with ideas. They were also meant, by his own admission, 'to prolong childhood and to mock the pretensions of *responsible* people – adults'. Humphries' subsequent flirtation with repertory theatre was seen by him as 'merely a postponement of that *awful* moment when I had to confront what I *really* wanted to do'. In time, Dame Edna would allow Humphries to be perpetually at play in the world. 'I suppose I'm still a Dadaist,' he says. 'Still finding the shock threshold which shifts such a lot, doesn't it? I still succeed in horrifying my countrymen.'

'You can come in, John.'

Humphries is dialling another number, speaking, as I enter, to my reflection in the left-hand corner of his dressing mirror. 'They want me to close the Prince's Trust performance at the Palladium. Frank Sinatra, Sammy Davis Junior and Liza Minnelli are on the bill too.'

The ringing at the other end of the line distracts him. He waits for the connection, holding up his hand to stop conversation like a traffic cop halting a car. He listens gravely, and then, when his turn to speak comes, he says, 'I've been having a most stimulating conversation with your phone machine. Perhaps you can call *me*.' He puts down the grey receiver and turns to face me: relaxed, excited, already watching Edna's persona go by. 'I have to come on late because of my show. I suppose I'll do "My Public", and change the lyrics. But what about them? I don't know too much about them.'

'Well, Sammy Davis is black, one-eyed, and Jewish.'

Humphries' eyes drift away into thought. He mumbles a snatch of song. 'I'm better off than Sammy.' And then, with a clap of high-pitched laughter, he turns back beaming. ' "I may be over-tired and fluish/But at least I'm not one-eyed and black and Jewish." Dare I sing that? They'd never allow it on television.'

The phone rings again. 'Hello, Stephen.' Humphries launches into the description of a dress seen in a Parisian revue that he wants Stephen Adnitt, his designer, to copy. 'It had mirrors on it. Actually around the neck. A kind of V-neck or a yoke of mirrors. But they weren't just smallish. They were rather chunky, like tiles almost. No . . . but you can imagine what happened when the lights hit them because they were separate and moved with the fabric a bit. They sent these rays straight out into the audience

51

. . . Well, no . . . they were sewn on, appliquéd. They belong with the fabric. It was just like a kind of yoke. But it looked very effective because they were largish. They were an inch square or something. Then it threw separate beams into the audience like a mirror ball. Very exciting. It might be nice to have something like that. Also remember on the bill are Liza Minnelli, Sammy Davis, Frank Sinatra, Kiri Te Kanawa – I have to excel them *all* . . .'

While Humphries talks and smiles at Stephen on the other end of the phone, I move away from the dressing table toward the back wall where Katie is hanging up Edna's white evening dress. Edna began life in the late 1950s dressed from Opportunity Shops. But as she has progressed in confidence and class, so too have her costumes. Humphries has always considered fashion as part of modern art, even his essay in *The Melbournian* mentioned the innovations of Schiaparelli and Dior along with painters and philosophers. Dame Edna is a reflection in Humphries, both of his *flaneur*'s fascination with the surface of life and of his caricaturist's ability to capture quickly the essence of its passing show. When Punk hit in the early 1970s, Dame Edna decked herself out in leathers and 'Zandra Rhodes safety pins' to sing 'S & M Lady':

Shave half your head, paint your legs green,
No one's too old for the S & M scene.
Drive them insane, frighten the vicar,
Swing that chain with a big swastika.
S & M Lady, let 'em all go to Hades.

In the late 1970s, when tennis was the rage, Dame Edna was in tennis clothes. At the moment, bowing to the brouhaha over animal rights, she has eschewed her 'pre-conservation mink' for 'humanely culled acrylic'.

Humphries' ever-changing satire on modern manners is inevitably a satire on modern fashion. In the last twenty years, Edna has turned into a clotheshorse of many colours. Edna herself explained the transformation to the *Sunday Telegraph* in 1987, 'As late as the early nineteen seventies, I was still really dressing like a tourist, buying off-the-peg in Oxford Street. I wore a tweed overcoat which may have come from C & A, white vinyl Courrèges-style boots, a hangover from the 1960s and a felt hat in autumnal colours.' But since the late 1970s, when she declared herself a superstar, Dame Edna has had to become the 'glass of fashion and the mould of form'. 'Sometimes the clothes have to be satires on modern styles,' Humphries says. 'In the mid 1970s, Edna appeared in a denim dress. So Edna was wearing things that some of the most fashionably dressed women in the audience were wearing. Suddenly there was the feeling: "Oh we're not laughing at her dresses any more. She's wearing *our* clothes. If anything, she's wearing clothes we can't quite afford." '

Edna's clothes have sometimes been known to bring the house down. 'When I did "The Song of Australia" with Carl Davis, which is the history of Australia set to music, I had a special dress which had a panel that opened up in front revealing the Australian coat of arms *lit up*, flashing. A kangaroo and an emu holding a shield,' says Humphries. 'Also there was a cape that folded up behind the dress. A stagehand pulled a gut in the wings, and the whole thing unfolded behind Edna like enormous wings, which added decibels to the applause. Everyone was cheering and suddenly, at a given signal, the wings went up. The whole pitch of the ovation changed.' Edna has also attempted (and failed) to crash the Royal Enclosure at Ascot wearing a behemoth hat in the shape of the Sydney Opera House, with a shark-infested bay as the brim. She has worn a mini-skirt with appliquéd hand-beaded eyes that wink, a gum-tree frock whith a koala-bear pocket, and a jacket appliquéd with lips. She has worn an Australian flag dress with shoulders in the shape of the Opera House ('our famous facility') and another with gladioli over the shoulder. Dame Edna, who assumes she is the role model for womankind, confesses to one dress tip given her by the Queen: 'Never wear anything that arouses envy in your subjects.'

'. . . And Stephen,' says Humphries, 'the dress actually ought to do something. It'd be very nice if there was something that could be hooked on to a wire so that actually a *huge* cape opened up behind me. But I think the time I've got rushing to the theatre to get miked up is going to be enough trouble. So you know, Stephen . . . That's good, Stephen. Well, have a bit of a think. But, I suppose, it has to be the finale frock to end them all . . . Lovely. Thanks. Good. 'Bye.'

Dennis Smith and the stage manager Harriet Bowdler come into the room. Humphries looks up and starts to sing: 'I may be slightly over-tired and fluish/At least I'm not one-eyed and black and Jewish/Though my hands are hot and clammy/I'm better off than little Sammy . . .' he breaks off, directing his eyes at Dennis. 'You think that might be funny? Why not? Mmn? He goes on about himself, doesn't he? *Ad nauseam.*'

'In superb taste,' says Dennis, who bears a handful of opening night telegrams and a memo about the Prince's Trust performance.

'We've got to have a few references to the people who are there. Little Kiri,' says Humphries, his eyes bright, thinking. 'Of course, they might drop out . . . Well, they won't drop out of this, will they? The Prince's Trust.'

Later, as Humphries freshens up in the bathroom, Harriet turns the sofa into a bed. 'I wonder how many changes of sheets he'll want?' she says.

The pre-opening orders to the ushers from the Drury Lane stage sound through the loudspeakers in Humphries' dressing room. 'They've adjusted the speakers,' Harriet says. 'Barry gets most upset if we play a theatre and the show relay doesn't come back to the dressing room. He likes to hear the audience.'

'He often says "Listen to them, listen to them,"' says Katie, scuttling into the dressing room with Sir Les's padding.

' "Is it a nice crowd?" he'll say. "Who's out there?"' says Harriet. 'He likes to know people are waiting. Sometimes he just needs to know they're waiting.'

Humphries comes out of the bathroom and sits on the edge of the bed. 'I think I'm going to have a ten-minute nap, John.' He pulls down the coverlet. 'It'll go all right tonight, don't you think?'

3

Dame Edna Plays Possum

Superstars may come and go
But there's no other
That folks identify with their own mother;
To think there's people in this room
Who wish they'd sprung out of my womb
That's what my public means to me . . .

Barry Humphries, 'My Public'

The postcard from Ian Davidson says, 'Re: Edna and Embarrassment. Forget embarrassment and class. We failed to mention the terrible embarrassment felt by the child for its *parents'* antics. Not so a *Lahr* perhaps, Dad being licensed – but for the rest of us, very powerful. Regards, Ian D.'

There are other things in my satchel besides the card. A list of questions to ask Humphries. A copy of *Against Nature*. The letter from Humphries agreeing to be interviewed backstage during the Drury Lane run. But I can only focus my attention on one acid thought: where is Humphries? I expected to begin asking him my questions on Friday the day after the opening. We agreed to meet at 7 pm. The show begins at 7.30, but at 7.20, with the rumble of the excited audience already coming over the loudspeakers, he is still nowhere to be found.

Katie bustles in carrying Humphries' overcoat. 'Sorry,' she says. 'It doesn't look good.'

'Did you tell him I was here?'

'He said to tell you sorry he was late.'

On Saturday Humphries drove himself to work, but a bomb threat in central London delayed his arrival until 7.25. Now on Monday, still without an interview, still in the same place at nearly the same time, Harriet sticks her blond head into the dressing room and is startled to see me. 'Didn't Barry's secretary get you? He's got flu,' she says. 'He's a bit of a ratbag about interviews. He's always like this. It's not you.' And then she adds, 'It happens to the stage management too. He's known in certain circles as the "megastar of hollow promises".'

When Humphries does arrive, feeling ill, he's with Lizzie Spender. They carry two of his bright Impressionist landscapes to hang in the dressing room. Liz is in blue jeans and sneakers. 'I don't want resentment time. I'm under a lot of pressure, John,' he says, speaking of Edna's autobiography, which has to be written within the month. 'The publisher's driving me crazy. Today, we lost a few pages on the computer while recopying.'

Katie brings Humphries a mug of thyme tea for his throat. 'Tell the girls please . . . oh, look, have you got a fiver? Tell the girl at the stage door that Matthew Spender — that's Lizzie's brother — is coming at the interval to do some drawings. So do the Lesettes mind if he pops up there and does a few sketches?'

Humphries looks through his mail as he undresses. 'Charity requests,' he says. 'They have phrases like "We realise you must be very busy" or "This will not take up more than a day of your time." I wonder if there'll be a time in the future as I sit in the old comedians' home which I've helped perhaps to wallpaper from a midnight matinée where I'll think, "If only I'd accepted that . . ." or "If only I hadn't thought I was too grand and busy. If only I'd had the time for *all* of these people." '

'If you could free-associate Melbourne in the early nineteen forties and fifties. *Your* Melbourne,' I say, hoping today to be one of the people for whom Humphries has time.

'It's very much to be found in the monologues of Sandy Stone. Suburban gardens. Sprinkler systems. Very ordered. Well, a kind of dullness. Only when I went to Sydney as a student actor in the mid-fifties did I meet a new kind of Australian who you don't find in Melbourne. I met descendants of convicts, a much more raffish society. It came as a jolt to me, living as I had in a rather protected society. My father was a builder, mostly of suburban houses. My mother was a housewife with plenty of people to help her. There was a kind of genteel prudery. There was a variety theatre in Melbourne called the Tivoli, but we only went there a couple of times. My parents disapproved of it because it was the home of *blue* comedians. No one ever knew an actor. One never met one. I think it was vaguely hoped that I might be an architect or something of that kind. And I think later on that was expressed rather more overtly. But the theatre wasn't considered. One only went occasionally to *The Desert Song* and things like that. Revivals and musicals . . .'

Dennis Smith and the production manager Nick Day lurch into the room and into the middle of the interview. 'We just discovered that the Sandy Stone cassette player we use on stage has been knocked off.'

'That means we'd better be very careful,' says Humphries. 'Knocked off? Well, that was on the cards.' He turns to the production manager. 'I tell you what else is worrying me, Nick. Last night when I was Edna, the smoke was fine except that a third of the stage was bare. It's a rotten, rotten look.'

'Bare?'

'No smoke on it. And the smoke was very uneven. Now it seems to me there must be an intense draught coming from the scene bay. They must close it off. There's a vertical curtain there. That could be dropped to start with. Let's do everything we can to get an even carpet of smoke. Happens in every other show you see, I don't see why we can't have it. I mean, it looks very bad just to have a bit of smoke. It spoils the whole effect. It really has to be . . .' Humphries takes an intake of breath to indicate astonishment. 'I'm more and more convinced, Dennis, that the box is the wrong box for the stunt. It doesn't have the same effect on the audience, *at all*. I'm not satisfied with the explanation that it's too dangerous. I really think, although it's a bit of a bore and we'll have to shuffle people around a bit, it should be the upper box.'

'The closest to the stage?' says Dennis Smith.

'Can anything be done about that?'

'First and foremost, I have to talk to the box office about that.'

'Well, let's talk to the box office quickly before we open up another box plan,' says Humphries. 'I don't think it's working, you know. It's a feeling I have. I must be in a very good position to get such a feeling. I'm up there when it all happens.'

Humphries' staff exits sharpish with their orders. Lizzie Spender props her long leg on a radiator and begins doing stretching exercises. I resume.

'Has Edna become an alter ego?'

'No. It's a portrait of a certain type of person which has become stylised and invested with its own life. The character was conceived out of indignation at the stultifying atmosphere and genteel bigotry that I sensed in my youth. My nanny was called Edna. She was with me up until I was about five. Very nice she was too. And I had an Auntie Frances. She said to me once, "You'll never guess. My hairdresser calls me Edna, after your character." I began to apologise. She said, "Isn't it marvellous. I'm very flattered." Mind you, I never consciously modelled the character on anyone. I was working out of the unconscious. So many people in Wales, Tasmania, Hong Kong, even America have said, "Well, that was my mother up there." '

From the loudspeakers, Katie's voice coos, 'Lesettes. Lesettes. On stage please for warm up.'

'As I rushed to the stage door tonight, there were people waiting who had stuck into books photographs of me to be signed,' says Humphries. 'And I've noticed that type of person is not very, well . . . highly intellectually endowed. I had only time to sign one.' Humphries slips into his sweat suit . . . 'You want to warm up, John? This is the only way I'm going to get any energy.'

I demur, and choose this night to leave Humphries to the mysteries of his preparation and his performance.

'Your attention please, ladies and gentlemen. Contrary to the television broadcast you have just seen, we have received word that a world-famous woman is speeding to this theatre under police escort in the Ednamobile. The management have little doubt that if this proves to be Dame Edna and that she has indeed decided to keep faith with her devoted public and give you a show tonight, the generous-hearted men and women of good will in this audience

will give this courageous woman and widow a standing ovation rarely witnessed in the annals of the British Theatre.'

A crash of cymbals. A spotlight. And there, at the front of the stalls, is Dame Edna in her widow's weeds. 'Hello, possums!' she shouts, waving and smiling and vaulting up the stairs to the stage with her slightly bow-legged gait. 'Hello, darlings! Hello, possums!' she beams as she crosses to centre stage.

A woman wrapped from head to foot in bandages emerges through the centre of the curtain with a bouquet of gladioli.

'Madge Allsop, what are you doing on my stage? You look like the Phantom of the Opera. Or the Phantom of the Oxfam in that outfit. Off with you, Madge, you're ruining my show . . .'

Madge turns on her heels and exits without a word.

'. . . Madge, sorry, don't take offence, woman. Oh, my fuse is so short tonight. But I'm glad I stepped on to the stage now, possums. I am. I am. When I first heard that Norm had been axed by the Big Rupert Murdoch in the sky, I phoned up my shrink in L.A., Dr Marvin K. Schadenfreude, MD. I share him with Little Elton John, Little Michael Jackson, Little Madonna and Big Sylvester. I said, "Doctor, what am I going to do?" And he said, "Let it all hang out, Edna." I said, "That's what Norm did. And look where it got him!" He said, "Time is a miracle healer. Only Time can heal." And he was so right. Because that was, what? four hours ago. And already I'm feeling *marvellous*. I am . . .'

Edna originated as a totem of Humphries' sense of displacement both from his milieu and from his parents. 'I invented Edna because I hated her,' he said. 'I suppose one grows up with a desire to murder one's parents, but you can't go and really do that. So I suppose I tried to murder them symbolically on stage. I poured out my hatred of the standards of the little people of their generation.' Humphries went further than that. He mocked motherhood, turning Edna into a virago of impoverishing niceness. Edna was also the first Australian comedy turn to mock the suburbs, which his father had helped to build. As a comic caricature, Edna allowed Humphries to turn the infuriating fears of his parents against them. 'When they looked at me,' says Humphries, 'they saw someone who was interested in things that seemed very strange. They had a permanent anxiety about what the boy would be, what his profession would be.'

Humphries became his parents' nightmare: the embodiment of the shame and waste and impropriety against which their upwardly mobile life was dedicated. As Edna, Humphries was a cavorting vulgarian consecrating life to frivolity not useful work, a freak of comic excess calling attention and humiliation on himself by dressing up as a woman. Edna's noisy celebration of self turned back on his progenitors their parental ambition and disappointment. *They* had produced *this*: a housewife/superstar.

Edna is a creation of Humphries' imagination, but she contains among other things a son's disturbing view of his mother. Edna talks but never listens. She asks questions only to double-bind her interlocutors. She is a queen of control. 'You're tired. You're over-excited,' she says, turning fiercely on her infantilised audience. 'There'll be tears before bedtime!' What Edna claims about herself and what the audience receives about her are a different matter. She is 'approachable' and devastating, 'nice' and devouring, 'caring' and callous, 'intimate' and detached. She contains a son's envy of his mother's power to be at once the agent of joy and of eradication. 'Don't twist my words!' says Edna to the laughing audience, who get her innuendo. Edna puts on to the audience what rightly belongs to her, just as Humphries' parents put on to their first-born the responsibility for fulfilling *their* potential. In Edna's side-splitting contradictions, Humphries literally *ex-presses* the sense of disconnectedness so confusingly inherited from a family in which he couldn't make himself known.

'My father became very successful,' says Humphries. 'I didn't see a great deal of him. He was always very, very busy.' Humphries pictures Eric Humphries surrounded by drawing boards, set squares, drawing pins, which were the tools of his building trade and the source of the increasing wealth which helped him move from Oldsmobile to Buick to Mercedes in the 1960s. 'My mother, Louisa, was a distant figure as well,' he says. 'I think she had some period of illness. I think she was sent away for a bit. It might have been as little as a fortnight, but it seemed months to a child.'

Outside in the spacious world of herbaceous borders and rolling lawns that surrounded their two-storey neo-Georgian cream brick home in Camberwell, the most fashionable new suburb of Melbourne, looking down Marlborough Avenue to the Golf Links Estate, Humphries sensed an 'unneighbourly feeling'. His parents 'didn't fraternise much with the neighbours. It was thought not altogether "nice" to know people very well,' Humphries says about the general 'lack of intimacy' which extended also to the world inside his house. By the age of six, Humphries was withholding explanations of his deepest hurts from his parents. 'I was puzzled even then by this mysterious lack of rapport which seemed to have grown up between parents and child.'

The incident which prompted this recollection was a schoolyard quarrel at the dreaded South Camberwell State School ('I still drive past in order to see if I can revive my hatred of the school: I do so without any difficulty') which Humphries briefly attended before going to Camberwell Grammar. In his account of the event, Humphries linked feelings of humiliation to a desire for revenge. 'Once a whole crowd of bullies set upon me in a corner of the arid and ashen playground because I had a toy submarine they envied,' he recalled. 'They'd seized up handfuls of gravel to pelt me; and in self-defence I threw a handful back at them and was immediately reported for throwing stones to Miss Jensen, the woman in charge of our class.

'Miss Jensen preferred to take their testimony against my own, and she threatened to take me to the headmaster. Waiting to see the headmaster, I was placed in a corner of the classroom in front of everyone with a note on my back. "I am a bully," said the note. "I am a bully." So I was subjected to this humiliation; and after that I broke down and confessed that in fact I had been culpable, when of course I knew I hadn't really, to avoid the ultimate vengeance of a confrontation with the headmaster. This filled me with very uncomfortable feelings for many, many years. I've often thought to this day of taking some form of revenge upon Miss Jensen if she were still alive, some kind of incomprehensible vengeance; to

61

find her in some place of retirement and inflict upon her some mild punishment, some bewildering punishment. It would make me feel a little better.'

As Edna, Humphries discovered he could call out himself the unacceptable feelings that haunted him and let them haunt his world in the acceptable form of laughter. He found impersonating Edna 'very therapeutic and liberating'. Says Humphries, 'I was finally more comfortable as Edna because I was more heavily disguised. I could relax in the character. It was like a girl who suddenly discovers she has a career in prostitution. On the one hand she suddenly thinks, "Oh, I've got a job"; and on the other hand, "Well, actually it's a job my parents aren't going to be too happy about."'

Louisa and Eric Humphries were vociferously disapproving of their son's vocation. Humphries caricatured his father as Colin Cartright on the record *Sandy Agonistes* (1960). 'He actually repeats things my father said to me. "A man does all he can for his kids and what does he get for it?" And "I've come to the conclusion you can give kids too much".' The point of the sketch was that the giving of things was the businessman's substitute for the giving of attention. 'Things were going well for *him* professionally, then suddenly I seemed to be what Vance Packard called the "slip generation", the one who was going to blow it all. I shared his anxiety but didn't let on to him. What indeed would I be? I was tortured with wondering. It certainly couldn't be anything I was good at or enjoyed, it had to be something else.'

The father looked upon his son's education as an investment in a blue-chip future that would reflect his own accomplishment. But as an embodiment of upper-middle-class status, Humphries was proving a bust. He got no parental support for his artistic interests. 'It was hoped', says Humphries, 'that if I wasn't given too much encouragement in this area, it would go away.' When it didn't he was sent to a vocational guidance counsellor for tests. 'They finally told me, after lots of tests, that I would make a good vocational guidance counsellor.'

Eric Humphries was the third generation of builders in the family. He had taken the known routes; but his son seemed intent on making his own path. Even as a child, Humphries was indifferent to the conventional boy's toys with which his father showered him: boxing gloves, a cricket bat, a train set. 'These were things that middle-class kids were supposed to want. I was really interested in magic and tricks. I identified with Mandrake the Magician because of his unerring ability to make people disappear.'

In time Humphries disappeared inside Edna, who subverted the *nouveau riche* values of his family. 'My parents didn't come to my shows,' he says of the early years (and even with success his mother refused to see him perform his priapic Les Patterson). 'Only later did my father come. He went to a theatre in Melbourne. The box office lady said to me, "Oh, your father's such a nice man." I said, "When did you meet him?" She said he'd come that morning. He wanted to buy all the tickets in the theatre and give them to his friends. He was very surprised to learn they were sold out. He was convinced no one would come.'

To his mother Humphries was, according to him, 'guilty of letting down the side, a frequent crime'. An elegant woman, Louisa was adored and spoiled by her husband, whose preoccupation with his business left her ruling the roost. 'My mother wasn't a particularly warm woman. She was an interesting woman and an intelligent woman. She had artistic qualities which were *all* suppressed,' says Humphries, who in public draws a curtain over their frequent rows and concentrates on filial respect. 'She used to make her own clothes. She devoted a lot of time to the decoration of her own house.' Ian Davidson remembers her as 'lugubrious and rather long-faced'. Louisa was judgmental and could make her disapproval felt. When Humphries told her he'd met the Queen after a Command Performance at the Palladium, she replied, 'I hope you were wearing a nice *suit*.' Humphries wasn't. 'She had a very oblique way of paying you a compliment, always very recondite,' says Humphries. 'She was the master of the recondite compliment. It didn't seem necessary to inform her that I was wearing a dress.'

Louisa compounded Humphries' sense of displacement by producing two other sons (Christopher and Michael) and a daughter (Barbara). 'I think the first four years were my happiest days,' says Humphries. 'When I had my parents' total attention and didn't have to share the bill. I gave my sister a bad time. I've since apologised.' Humphries also frequently had to send flowers of apology to Louisa. 'There are some things to which human beings have difficulty in making a response, things of such a moral and semantic upheaval that they just can't manage it,' he says of his mother's reaction to his chosen career. 'They just have to say something like "Oh, Barry, you're being silly. Why are you doing this?"'

But even before acting and Edna, Humphries had great difficulty in making his mother see him for himself. She once asked him to return the gift of a pair of earrings he'd bought for her. 'This was a very wounding experience as a child,' says Humphries. The problem of being properly received remained an issue between them into adulthood. Humphries tells of returning from London to Melbourne to show off to Louisa his newborn son Oscar, the first child of his now dissolved third marriage, to the painter Diane Millstead. 'She had not met her grandson,' he recalls. 'As I arrived, I noticed my mother listening to the transistor radio. I came forward to present my son to her, she was cautioning me, "Listen! Listen!" It was a typical Australian disc jockey on a phone-in programme. He happened to be talking about me. Was I good for Australia or not? It was generally felt that I was doing Australia a great disservice by my impersonations, particularly that of Sir Les Patterson, this anachronistic figure. My mother was saying, "Sssh . . . sshhh . . . listen . . . !" People were ringing up and saying things like, "Well, I haven't seen one of Barry's shows, but from what I've heard, it's a disgrace . . ." This man by impugning my patriotism was inflating his own reputation. My mother said, pointedly, "You see. That's what they think. That's what they think of you!"

'I was so incensed that I should come home and that my mother should be listening to this rubbish and not dismissing it instead of greeting me and her grandson that I went into another room. I telephoned the radio station as Edna. I got through using the voice of Edna. I said that this was Dame Edna and I was on a brief visit to Australia and I was listening to the programme about Barry Humphries and I heartily agreed with these women. I said, "Not only do I agree with what these women said about Barry Humphries, but I happen to know that Barry Humphries' own mother thinks *exactly* the same." I knew that within a few inches of brickwork from me, my mother was actually hearing this. I thought it was an amusing way to get through to her and to syphon off my extreme anger.'

Dame Edna is out of widow's black now and into iridescent celebrity red. 'Eat your heart out, Tina Turner!!' she shouts, unveiling the short, fringy dress in which she hymns her public and her professionalism. The audience is in a party mood. Someone hidden in the shadows of a box to the right of the stage throws a chartreuse-and-yellow card that lands with a clatter at Edna's feet. She kicks the missive off stage, where Harriet retrieves it. 'I LOVE YOU,' it reads. 'Hays: known as "Hayseed" from Kentucky. First bloke in first box on left.'

Edna, too, is talking of love: 'I love to hear laughter. I call it Vitamin L, what an essential part of our spiritual diet it is, isn't it, possums? Norman and I, oh we used to love to laugh! We were always playing little jokes on each other. And it's not easy, is it?, playing jokes on institutionalised loved ones. But every April Fool's Day we had a little jest with each other. I remember last April the first . . . ha! . . . we pretended to Norm . . . ha! . . . he was going to be discharged from hospital. Ha, ha! Isn't that gorgeous? You could do that with a loved one. The matron helped too. She packed his little case so he could watch her doing it out of the corner of the mirror above his page-turning machine. He's had *The Thornbirds* open at the same page for the last seven years. (Who hasn't?) Anyway, they got him into his dressing gown, and he shuffled down to the front of the hossie where I had an ambulance ticking over. And just as Norm was about to fall into the ambulance . . . hee . . . hee . . . *it whizzed off down the driveway*! Ah, ha . . . ha . . . ! He fell flat on his face in the gravel. And all the doctors and nurses leant out of the windows and said "April Fool!!!" Ha, ha . . . I wish Norm could have laughed at that . . . Oh dear . . . Oh, but I'm a lucky, lucky

65

woman because I was born with a priceless gift. "What gift is that, Dame Edna?" I hear you saying ... The ability to laugh at the misfortunes of others ... And, you know, that keeps me cheerful twenty-four hours a day. It does!'

He was born John Barry Humphries in the Melbourne suburb of Kew on February 17th, 1934. Although it would be wrong to consider Edna as merely Humphries' alter ego, it would also be wrong to consider her just 'that woman you inhabit', which was Graham Greene's description. Humphries has created many memorable characters – Sandy Stone, Sir Les Patterson, Bazza McKenzie – but as Edna his performance has a peculiar urgency and theatrical invention because of the deep childhood feelings the character touches and transmogrifies. In Edna Humphries is able symbolically to control both his mother and her judgment of him.

Edna frequently criticises Humphries in public and in the press. (Writes Edna in her autobiography: '*BARRY HUMPHRIES.* Still my manager, but under solicitor's thumb. His contributions to our show getting smaller by the year.') But instead of shaming Humphries, Edna's put-downs about his lack of talent only add to his legend and his mystery. In explaining Edna to the public, Humphries, like all dandies, obscures his depths and his roots. 'If England is the Motherland and Germany is the Fatherland, Australia is certainly Auntieland,' he told his friend the actor/writer John Wells. 'I had a lot of aunts, all very nice, but they were there, all the time. So I was pretty good at giving an impersonation, certainly, of a kind of synthesis of these women. And also of their obsession with domestic detail, seeing the whole world through the venetian blind of the kitchen window: seeing everything in terms of household arrangement, cleanliness, all that stuff.' But, in his first appearance as Edna, Humphries wore his mother's hat, and also sported some of her bigotries.

Louisa Humphries looked on her first-born with bemusement. 'Where did you come from?' she used to say to him. 'We never knew where you came from.' 'My mother would very frequently express surprise at me, which reinforced my adoption fantasy,' says Humphries. 'We had a neighbour whose daughter was adopted;

and one became acquainted with the idea that there were some people around in the world who thought that they had parents when they turned out to be adopted. This seemed to explain my feelings of being slightly alien to the milieu to which I was born. It was just possible I was adopted; and my parents' denial of this was proof positive. They looked like very bad liars when they told me I wasn't *adopted*.'

Humphries puts the feeling into Edna and lets her both admit and play with his sense of estrangement in *My Gorgeous Life* when Edna confronts her mother in a Twilight Home for the Partially Bewildered. 'Oh, Brucie,' says Edna's mother, confusing her with her husband, 'do you think Edna is really ours? Could there have been a mix-up at Bethesda?' Later, Edna confesses to Humphries' own adoption fantasy:

I began to get the feeling that I too may have been adopted because I felt so different from my own family, a bit of an outsider if you like. I have since read biographies of Mozart, Shakespeare, Vlad the Impaler and Mrs Thatcher and discovered to my relief, that they all entertained the same scary fantasy. Expressed bluntly it was: 'How could a brilliant and gorgeous person like me have been born to a stupid old boring couple like you?' It sounds awful, doesn't it, Readers? But that's how I felt and if this book isn't honest it is nothing.

Edna's mischief began as Humphries' antidote to the tedium of Australian suburbia; one of many discoveries Humphries made over the years to nourish himself in an unstimulating environment. 'I certainly didn't enjoy my childhood tremendously in Australia,' he told the press in 1976. 'Unless children like jumping about in the water, rolling around in the yellow grit called the beach or injuring themselves on the football and cricket field playing absurd sports; in other words, if you're slightly simple minded, Australia is ideal. I think children miss out on a lot of things. There's very little cultural recreation for children.' Edna's arrogance and ignorance ('I just love Edvard Munch's painting *The Scream*. I've got reproductions of it all over my exquisite home in Melbourne, so that you keep coming across it where you least expect to') hold all Humphries' anger at not being properly nourished throughout his childhood. There were few books in the Humphries' house. 'My mother was a great student of the *Australian Women's Weekly*,' Humphries said. Their tidy and comfortable home was as free from the infection of ideas as it was from dirt. 'There were just standard books. *The Family Doctor*. An encyclopedia bought from a travelling salesman. Very few novels. My uncle (my mother's brother-in-law) had been in France during the First World War. He had a lot of books and gave me some. My father bought me whatever books I wanted. I was never prevented from reading whatever I wanted, although a copy of D.H. Lawrence was seized by my mother.' Humphries also had two uncles who painted. 'They did very large pictures of the River Nile at sunset and of lions in their lair.'

Accompanying the banality of Melbourne life was also its silence, which seeps into Sandy Stone's catalogue of uneventful days and Edna's manic caterwauling. 'Behind the sunshine and the bustle and the gregariousness, there is the silence and the sad loneliness,' said Humphries of Australia. His own childhood isolation was compounded by having few friends in the neighbourhood who went to his school. 'One problem with "friends",' he says, 'was that one only had two days off school a week, Saturday and Sunday. My parents observed the Sabbath. So I was not allowed to play with other kids on Sunday, which was consecrated to Church and Sunday school and a kind of gloom. The Melbourne Sunday anyway is notoriously dull; and it's made even duller if you can't see friends. Very often Sunday afternoon was spent visiting relations (one had a lot of them), and on drives. What Sandy Stone calls a "spin".' Humphries' parents enjoyed looking at newly constructed houses. 'So you'd drive to the outer suburbs where there was a stylistic jump from the California Bungalow, Spanish Mission style of the nineteen thirties to the houses of the forties and early fifties with their cream-brick veneer and feature chimneys. There was a lot of looking at these houses, driving very very slowly past these new lawns. This intensified the boredom.'

It was not just the deadly tedium of the Melbourne suburbs

which so powerfully affected Humphries, but the silence inside his own house. 'It was quiet. Only at my insistence was a gramophone obtained. I started collecting records seriously even then.' Music partially answered his 'hankering for somewhere else'. 'In the early Melbourne days sitting in Camberwell wondering what I was going to do when I grew up . . . I mostly listened to English music: Vaughan Williams and Delius in particular, romantic "pastoral" music . . .' The Humphries' brown bakelite radio also abetted his yearning for 'moister climates' by bringing him into contact with British music-hall comedians and the notion that people told jokes for a living. Humphries was about ten and laughter seemed to hold out to him a power comparable to his fantasy of being a magician and making people disappear. 'I wanted to exercise power over people. I wanted to control their access to me, too.'

In a mock-novel about 'an androgynous and eldritch child' named Tid, Humphries wrote in 1961, 'Tid's main thing was trying not to be seen. You can't imagine how hard this job was . . . He just wanted ladies and men to accept the fact that he wasn't there when he was there.' At the finale Tid becomes King. Wrote Humphries, 'Tid hides in the world and is King of it.'

Dame Edna engineers Humphries' persistent daydream of omnipotence. Not to be understood or contained or believed or known in his family made it intolerable for Humphries to be *him*. He was compelled to become *her*. Dame Edna was both a brilliant display of his mastery and an exercise in mystification. Through her Humphries could enthral the world, at once captivating it and keeping it at arm's length.

Dame Edna scowls at the audience for laughing at the notion of her as 'Saint Edna', a model of nurturing self-sacrifice. 'Please! Don't laugh. I've had a tip-off. I can't tell you who told me, but he's Polish, single and lives in Italy. That's *all* I can say.'

But later, after her monologue has meandered through accounts of her 'regular exploratories' and her Swiss financial advisers, Dame Edna returns to her latest claim for herself as a mother. 'I'm an upmarket Mother Teresa. I am. I am. And Mother Teresa comes to see me too. Every time she comes to London. (She comes to London once a year for the Harrods sale.) It's not . . . no . . . it's not for the merchandise. She just loves sleeping in the street. She *loves* it. She said to me, "Edna, those Knightsbridge gutters have got the edge on Calcutta." She came backstage with her little programme, holding a little gladdy she'd caught. And I said, "Did you enjoy it, Tess? Tell me" . . . And she said, "Edna, I came out of your show feeling another woman!" '

The audience roars, and Edna compounds the laugh by ignoring it. '*Mother Teresa* said that to me! I mean, compliments like that don't grow on trees, do they? Could you imagine Mother Teresa saying something like that to you? Ha, ha . . . *Not in a million years!* But she said it to me. To me. Me, me!! Mother Teresa said it to *me*!

'And that is why everyone is admitted to my beautiful shows. We don't turn anyone away . . . except lepers, that's all. And only . . . only because we've found they're very poor clappers. No, no . . . I mean . . . don't misunderstand me . . . I mean they're very *careful* clappers. Then they're looking for things on the floor . . .'

Dame Edna turns to the pianist behind her. 'I said to you, "They couldn't have spilt that many Maltesers," didn't I? We had a big party in when I decided to put a ban on it. Where were we?'

'Leeds and Liverpool,' says the pianist.

'In Leeds and Liverpool. Oh yes, particularly in Leeds we had that big party of lepers in. I think it was a convention. Or it might have been their airline. Lepair. I don't know. That's the one with one wing. But they were all sitting there. They were beautifully groomed, do you remember? Beautifully groomed. I think they were yuppies . . . Or luppies. There was a young chap down there beautifully dressed. Immaculately dressed. I think he was an executive leper . . . I remember this *so* vividly, possums. He was just there, and he waved. He waved. I thought at the time: that's a bit vigorous. You're waving too vigorously. I was up here going, no, no, no, no. And sure enough . . .' Dame Edna strides across the stage, tracing the trajectory of the leper's hand with the arc of her own. 'A woman all the way over here was grievously goosed. She was. It was a freak accident. This woman was horrified. Not so much by the finger, I think, as by the total absence of follow up of any kind. It was as though . . . it was as though she had been violated by a heat-seeking missile . . .'

For both Humphries and for his audience, Edna's laughter is a liberation from a life that must necessarily be lived under wraps. 'There's a kind of camaraderie about laughter,' says Humphries, seated a few days later beside his dressing table in a purple and blue striped bathrobe. 'It's a unifying experience. It's one of the few things that a very heterogeneous group of people do together. They decide to put aside many of their prejudices and preconceptions and to participate, if only partially, in someone else's view of the world. That's a very strange thing for them to be doing, isn't it? But it seems to be important for people to do.' Edna's act works not just because the public enters her world, but because she taps into the audience's unconscious. This gives the character a terrific power and liberty. Edna claims to be a bit of a swami; and in this sense, she is. In her viciousness Edna allows the public to admit in laughter its own repressed cruelty, which defends against anxieties of humiliation and annihilation.

'If there's anyone tonight who came on wheels,' she says at one point on the issue of disablement, to howls of laughter, 'anyone with a hint of chrome about them, anyone with a touch of Richard the Third, I'm not a healer. I wish I could heal. But I cannot heal. So don't bring your sore bits around to me later. Though funnily enough we found a battered crutch under the seat the other night. So someone must have walked home laughing, mustn't they?' The danger and exhilaration of Humphries' laughter is that it takes the paying customers to places in themselves they didn't know existed or were afraid to go. Dame Edna engineers a holiday from conscience.

On a yellow piece of paper taped to the dressing-room mirror, Humphries has scribbled notes for the rewrite of 'My Public' which Edna will sing for Prince Charles's Trust at the Palladium: 'Makes me go all goose-bumpy and clammy/To be on the bill with darling little one-eyed Sammy/And nothing could be nicer than . . .' He is planning a comic surprise; trying to frame a joke so that it winkles out from an audience both shock and delight. Dame Edna says the unsayable, and the response – half gasp, half laughter – subverts the climate of puritanism which was a strong and restrictive childhood influence in Humphries' family.

'I made a very specific observation once as a child,' he says. 'In a seaside resort garden in Melbourne, they'd reproduced in crude cement the Mannikin Piss from Brussels. I had never seen any kind of sculpture or artistic reproduction of this simple human activity. And there he was on a little fountain. I saw him, this little pissing figure. And I saw adults turning away with very strange little crooked smiles. They were actually smiling behind their hands. They were embarrassed smiles, and they were embarrassed to be seen smiling. And I remember the same response when my parents on one of those very rare occasions took me to the Melbourne Tivoli, which was consecrated to vaudeville and deeply disapproved of by them. My parents were rather puritanical to say the least. We went to see Tommy Trinder, whom I later used in the second Barry McKenzie film, *Barry McKenzie Holds His Own*. Trinder wasn't one of those dirty Aussie comedians. He was, after all, Tommy Trinder, and there'd been photographs of the Queen shaking hands with him. In fact, the show was a rather "blue" show. There were lots of jokes I didn't get, and the adults were rocking with laughter around me. My parents were more or less unsmiling throughout. In one scene, Trinder asked a member of the audience to guess the song title that the sketch acted out. There were a couple of parents sitting on stage reading a newspaper and knitting. Then, in comes the girl with a cushion under her dress. It was a very simple infantile game with the audience. I guess the people who yelled out names were planted in the audience. Someone right behind us called out, "I Didn't Know the Gun Was Loaded".

'I didn't know what that meant. I don't get the point of it now, really. The audience all went up. My father actually exploded with laughter. It was, in fact, an explosion of laughter. There was a reproachful look from my mother, showing that she too got this esoteric point. I realised that this was a kind of sexual joke. And that everybody had laughed, and my father had laughed as well. The intensity of laughter has something to do with the fact that we were sitting in the dark, in the theatre, looking toward the stage and not at each other.'

In time, as Edna, Humphries would become master of the pole-axeing innuendo whose impact surpassed even the astonishment he'd glimpsed as a child at the Melbourne Tivoli. 'Barry Humphries is the heir to Max Miller's territory, but his eavesdropping androgyny gives him the edge,' wrote the playwright Peter Nichols in celebration of the old king of British music-hall rudery. 'The energy, unpredictability and popularity are the same (or greater), but the scope's wider and deeper, the outrage far more telling.' Edna, who once offered coffee to the TV presenter Joan Bakewell saying, 'You look like a girl who needs something hot inside her,' releases the public happily from the gravity of its propriety.

'Innuendo', says Humphries, 'is a great release, you know. It's a perfect way of releasing an audience.' The risqué manoeuvres that he gleaned from Firbank's collision of vulgarity with artifice and from music-hall turns tease out from an audience the awful recognition of its secret sexual aggression. He says of the guilty hilarity he can inspire, 'The body language of audiences is very interesting. People who are laughing turn all the time to whoever's near to them to see if they got it. Did they enjoy it? It's a very strange language they speak. It means, "Was it good for you?" Having once established the character, whether Edna or Sandy or Les, the audience is secure with the type of person it is; and you get to go on little satirical jaunts, little moonwalks, as long as you come back to the character. Edna, after all, the housewife, the mother, the successful actress, would not talk about lepers. In a way, that's someone else's material. It's a bit inappropriate, a bit of a cheat. But you can go on a little foray like that outside the character, as long as you come back into it and don't disappoint the audience.'

'Beginners,' says Harriet, sticking her head brightly inside the dressing room and giving Humphries his half-hour call before showtime. 'Dennis apologises. He's locked in his flat.'

'Is he?' says Humphries, his eyes shining. 'Ring him. I want to speak to him. Ring him. Ring him. He's locked in his flat?'

'It's my fault,' says Harriet, dialling as she talks. 'I've sent somebody over to get him out. The flat's got a real dodgy lock. When I left, I slammed the door.' Humphries holds out his hand for the receiver. 'Hello. It's Harriet. Barry would like a word with you.'

'What is this excuse?' says Humphries. 'I told you last night you shouldn't be staying there. I mean, really, trying to save a few bob. You've got a quid or two, Dennis. What are you actually saving up for? Just sit there and watch television. You'll be disappointed to hear the show is going to go on perfectly well without you. You may never get out of there, Dennis. I hope it doesn't get spooky in there. I hope there's not a fire, or anything, Dennis. I said to Harriet, "Where's Dennis?" She said, "I don't know. Oh yes, that's right," she said, "he's locked in the flat." So I hope she remembers you're there. I better go now.'

'Barry,' says Harriet, 'sorry to keep intruding, but Eddy hurt himself in the stunt last night. He's not doing it tonight, Jazza is.'

'How did he hurt himself?'

'Well, the bottom ledge at the Strand used to cut into his stomach, so his legs swung free. But here, it cuts the legs. He's very badly bruised.'

'What can we do?' says Humphries. 'Pad it somewhere?'

'No, not really. Not much that can be done.'

'Hello, Barry.' The girl standing on the threshold is the 'plummeting pauper' who does the stunt with the injured Eddy. Humphries has summoned her.

'Look,' says Humphries, 'can you scream more?'

'Yes,' she says. 'Last night I got lost a bit.'

'Trouble is,' says Humphries, 'it won't alarm the audience unless we really hear the screams.' He turns back to me, as the girl exits. 'Poor Eddy,' he says. 'Oh dear.'

One way or another, Edna is meant to terrorise both people in Humphries' audience and in his past. Even Edna's 'paupers', who perch rather expensively for such a sobriquet in the Upper Circle, are turned by the power of Humphries' comic invention into personifications of a smugness which echo his 'embarrassment at the *nouveau riche* gentilities' of his parents.

74

Katie posts a yellow note on the dressing mirror in front of him. But Humphries is warming to the conversation now and hardly notices her. 'In Edna's autobiography, Edna's description of driving through the slums of Melbourne is as close to any childhood experience I had,' he says. 'The father says, "I'm going to show you how the other half lives," and they detour, after a pleasant Sunday afternoon perhaps going up to the hills, to buy an azalea. They would drive back through the poorer areas called the slums. I think if we saw it today, we wouldn't exactly describe it as a slum in the sense of Harlem. Certainly Edna would be looking through the glass window, and the father would say, "Look at that. You kids don't know how lucky you are." Indeed, that was what my father did say. And Edna's mother would say, "See how polished that brass door handle is. See how clean that window is. You see, even if you live in a slum, you can still have your pride." I've reproduced some of my own parents' dialogue there. And my fascination with the slums. It really rang a bell when I heard that it was quite fashionable in Wilde's period to get into a hansom cab and to go to the East End and *look*. I was appalled and fascinated by the stews. The louche, the raffish, the carnal. At the time it was just, "You don't know how fortunate you are. Look out the window." '

Edna exaggerates Humphries' parents' habit of invidious comparison and turns it into a star turn. But in her autobiography Edna's description of the drive into the slums allows Humphries both more satire and more seriousness than his backstage recollection. Humphries emerges subtly out of Edna's story. Edna's buoyant smugness admits its origins in the parents' game of measuring the distance between themselves and others, while Humphries obliquely admits his own barbed sadness at the distance between his parents:

I was fascinated by the poor – and still am! Whenever we were on a Sunday afternoon 'spin' in the car I would exhort my father, 'Pl-ea-se, Daddy, take us past the paupers.' He started it. Even if we had been up for a Devonshire tea or to pick up an azalea or two in Melbourne's world-class Dandedong

Rangers (a lovely aboriginal word meaning something), my father would insist on driving back to Moonee via Dudley Flats. This was a ghastly slum, long since replaced, thank goodness, by condemned high-rise council housing . . . Unless we went for an afternoon 'spin', I can't say Sunday was ever my favourite day of the week. There always seemed to be an atmosphere of tension about it and I think that it had a lot to do with the fact that it was the only day of the week when my parents spent any time together . . . Even today I get a funny, empty, worried feeling on the Sabbath which harks back to my childhood, when my parents were forcibly reminded that they were married to each other.

Katie sticks a second note on his mirror. Humphries glances at it, then looks up at her, his face tightening. 'Why didn't you tell me?'

'I did,' says Katie. 'I put two notes in front of you.'

'I'm going to have to hurry,' says Humphries, looking at the clock which says 7.27 and stepping into Sir Les's paunch with its 'enormous encumbancy' dropping down below the chair as he turns back to do what he calls Sir Les's 'neo-impressionist make-up'. 'It's as though my face is formed by a swarm of multi-coloured locusts,' says Humphries, marking his forehead with red, pink and carmine dots and then highlighting them with white underneath. 'Are you in tonight?'

'Yes.'

'It's only about ten minutes before I go on stage I get a bit introspective,' he says, blending carmine dots on his forehead. 'It's not that I think "Now's the time I have to concentrate." It's a process which automatically starts taking place. It's a kind of withdrawal before this tumescence. If you'll excuse me, John.'

Six minutes later the doors to the green room bang open, and Humphries scurries out in Sir Les's blue tuxedo coat, ruffled shirt, platform shoes, and dentures. 'I'm late! I'm late!!' he calls as he sweeps by Harriet at the prompt desk. 'You shouldn't have done this to me!'

Harriet laughs as Sir Les, with Katie guiding him with a flashlight, steps carefully through the cavernous shadows toward the other side of the stage from where he'll make his noisy entrance. 'Whose fault is it if he's late?' Harriet smiles, a veteran of two years of the show and of Humphries' occasional outbursts of temperament. 'He comes out saying "I'm late" as if it's someone else's responsibility. It's a traditional thing: calls are a courtesy. Anyway, we set his clock five minutes fast. But don't tell him.'

Les is on form tonight, but Edna is hot. From the wings, the audience blurs into a wave of heaving bodies lashed forward and back by great bursts of laughter. Often, the grimacing faces hold their hands up to their mouths as if appalled and thrilled at what Edna's jokes allow them to admit. Edna is spinning a yarn about a letter she's received from a woman in Shepherd's Bush who'd been to one of her shows. 'She said "Dear Edda" . . . she couldn't even spell my name. *The stupid woman!* I nearly stuffed the letter down the waste disposal. But something made me read on . . . A power greater than myself made me read that stupid woman's scrawl . . . "When you were last in London, a friend of a friend gave me a ticket." This woman has no friends, you see. Just friends of friends. And she said, "I came on a Saturday night in the beginning of April." Isn't that spooky? She said, "I was the woman sitting in the first six rows that you chose that night . . . as you always do . . . choose a woman . . . to do the nude cartwheels on stage." '

Edna paces the stage and looks down into the front rows. 'And now the mood has completely changed, hasn't it? I don't know what you'd call it. Blind terror, I think, don't you? I think these yups want to be up with the paups, don't you? *I think they do.* But don't be nervous. Please . . . supposing I chose for argument's sake . . . *You!* In the third row . . . as I almost certainly will. Hello? What's your name? You. Yes. Yes. What is your name?'

'Emma,' says the middle-aged blonde faintly.

'Hello, Emma,' coos Edna. 'Have you done much nude cartwheel work? Don't worry, Emma. We've found audiences prefer an amateur nude cartwheelist, they do. They have a way of falling over which is vulnerable . . . and, well . . . strangely appealing. So don't be nervous, Emma. Don't scratch your eczema, Emma.

Because you will not know you're doing these cartwheels, Emma. Do you know why? You'll be in deep shock, Emma. You will. Because whenever we women are very very frightened, our bodies do a funny thing. We secrete an enzyme at the same time. So you'll not only be in your birthday suit endeavouring to do cartwheels and failing. But you'll be secreting an enzyme at the same time. I hope that's reassuring. You know much about your own female anatomy, do you, Emma? Did you know, Emma, that we women have a little wee gland about half the size of a little fingernail tucked in an intimate nook. Did you know that, Emma? This is a bit of a first, isn't it? This is the first time this intimate woman's gland and its nook have been freely and exhaustively discussed in a popular show. There is no reference to this gland in, well, *Starlight Express* for example. *The Phantom of the Opera* doesn't touch on this gland . . . Ha, ha . . . *He'd like to, but he doesn't.* I'm going to drag it out into the open, Em. Or as far out as it will come. This gland of ours, Emma, has a *duct* joined on to it. What has it got joined on to it . . .?'

Emma, who is tearing with laughter, is wrong-footed by Edna's schoolmarmish question. 'Duct,' she says finally.

'A duct, that's right. A duct. And whenever we women have to do something a little, oh, unacceptable or even a little bit yukkie, Emma, you know what this funny little gland of ours does? Do you? It squirts. It squirts. And it oozes. And drips. And we black out, Emma. Because . . . It's called the Honeymoon Gland because that's when it mostly comes in handy. But more to the point, *DO YOU KNOW WHAT YOUR GLAND IS DOING RIGHT NOW!!!* It's going berserk, Emma. So when you do the nude cartwheels, you'll be in a transcendental state like the tinted folk who walk on the red-hot coals, and they don't even know they're doing it until they fall over screaming and tweaking at their charred stumps. And that'll be you. You will literally not know that you've been tonight's cartwheel girl until you're leaving the theatre and you notice people are pointing and laughing at you. And saying things like, "She wasn't a natural blonde, was she?"'

In Dame Edna's act, Humphries moves the audience into all sorts of taboo areas: sex, death, handicap, attacks on personal taste.

'She's leading the audience into this labyrinth where they bump into these clammy objects,' says Humphries, who knows better than any modern comedian that games are best when tense. 'It's rather like a funfair. It's a bit spooky and frightening. It's like the roller coaster: sometimes you feel near death but in the end you come out and you want another ride.' For Humphries the exhilaration is, in part, the raising to the level of laughter the areas of life which his prim parents kept hidden. 'Death was not discussed,' he says. 'Sex was not discussed. Serious illness was not discussed. For example, after I was grown up and working in London, I came back to Melbourne to find my mother had been ill. "Why didn't you tell me?" She said, "We didn't want to worry you." I then made up a joke about someone coming back to Australia and finding other people in the house. "Where are my parents?" "Oh, well, they died, but they didn't want to worry you." No one wanted to worry you. Religion was not discussed at all, although there was regular religious observation. My mother was always hostile to the vicar. I think she found religious observation boring and incomprehensible. She occasionally evinced slightly anti-Semitic views. Anti-Semitism was something I knew nothing about, and yet it exhibited itself in that kind of Australian community where my father was doing business with Jews. He had a friend in the timber business called Friedman. I can remember one anti-Semitic outburst of my mother's. "Well, you will deal with that man Friedman. What do you expect?" I remember as a child being appalled by this. It was clear that my father liked him. My father was much more tolerant and liberal. Melbourne owes its musical life, its cakes, its coffees, particularly to the Viennese Jews who came. They made chocolates. They made shoes (Kurt Geiger had his first shoe shop in Melbourne). The photographer Helmut Newton is from Melbourne. I have memories of Jews coming to Melbourne, a group with whom I've always sympathised and identified with. I felt envious of that kind of hermetic culture. Community. Family. Even persecution.'

Dame Edna sports with these bigotries. In the opening sentence of her autobiography, she announces, 'I am probably Jewish', but in the next breath speaks of 'Red Sea pedestrians'. As Edna, Humphries once asked his audience to take their gladioli and hit the Jew next to them. 'It was chilling. The joy went out of the occasion,' he says of a show he characterises as 'about as democratic as a Nuremburg rally'. 'So I changed it to something satiric. "Hit the nearest Presbyterian." That got a big laugh because it could mean "Jew". "Presbyterian" didn't carry such emotive force as "Jew", and so the audience was able to enjoy it firstly as a joke and secondly as Edna telling her public how much power she's able to exert over it. I was reminding them to what extent they'd delivered themselves into my hands.'

Edna is a confection of intolerance through whom Humphries teases both parochial bigotry and puritan liberalism. 'Today the Puritan has never been more numerous or influential,' he wrote in 1984, celebrating his fiftieth birthday in print, recollecting his original mission both 'to shock and goad the humourless'. 'Institutionalised puritanism, masquerading as humanism, can be seen at its least appetising in the Anti-Discrimination Board . . .'

Tonight, I'm watching Dame Edna from the mesh window cut into the curtain. 'Oh, darling, aren't we getting on well?' Dame Edna says to Emma. 'I need your help, Em, as I've never needed anyone's help. I'm redecorating one of my homes. I don't mean this in an elitist way, Paups and Budget Budgies. But I do have a number of homes. I've got a house in Malibu. In Mustique. In Montreux. And in Melbourne. I'm an Australian, incidentally. My Melbourne home is now a museum. Which is a big compliment to me, isn't it? I'm redecorating it. Japanese tourists go there. They don't know why, but they do. (Between you and me, I don't think they know why they go anywhere.) They just follow a little Nip with a flag.' The audience rolls with laughter, and Dame Edna demurs in her most punctilious falsetto, 'I mean that nicely. I'm not being Nippist. Don't accuse me of Nippism . . .'

Dame Edna began as a less strident voice from the back of the Union Theatre Repertory Company touring bus taking *Twelfth Night* on one-night stands through Victoria in 1955. It was

Humphries' first year as a professional actor. He was twenty-one. Having dropped out of Melbourne University two years earlier, he had been earning his way by working at EMI as variously a wholesale record salesman and breaker of recently obsolete 78s. 'This latter chore', he said of days spent in a windowless room in an 'inane frenzy' destroying piles of Mahler, Sibelius, Debussy, and the Ink Spots, 'produced a more acute form of nervous exhaustion than I had experienced in my less compulsory Dadaist activities, though it bore an ironic resemblance to them.'

Humphries' Duke Orsino, on the other hand, was less than smashing. 'He wasn't a swell leading man. Clearly he didn't concentrate. He couldn't stay in a role. You thought, "He can't possibly be an actor," but I knew he'd be something. He had such an extraordinary mind,' says Zoe Caldwell, who played Viola. 'His legs were too thin. When he came on, he got a laugh.'

To entertain themselves from one country town to another, the cast sang songs, told tales, and recited verse. Humphries' party piece was Edna, who had 'the unmistakable voice of the genteel Melbourne housewife' and who was also a 'flashback, really, to my earliest university days . . . and the Melbourne Dada Group in which we attempted to ridicule the fellows who we felt were terribly stuffy, and indeed we were right in thinking so'.

Edna allowed Humphries to show off his gift for caricature and his desire to shine. 'I found that I had a good falsetto voice, and I invented a character to go with it – a female character – because, you see, every night when the curtain fell on *Twelfth Night* the local lady Mayoress or the ladies' committee would invite this distinguished cast from the city of Melbourne to what was called a "bun fight": cups of tea and wonderful cakes such as only Australians seem to make – plates of lamingtons and iced vovos and butterfly cakes all stuck together with cream and cocoa. They used to give little speeches about how wonderful *Twelfth Night* was. I had a knack of anticipating some of the ladies' speeches very, very well as my funny little character in the back of the bus.'

Edna was encouraged by the company's resident writer–director

Ray Lawler whose *Summer of the Seventeenth Doll* in the late 1950s was the first Australian play to win international notoriety and, along with Humphries' characters, sound a new theatrical note of Australian self-awareness. 'When it came time for the annual revue *Return Fare*, which Lawler was directing, Ray said, "Why don't you write a sketch for that character you did in the bus? What's she called?"' Humphries recollected. 'I plucked the name out of the air: "Edna", I suggested, since I'd once had a kind nanny called Edna, of whom I was very fond. I said, "Her name is Edna, and she comes from Moonee Ponds." I thought I daren't say Camberwell, or my mother will think it's based on her. Indeed, Edna is more a Camberwell character than a Moonee Ponds character. Moonee Ponds is a suburb of Melbourne I'd never been to at the time. The name was chosen partly for its association with a famous poem by Kendall called "Moonee". It also had a good euphonious name, and it is still a wonderful name: it's evocative, and has a hint of something elusively humorous about it. "Well, if I write a sketch for this character," I said, "who will play Edna? Will I do the voice from off-stage?" Ray said, "You do it yourself." "Can't Zoe [Caldwell] be Edna?" I asked. He said, "No, you be Edna. Do it like a pantomime dame . . ."'

On December 19th, 1955, propitiously positioned next to closing, Edna Everage made her stage debut. She wore no wig, no spectacles, and no make-up. 'She had shortish brown hair which was in fact my own longish hair combed down,' says Humphries. 'She always wore a hat, a voluminous skirt, flat shoes, sockettes, and a rather large handbag. She looked somewhat gauche and nervous and spoke in a high, genteel, less vigorous and confident way than she speaks now. She was, after all, someone who merely strayed from the kitchen on to the stage.' The sketch was called 'The Olympic Hostess' – a title as up to the minute as the detail of Edna's palaver. The 1956 Olympic Games were to be staged in Australia, and already there were advertisements in the local newspapers asking for 15,000 beds to put up the athletes. In the sketch, Edna attempted to offer her Moonee Ponds home for the games, an opportunity not so much for hospitality as for house-pride. 'There were not many traditional jokes in this piece,' Humphries wrote in an article on *kitsch*. 'The real joke turned out to be her lovely home itself.'

MRS EVERAGE. There's one bedroom, one – then there's the lounge and dining room. If you open the double doors – little Kenny – that's my youngest – always calls them the reindeer doors because of the sand-blasted reindeers on the glass – if you open the double doors it's a lovely big room. We pushed back the Genoa couch and rolled back the burgundy Axminster squares for Valmai's twenty-first, and the young people had the time of their lives – . . .

HOPECHEST. Now, Mrs Everage, is there any particular nationality you would prefer? . . .

MRS EVERAGE (*confidentially*). Look, little Kenny would really be tickled to death if you could let us have a real Red Indian . . .

Hopechest suggests New Zealand. Edna phones her mother for final approval.

MRS EVERAGE. Hello – hello, Mother? The gentleman has just suggested New Zealand. I believe they're a very nice type of person. What, dear – a tattoo? Where, dear? . . . But how would *you know* . . . *Really*? Well, of course, Valmai's married and out of danger's way now, but I wouldn't like to think of little Kenny being contaminated, and I'm not even sure how Norm would feel about that sort of thing – all right, Mother, all right, we won't take any chances . . .

After rejecting Sweden, Hopechest goes down his roster of nationalities while Edna repeats them to her mother, who has an atlas to hand.

HOPECHEST. Zulu
MRS EVERAGE. Zulu
HOPECHEST. Serb
MRS EVERAGE. Serb
HOPECHEST. Portuguese

MRS EVERAGE. Portuguese

HOPECHEST. Dane

MRS EVERAGE. Dane

HOPECHEST. Alsatian

MRS EVERAGE. Alsatian. What, dear? . . . Of course, dear. (*To Hopechest*) Mother would like us to take it slower so that she could look up her atlas. What were the last two you gave us?

HOPECHEST. A Dane and an Alsatian.

MRS EVERAGE (*puzzled*). A Dane and an Alsatian, dear . . . (*To Hopechest*) Mother isn't certain how a Dane and an Alsatian would mix with two Australian foxies . . .

At the finale Edna's mother reminds her that friends from Tasmania are coming to stay for the Games. Says Edna to the fulminating Hopechest: 'She says if we've got to have anyone in the house, Aussies will do her. And you've got to admit she's right, you know, remember the White Australia Policy! Sorry to have troubled you – ' Edna exits 'with a fine suburban shopping-bent sweep'.

The response was rapturous. 'You could hear the whoosh of laughter,' says Humphries of the audience's shock of recognition. Even the cast was surprised by the sketch's impact. 'No one had really talked about Australian houses before,' says Humphries. 'Since my father was a builder and the creator of a number of substantial Melbourne houses, in jazz moderne with manganese bricks, or Spanish Mission with the barley-sugar columns and little grilled windows, I was interested in houses. I found that I'd discovered something I could write about, not by putting the telescope to my eyes and trying to write something in the manner of Coward or Alan Melville, but by just looking through the venetian blinds on to my own front lawn. So Edna was born. Edna Everage as in "average", husband Norm as in "normal".'

Humphries hands me a snapshot of an open-topped red London double-decker bus chock-a-block with gladdies, refurbished with wicker furniture and parked directly opposite Westminster Abbey. On the side of the bus it reads: 'AUSTRALIA. THE MIDDAY

'This was Fergie's and Andrew's wedding. Edna was reporting it for Australian television.' He hands me a second photo. 'Edna was part of the royal pageant.' Edna is beaming at the camera in a broad-brimmed white straw hat, huge gold earrings, and a canary yellow frock with a short white waistcoat and matching lapels. 'The royals all gave me huge waves,' says Humphries, dealing me his trump, a picture of Princess Anne in the royal carriage smiling up at Dame Edna and giving an unmistakable semaphore of greeting. 'Well, after all, Edna is part of the Australian royal family.'

'It's very funny. Edna's presence turns these occasions into a sort of masquerade.'

'Yes,' says Humphries. 'That's right.'

'In an epigraph to your collection of early sketches, you quote from Joseph Hergesheimer's *Java Head*: "Men even at the end of many years never definitely lost connection with their early selves, there was always a trace of hopefulness, of jaunty vanity – sometimes winning and sometimes merely ridiculous – attached to their decline."'

'It's an attitude of mine,' says Humphries, who refers to his most recent collection of monologues, *Shades of Sandy Stone*, as 'this street directory to my youth'. 'I am still re-examining my own past and the texture of my childhood. That's all we've got, isn't it?'

'*Lesettes. Lesettes. On stage please for warm up.*'

'C'mon, Barry, do your warm up,' says Lizzie Spender, who makes a statuesque appearance at the threshold of the dressing room. 'This is an important part of the day.'

'C'mon, Johnny.'

Out front the audience is laughing at slide projections which are warming it up for Les Patterson's raucous opening turn. Backstage Humphries is warming up for the audience. 'Swivel head to the right,' says Jane, the busty and bubbly Lesette, who leads us through the routine. 'Swivel head to the left. How's the book going, Barry?'

'Edna's just won the lovely mother contest. To my alarm, in the autobiography certain facts don't match up.'

'Like what?'

' "The Migrant Hostess" sketch. It was first called "The Olympic Hostess", but the Olympic Games were no longer current. It was done as a woman who was going to be billeting migrants, a big new thing in Australia.' Humphries turns to me as he swivels right. 'Do you think it's serious?'

'No.'

'She's offering her house to a shotputter from Lapland. A few *aficionados* are going to say, "Hang on. Brucie's only three, and in the stage version he's engaged." '

'Have a disclaimer.'

'Good,' says Jane. 'Now the arms. Rotate right. Left. Right. Left.'

'Something like "There have been other things which have been published without my authorisation. Scholars must not be confused. This is the real story," ' pants Humphries. 'The lovely mother contest, I've decided, has a prize that sends her to England. That'll get her there as a winner. She comes in as a winner. She will already have done a little bit of stage work. She'll leave her family behind. Not with much difficulty. With about as much difficulty as Fergie encountered.' When Jane gets to the jumping jacks, the inspiration of Dame Edna's 'dancing' becomes clear. I stop at sixty. Humphries keeps twisting and turning to the count of eighty.

On the way back to the dressing room, Lizzie says, 'The book just pours out of him. He speaks it in paragraphs to his secretary. Sometimes sixteen or seventeen pages a day with only a few corrections of grammar.'

Until Edna's début, Humphries had been 'the boy in the rep who was worst at learning his lines and was getting smaller and smaller parts'. Edna's success made him the star of the revue. But the slog of repertory did not easily agree with a performer who had already taken as his credo Francis Picabia's maxim: 'Art becomes a pleasure.' As Humphries put it many years later in his 'Ode to the Melbourne Theatre Company':

When told how old this Company is, I scarcely could
    believe it
For it only seems like yesterday that I was asked to leave it.
I couldn't learn my lines, you see, which wouldn't do at all.
So I was driven into a sordid life in the sleazy music hall . . .
Although I but a comic be, I don't envy real actors.
Of bitter dregs I've drunk enough; of fame I've sipped
    the cup,
They still have lines to learn by heart, I have to make
    them up . . .

According to Peter O'Shaughnessy, Humphries' frequent sketch-writing collaborator and main director in these formative years, 'Ray Lawler seemed to think Humphries was lacking in "esprit de corps", and his talents might be better fitted to revue.' Lawler made some enquiries which led to Humphries getting an eighteen-month engagement in revue at the Phillip Street Theatre in Sydney. 'I found, to my great pleasure,' says Humphries, 'that the Olympic Hostess sketch was popular there, and Mrs Everage was by no means unknown in New South Wales.' But Humphries had no ambitions for the character. 'It was just a bit of fun,' he says. Having discovered Edna, he promptly put her in mothballs. Edna made her Sydney debut in *Around the Loop* (1956), but she didn't reappear on stage in Melbourne until 1958, first in Peter O'Shaugnessy's *Lunch Hour Theatre Revues* and later in *The Rock 'N' Reel Revue*. Edna performed the rewritten version of her original incarnation in *The Migrant Hostess*. 'The sketch still had some life in it,' says Humphries. 'These new people were coming to Australia, a kind of *Arbeitleute*. No one ever suspected they'd end up pretty well owning it and running it. They were variously called "migrants" or "Balts" because many came from the Baltic States. "Balts" is never used now; later, they became the "new Australians". The two-hander again registered the patronising attitude the Australians had to foreigners. There's a kind of bracing unselfconscious xenophobia about Australians which I regret having been displaced by a terrible bogus liberalism. Like "we're really all the same", when we're obviously all so different.

I've always felt that the variety of the human race is the interesting thing about it. The thought that black people and white people are really exactly the same except that they're different colours seems a rather abhorrent, indecent, and fundamentally racist notion. As it was, Australia wasn't yet threatened by a *tinted* invasion. It was largely people from strange places who did strange things.'

Edna too was doing strange things. For the first time the preternaturally shy and gauche Edna looked directly at the audience and talked to it. Edna recited 'Maroan', in which she expounded on her notion of 'the colour question', and Humphries poked fun at the tenacious insistence of Australians to mispronounce 'maroon'.

> All our family loves it and
> You ought to see our home,
> From the bedroom to the laundry –
> Every room's maroan!
> When we bought our home in Moonee Ponds
> It didn't have a phone
> But it had one thing to offer:
> The toilet was maroan . . .

Edna also talked to the audience about the winning Danish design for the Sydney Opera House. 'I wrote a sketch the same night the thing was announced, in which Edna lamented the fact that the design hadn't incorporated crèches and rest rooms for old people,' says Humphries. 'Edna felt that it really needn't be used for opera at all. You know, "It's all right to have an opera house but can movies be enjoyed there?" The opera proved to be as Edna had supposed; and indeed was wrenched out of the hands of the Danish architect by Australian bureaucrats in order that all of these rather irrelevant amenities that Edna had *satirically* prophesied could be installed.' The sketch was only performed a few times. 'I think it was thought tasteless by the Sydney group, considering how much time and money had gone into the opera house. Later it became a national joke, but then it was very bad form.' None the less, Edna scored with her public. 'It was mystifying, but people were amused at this little figure standing on the stage doing it,' says Humphries. 'It was in a slightly different tradition than the Sydney writers who wrote apposite material: jokes about socialites and hairdressers or well-known political figures. But this was a person from the wilderness from which no theatrical bloom had ever sprung: the suburbs. It was sort of regional stuff. It was specifically Melbourne and always seemed, even to those Sydney people, a little foreign.'

Edna was the first flowering of experiments begun as early as the Melbourne Dada Group to elevate suburban banality to fiasco. With his friend John Perry, Humphries had tried to tease amusement out of the Australian idiom in sketches for *Call Me Madman!* Together they 'improvised certain dialogues and monologues in which characters addressed each other as if over a suburban fence in very stylised ways about suburban obsessions – the football match, shopping, school. They were deliberately banal and boring. They went *on* for a long time.' In *Hello, Jim* two characters with the same name greet each other so that colloquial clichés becomes 'abstracted and non-realistic'. On stage (1952) and on record (1953), Perry recalls, 'we assumed "comfortable" and confidential voices. The very act of uttering the bizarre expressions was intoxicating.' The sketch foreshadowed the seeds of Edna's fun and her focus, if not her style.

JIM A. Oh, hello, Jim. What's the score? I haven't seen you in donkey's years.

JIM B. Put it there, Jim. I'm not so bad. How's yourself? I haven't seen you since you went up north. How's Marj these days?

JIM A. Well, to tell you the truth, she's only just so-so.

JIM B. Oh! I'm sorry to hear that. Such a clean living kid too – a good church-goer.

JIM A. Yes, she caught a cold when she was down at the market, stockin' up on veggies.

JIM B. I see. And talkin' of veggies; up our way we got some lovely spuds.

JIM A. Are you fair dinkum? They are scarce now and real pricey. We just got a beaut. Good-eatin' cauli.

JIM B. (*making appropriate gesture.*) Like a fag?

JIM A. I don't mind if I do. (*He takes cigarette with which he then lights his own. Hands back Jim B's cigarette.*) Ta. How's the kids?

JIM B. Okey-dokey. Merv's at Oakaleigh Tech. And we got Norm boardin' out at Wagga Wagga School.

JIM A. Lummi! That's far enough away, isn't it?

JIM B. Oh, yes and no; it depends on the people.

JIM A. Yes, you've hit the nail right on the head there. My Shirl's at Pra'n Tech, and she's getting along like a bomb, and our Jacky's up at Box Hill and going to Dookie next week.

JIM B. I saw Jacky the other day, at the trots. She was with Irene and is she a beaut. Fast sheila with that new pancake make-up over her dial. Jacky looked a dandy too; all dolled up like a sore toe . . .

Edna's success in *The Rock 'N' Reel Revue* coaxed Humphries into writing monologues for her. Until then, Humphries had only conceived monologues for Sandy Stone, a character invented for a gramophone record who he admits had strong similarities with Edna's story. 'Sandy was Norm, wasn't he? In a sense Sandy and Edna were two sides of the same coin. But I thought Sandy had more of a treasure trove of material to draw upon,' says Humphries, of the sad, childless, credulous Australian Mr Pooter. 'Edna seemed to be one joke which was merely reiterated until I decided to develop Edna's family and the family took on a life of its own outside the theatre.'

In time these characters turned Humphries into a regional monologuist. 'All great British comedians have provincial backgrounds, whether the province is East London or Lancashire. Their humour is regional humour that has a metropolitan following. In Australia, before me, most comic stereotypes were kind of rural people: hayseeds, hillbillies. If you could think of Melbourne and Sydney as the Home Counties in the Pacific, a kind of Oceanian British province, which it is, the Australian public weren't used to that novelty.' Edna, an amalgam of the suburban Australian 1950s, as well as an embodiment of a nascent spirit of critical self-awareness, was conceived as a rebuke and an essay in naturalism. To a society used to defining itself in colonial terms, Edna was both a shock and a revelation. 'In the back of the Australian mind,' wrote A.A. Phillips in 1966, coining the phrase 'cultural cringe' for the then pervasive Australian sense of cultural inferiority, 'there is a minatory Englishman.' Edna inverted the cringe, which saw Life as elsewhere. Edna was unabashedly Australian. Her look, her language, her obsessions owed nothing to any outside influences.

'There seemed to me no Australian comedians who actually tried *as accurately as possible*, without the use of jokes or even funny names, to discover something intrinsically funny in the way that *most* people really did live,' says Humphries. 'In refrigerators. In appliances. In the problems of parking the car. Sandy Stone was the first person to get a big laugh when he said in his cracked intonation in 1957 – "Had a bit of strife parking the vehicle." The audience used to laugh uproariously when it heard that because people called their cars "the vehicle". It was what people said when they couldn't park. It was just a sort of fresh interpretation of ordinary life. Whereas before, when you were identifying with Lucille Ball or Bob Hope or the Marx Brothers, you had to go through a very quick series of transpositions. First of all, you had to translate from the American into the English or Australian idiom. And *then* get the joke.' In Edna's case the joke was outside the Australian front door.

'In the fifties,' Humphries told the *Sunday Times* in 1987, 'Australian drama meant rep versions of Rattigan and Christopher Fry. Then, along came this lady from next door, talking about recipes and curtains; the blissful commonplaces.' The shock was not just of recognition, but of satire. Edna was an incarnation of the Australian Ugliness, so well named by the architect Robin Boyd in his best-selling book of the late 1950s. When monologues of Edna and Sandy finally found their way into the Australian mass market in Humphries' popular and influential record *Wildlife in Suburbia* (1958), it was Boyd who announced on the record sleeve, 'He has the modern Australian way of life stretched out and pinned down with needles. He has us taped in killing caricature: our accent, intonation, vocabulary, the shattered syntax, the activities, accessories, diet – and through it all the ghastly proprieties, the crazily clumsy genteelness of brick-area suburbia.' What Humphries caught in Edna's polite censoriousness was the whiff of puritanism spawned in the suburbs with, as Boyd wrote, 'its ever-increasing prudery on the surface, while the male community grew more ribald and appallingly blasphemous under its breath'.

Edna had all the distinguishing marks of this familiar Australian breed: an obsession with surfaces and colour, the love of advertisement, the dreadful language, the ladylike euphemism. With her emphasis on the sympathetic magic of niceness ('You may be black or tinted or have nought to eat but rice,' sings Edna in 'Niceness'. 'But if you clean your teeth three times a day the chances are you're nice. /And the World will be nice to you . . .'), she exuded the hectoring zeal of the prude. 'P is for prude in the great land of ours,' wrote Humphries in 'Edna's Alphabet'. 'Our culture, our history, I could go on for hours . . .'

Edna was the doyenne of philistine denial. She feared penetration of anything: germs, ideas, certainly sex. 'Although my childhood was in the midst of – at the very heart of niceness and decency and cleanliness and comfort,' wrote Humphries, 'I perceived the little dramas of Australian suburban life: the war against stains, and creepy-crawlies and the mysterious Outback; the knowledge that we didn't really live in Bournemouth or Wimbledon, but on the ghostly periphery of Asia, with no traditions or even ghost stories to palliate our fear.' Edna barricaded herself in the trivia of daily life, for which Humphries with his superb memory seemed to have total recall. She gave her listeners detailed baking recipes. She lectured the audience on Home Hygiene ('A drop of disinfectant in your kiddy's schoolbag could save a lot of heartache. A Pine-O-Clean rinse makes your rubbish bins *safe* to live with . . .'). She hymned the contents of her medicine chest: 'Calamine Lotion. Milk of Magnesia. Laxettes. Asprose. Band-Aids (flesh tint). Bicarbonate of Soda. Golden Eye Ointment. Rawley's Ready Relief . . .' Her fear of infection belied a mind without a thought, just the echo of brand names and the rhythms of their advertising slogans.

Advertisements were among Humphries' earliest memories and among the first words he learned to read. 'News was sad. Ads were happy,' he recalled of growing up in the late 1930s amidst the grim unreal topics of world cataclysm. 'News meant war. Advertisements peace, comfort, security.' Edna's presence called post-war Australian prosperity into question. She was an act of disenchantment in the guise of feverish credulity. Edna kept faith with consumerism, a theology of ownership made more virulent in Humphries' eyes by television advertising. 'The commercial break is our orison,' wrote Humphries, 'the singing advertisement our liturgy and Gregorian chant, the telly our icon and stained-glass window through which we glimpse a purchaser's paradise. When the ad man dies he will surely be fumbling with a rosary of video tape.' When evoking the heaven of her Melbourne childhood, Edna's purest and most poetic words for it are brand names.

> The Melbourne of my girlhood was a fine Rexona Town.
> Her smile was bright with Kolynos and Persil white her gown,
> Her Bedgood shoes with Nugget shone, she scorned inferior brands,
> And in her Lux-white gloves there slept her soft Palmolive hands . . .

In the catalogue for 'The Art Works of Barry Humphries' (1958), 'Dr Humphries', in black cape and fedora, was photographed hunkered down in a garbage dump holding a stethoscope to a trash can. This was supposed to be the 'Murrumpjubba Capsule, in which priceless fragments of sponge cake, ketchup and shoeware were discovered'. The image was apt. Humphries was picking over the detritus of Australian culture and reassembling something of beauty from the waste. Edna, too, was a found object. When Humphries explored his characters, as he did on one extraordinary taped improvisation of Sandy Stone's which later became part of the record *Sandy Agonistes*, he found a jumble of song refrains, street names, surnames. In these early years, Sandy and Edna were undifferentiated characters, and Edna had much the same habit of mind. In his cracked sing-song delivery, Sandy launched into a sibilant litany of trivia which went on for twenty minutes. What began as a free association ended as a kind of destiny.

Palm Court . . . Palmolive Toilet Soap . . .
NO NO NANETTE! . . . Naughty Marietta . . .
Nelson Eddy and Jeanette MacDonald . . .
The Desert Song. '*Mine alone. You're mine alone . . . Mine alone. You're . . .*'
The Maid of the Mountains . . . White Horse Inn . . .
Gladys Moncrieff . . . DOCTOR MORSE'S INDIAN ROOT PILLS . . . Phosphatine . . . Kolynos . . .

When Humphries spotted a mint-condition blue, black and gold 'Dr Morse's Indian Root Pills' hoarding on a Melbourne side street in the late 1950s, he celebrated his discovery as if it were an archaeological find. After a lunch at the Society Restaurant, guests and waiters bearing champagne were ushered by taxi to the sight. Humphries made a speech, and then glasses of champagne were passed around on silver salvers. 'To Doctor Morse,' he toasted. The assembled downed their drink and threw the champagne glasses against the brick wall. 'I really am a pioneer of Australian nostalgia,' said Humphries, whose characters too were a kind of walking time capsule. 'In my early shows the interval was occupied by showing coloured slides which I'd got from old cinemas, of furniture, houses. Goodness knows what happened to those slides. I should have kept them all. They were historical documents. They'd been thrown out, many of them found in rubbish bins. And the audience pissed themselves laughing, just looking at their past. I was one of the first people to actually say, "This material is so recent we don't pay it any attention at all."'

Humphries' fascination with signs fed his comedy. Edna's 'War Savings Street Song' (1962) emerged out of a passion for THIS

IS A WAR SAVINGS STREET signs. Qantas flew two signs free of charge to Humphries during his first stay in London. And Humphries nailed one of these signs outside 10 Downing Street in London, saying as he hammered, 'We aim to preserve all existing signs and re-erect those that have suffered from the corrosion of time and the apathy of peace. Our motto is "They meant something then – what do they mean now?"' He wrote to a friend, 'Naturally the new Melbourne suburbs present a problem. Many residents in Clayton, Highett, McKinnon and Nunawading may object that they can't get into the act. We are therefore preparing signs for them – THIS MIGHT HAVE BEEN A WAR SAVINGS STREET.'

But for Humphries himself there was no advertisement like self-advertisement. Edna gave Humphries the licence to make a spectacle of himself. And he did. 'Barry Humphries is, perhaps, the most gifted clown in Australia,' read his bio in the 1958 programme for *The Rock 'N' Reel Revue*. By 1959, Australian society had taken both the character and her creator to heart; and Humphries could leave it to others to make claims for him. Support came from improbable places. The novelist Patrick White, who would dedicate a play to Humphries, became a devotee of Edna and her rendition of 'Maroan'. Upon receiving a plaque as Australian of the Year after winning the Nobel Prize for Literature, White proposed dividing the plaque among the historian Manning Clark, the communist activist-ecologist Jack Mundey and Barry Humphries. Sir John Betjeman, later England's poet laureate, became a fan and friend after hearing *Wildlife in Suburbia*. 'We had a liking for dim poets in common; we liked them *because* they were dim,' recalled Humphries, who was urged by Betjeman to bring his act to England. 'Betjeman and I also appreciated old buildings.'

Edna's dissection of the Australian home also won Humphries the adulation of the Small Home Section of the *Melbourne Age*. 'ARE HOUSES FUNNY?' asked the headline in an article that explained: 'Not for years has there been a legitimate sophisticated national basis of general humour. Now one has been discovered. It is the suburban house, its design, furniture and landscaping. In a nation of avid homebuilders, no more fitting voice could have been made and it is now strange to think that our entertainers took so long to wake up to the inherent humour of our homes. The leader of new and startling movement is most certainly Mr. Barry Humphris [sic] ... Mr Humphris, or rather Mrs Everage ... is not only a successful comedian in the long lost Australian tradition, owing nothing to contemporary London or New York, but she is now the darling of Toorak.'

'Much to my own surprise, it seemed that houses were funny,' said Humphries. 'The more minutely I described in subsequent monologues and sketches the appointments of the *Australian Home Beautiful* – the gewgaws and kickshaws of gracious living from Laminex to lamingtons – the more the public laughed. High on the joy of self-discovery, they laughed at the very symbols and ornaments of their prosperity and dignity. Perhaps the stuff that mulgawood serviette rings and lounge suites were made of was also the stuff of jokes, even dreams. It was in the midst of these curious theatrical seances that the Spirit of Australia present palpably materialised and the conviction that Australia itself might be funny and therefore in some way forgivable.'

In February 1959 Humphries and Peter O'Shaughnessy gave a Testimonial Performance, 'as a review of some of their work over the past few years', so the programme read, 'and as a testament to their artistic intentions'. Over the previous three years, besides the revues, Humphries under O'Shaughnessy's direction had played Estragon in the Australian première of *Waiting for Godot*, Colonel Pickering in Shaw's *Pygmalion*, Bunyip in the children's fable *The Bunyip and the Satellite*. Humphries had also launched into the national consciousness two mischievous characters – Edna Everage and Sandy Stone – whose stories would continue to captivate audiences on three continents in performance, record, interviews and books. Edna would become a superstar; Sandy in both this life and the after-life would remain the same desiccated presence. Says Humphries, 'Sandy is the part of me that never left home.' But Humphries did.

In 1959, Humphries set off for England to test his talent in the more competitive arena of English theatre. In her chapter about the Australian leave-taking, Dame Edna recalls that Mother Teresa subsequently told her that true happiness comes from renunciation. 'I began my life of renunciation years ago,' she writes. 'I decided to renounce obscurity.' It was a big roll of the dice for both Edna and her creator. Humphries' arrival in London was noted in one paragraph of the *Evening News* with the headline: 'A STAR HERE?' 'That question mark haunted me for years,' Humphries says.

Barry is applying No. 5 and No. 9 panstick to his face in preparation for Edna. The show's limited season has been extended. Soon the man I'm watching powder his base make-up will look like the beaming matron in tonight's *Evening Standard* ad, which shows a grandfather telling his granddaughter that he didn't realise Dame Edna's best-ever show had been extended, and Dame Edna grinning at the bottom: 'Don't be like this foolish embittered old man, Possums. Call 240–7200, or buy tickets at the door. I may not come your way again for years.'

'The characters are getting even more exaggerated, aren't they?' says Humphries, glancing in the mirror at me seated beside him. 'I quite like the opportunity of writing the autobiography in order to actually reacquaint myself with Edna's milieu, her roots. I've always been a caricaturist.' He stops to finish highlighting Edna's face. Once powdered, Katie slips on the hair-net and starts to tape the microphone to Humphries' back. The battery pack sits in the small of his back; and the wire is then taped with microfoil along his shoulder line so it doesn't flow across or get seen in a gap in the dress. The microphone is then threaded up through the double hair-nets and sits just above his right eyebrow. Katie clips it in three places. Humphries is now ready to do his rouge and eye make-up.

'I've always been a caricaturist,' he says. 'I love the art of caricature, of achieving verisimilitude through exaggeration. Caricatures are better than the finest portraits. They have a better quality. Daumier, Lautrec, Hogarth – all somehow or other achieved more truth in their work. It's a spirit, a penetrating observation. It wasn't, in other words, their subject as the subject saw himself.'

His eyes done, Katie now approaches Humphries with Edna's natural wisteria wig made of yak's hair. 'Holds the set for two weeks,' says Katie. 'When it's dyed, yak has a more iridescent quality.'

'Great portrait painters, whatever they may tell you, are flattering their subjects,' says Humphries, as Katie pins and then tapes the wig in place so that the microphone is unnoticeable beneath the curl on Edna's forehead. 'Whereas the caricaturist is the outsider. He's not the friend of the subject necessarily, and is perforce detached in some way. I'm a theatrical caricaturist. Caricature is a creative distortion. Almost lying to get at the truth.'

Katie hands Humphries Edna's jewellery: her ankle bracelet, her diamanté rings, necklace and earrings, which have to be attached with wig tape because they're so heavy.

'I'm working on a new rhyme for "My Public",' says Humphries 'in honour of Glasnost. "Dad ... da ... da ... Mikhail and Raisa/I love to see my gladdies tremblin'/Soon they'll be tremblin' in the Kremlin." ' He looks over to me. 'Mm?' says Humphries.

'Not bad.'

'Get away with that?'

'I thought you were going to do something about the people you're on with.'

'I thought Sammy and Sinatra would be on the bill. But they're not. They're at the Albert Hall. That's a problem for me. At the last minute they might be coming across.'

Humphries starts doing Edna's nails with the nail-varnish pen. 'Lively audience.'

Humphries turns to the voice. 'Harriet,' he says, standing to get into his red dress. 'What's the house?'

'I don't have a figure on the house, Barry. I'll get one.'

'Where's Jack?' says Humphries, asking for the company manager, Jack Hylton. 'Look, what sort of house have we got?'

'I'm going to the box office and find out.'

'It is Monday. Does it look all right out there?'

'It does indeed.'

Humphries, now completely transformed as Edna except for glasses and mourning coat, crosses to Harriet, standing with clipboard on the threshold of his dressing room. They scrutinise a piece of paper on the clipboard. 'There are empty seats here,' he says, drawing a varnished finger over the page. 'Can you find out why? Do you think they haven't turned up, or are they just coming for Edna?'

'There's a guy here', says Harriet, indicating far left, 'with a swagman's hat with corks on it.'

'Uh oh. Don't get him laughing. He sounds mad. No one in Australia has a hat with corks on it. Where's the Fat?'

'Five rows back. Young woman,' says Harriet.

Humphries looks over to me. 'You see, John, it's so dark out there and my sight is going. As I peer into the audience, I can't always see as clearly as I used to. I hate to admit this infirmity. So Harriet has this interesting document.' Humphries beckons me into the circle. 'Look at it. Look what it's called.'

Harriet holds the paper up for me to see.

'Theatre Royal Drury Lane Victim Map?'

'And it says,' says Humphries, pointing to the map's legend and enjoying my astonishment. 'Look.'

'Who does the actual spying on the audience?'

'Oh, certain very trusted aides.'

'How do you remember it?'

'Well, I'm not going to remember it tonight with you trying to ruin my show,' smiles Humphries and turns back to Harriet. 'Show it to me.'

'Senior there. Fat one's five rows back.'

'Fat? Very fat? How far back?'

'She's fifth row three in. Yellowy-greeny colour. There's probably a better senior there.'

Humphries looks over at me. 'Because of the success of Edna's TV show, the audiences are getting younger. And it's harder to find faces to bring up on stage on whom life has left its mark.'

BACK WITH A VENGEANCE!

THEATRE ROYAL
DRURY LANE
VICTIM MAP

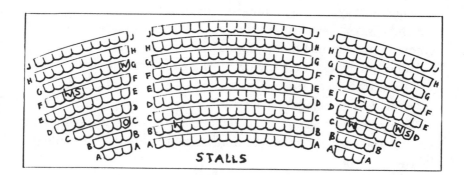

STALLS

legend

W	WOMAN	T	TINTED
F	FAT WOMAN	R	RED DRESS
O	OBESE WOMAN	S	SENIOR
C	CRIPPLE	PS	PATHETIC SENIOR

'This is really funny. Can I have a copy?'

'Also it's a warning, so I don't pick someone who's disabled. I have picked a crippled person before. They usually insist on coming on stage. It takes half an hour, during which time the audience falls very very silent indeed.'

'It's amazing that you can remember.'

'Sometimes I don't.'

Katie holds out the black coat, and Humphries buttons himself into it. He puts on the harlequin glasses, and the transformation is complete.

'Well, Dame Edna, thank you for letting me see the map. And visit, as we say in America. You'll be glad to know I won't be around for a while. I might just drop in and see the act next Thursday.'

'You're not ill, are you, John?' says Dame Edna in a rather husky falsetto, walking toward the stage with Katie and Harriet leading the way. As she pushes through the green-room doors into the stage house, she turns back to me. 'A thousand isn't bad, is it?' Dame Edna doesn't wait for an answer. 'Hello, Jim,' she says to a stagehand, as Katie leads her around the set to the left of house from where she'll make her entrance once the laughing from the filmed introduction about Norm's death dies down.

Harriet stands by the prompt desk and puts around her neck the headset with which she communicates to the lighting booth at the back of the theatre. She takes her position by the side of the stage. 'They've just extended the run,' Harriet says. 'I've got no idea whether ticket sales are stable. I know it's about a thousand for the next two weeks. Barry doesn't like that because it means no "paupers", and he has to use the Dress Circle as "paupers". Dennis gave me a crash course in what to say. Barry will say, "In the row for the house seats, there were three empty seats. Why?" And I say, "The tickets were sold, Barry. If they don't choose to come, there's nothing we can do about it." That's what I'm told to tell him.'

'I told him, "They haven't finished counting,"' says Katie, passing us on her way back from depositing Dame Edna for her entrance. 'It could have been thirteen hundred.'

Harriet laughs to herself. 'You know one of the stagehands

was killed at Covent Garden last Friday. Freak accident. Barry was asking me about it. "If it happens to me," he said, "make sure they're sued." '

At the sound of the drum roll and the announcer's baritone voice blaring '. . . *The management have little doubt that if this proves to be Dame Edna . . .*', Harriet turns abruptly away from the conversation, puts on her headset and mumbles something into the microphone. The pianist takes a quick sip of water. A stagehand settles back into Sandy Stone's easy chair with a copy of the *Sun*. And I turn away to take my leave. A bag lady in a tattered dress startles me. I take an involuntary step backwards. It's one of the Lesettes swathed in Madge Allsop's bandages.

I make my way carefully over the cables past the cherry picker with skirt, past Sandy's collapsible easy chair, past the columns with koala, past the rack of costumes for tonight's Victims, past Harriet and Katie and Andy and Jim, and all the faces that have become my life over the last three weeks. As I push open the grey exit doors, Dame Edna's clarion call resounds backstage.

'Hello, Possums!' she is saying to the boom of applause. 'Hello, darlings!! Hello, Possums . . . !!!'

4

Sir Les Patterson and the Chinese Year of the Trouser Snake

'In fiction as in history it is the shudder that tells.'

Edgar Evertson Saltus

Sir Les's bow tie has gone walkabout. A camera crew is setting up outside the dressing room to film Sir Les's TV greeting to the Melbourne Comedy Festival, of which he is patron. 'What happened to the bow tie?' says Humphries, padding up. He is not pleased.

'I always hang it here,' says Katie, starting to panic at the tight civility in Humphries' voice.

'How could it be gone?'

'I don't know, Barry.'

'The black will do.'

'I've got this, Barry,' says Katie, handing him a midnight-blue tie. 'Terribly sorry. It's elasticated. Goes over your head.'

Humphries fastens the tie above the ruffles of his blue tuxedo shirt.

Sir Les is a comic grotesque. The energy and joy of his creation is in confounding the boundaries of form: both the 'good form' of manners and the proper dimensions of the human silhouette. Sir Les bursts the seams of the real. He is a rollicking, tumescent theatrical creation whom Humphries has described as 'on a sort of bacchic trip'. His cock, a pendulous eight inches of padded cotton, dangles beneath Humphries' upholstered belly to his knees, making Humphries look for all the world like an Aussie Ubu. The archetypal Shakespearean fool held up a penis as sceptre and called this totem of the clown's rapacity a 'baubel' or plaything. The penis epitomised the clown's desire to create a

103

panic; and many of the great modern clowns goosed the world with some phallic vestige: Harpo's horn, Groucho's cigar, Chaplin's cane. Humphries belongs to this great anarchic tradition; and in the area of phallic fun Sir Les holds his own.

'There are literary allusions in Les,' says Humphries, 'but you're not really meant to get them. He is a music-hall character, very much a vaudeville figure, related to Max Miller a bit. The phallus is Aristophanic. But then he's also related to Mr Punt, that figure in an otherwise very boring play by Brecht, and to certain sorts of Shakespeare drunks, like Toby Belch. He's also very like, whatever they might say, a lot of people in Queensland.' Sir Les inspires a real sense of terror and elation in an audience.

'I can remember thinking, "Jesus Christ look at Les with that great dick. I was just absolutely flabbergasted,"' recalls Ian Davidson. 'The noise when the audience saw the dick! It was like someone stuck a fork into them. It was wonderful.' Sir Les's record *Twelve Inches of Les* and his book *The Traveller's Tool* all draw attention to his most salient anatomical feature, which he refers to variously as 'the pyjama python', 'the one-eyed trouser snake', 'my not-infrequently-felt-tip', and 'the enormous encumbancy which I'm holding down at the moment'.

As a character, Sir Les owes his unique endowment to an earlier 1970s Humphries caricature called Morrie O'Connor, a car salesman turned art dealer; he owes his vernacular vulgarity to Humphries' comic-strip cult figure of the late 1960s, the lantern-jawed Aussie innocent Bazza McKenzie. The penis itself, which is now a large lump down the inside of his trouser leg, Humphries owes to Katie. 'In the film *Les Patterson Saves the World* we had to make a discreet-sized one, apparently it was a bit unnatural on screen,' Katie told me one day while I waited vainly for Humphries to arrive early at the theatre. 'After the film, we decided to keep the body padding, but the appendage was now a bit small. So I had to do a penis transplant.'

'They just want Les to say good luck, don't they?' Humphries says, looking at his transformed figure in the mirror and still without Sir Les's stained snaggle-toothed dentures. 'See if Jane can come down. She can be sitting on my lap.' With Katie dispatched,

Humphries turns to me. 'Two of the most terrible things that ever happened in Australia in my lifetime were first the news that the aboriginal population was actually growing, which then brought a terrific wave of guilt because people had absolutely no idea of what to do about it. The second thing was the broadcasting of Parliament.

'When Parliament was broadcast for the first time, middle-class Australia sat down and listened to its leaders squabbling, *except* they had these untutored accents. They heard the liberal Prime Minister Sir Robert Menzies speaking in rather syrupy, sanctimonious Methodist preacher's English. The general feeling was: he's so beautifully spoken. The thing was to have *a lovely speaking voice*. There was still this admiration in Australia, certainly among Protestants, for the well-spoken person. That meant the person from the nice home, from the right school, whose "people" – "people" not "parents" – were, it was hoped, *comfortable*, that is to say: rich. So to be comfortably off, well spoken, and to have *nice people* was all very important. It was all part of the tyranny of niceness and order.

'So that when people heard the shattered syntax and garbled grammar on the radio there were a lot of protests. "Must we broadcast this? Are these our politicians? Is the country being governed by people who sound like street urchins?" (And who, in fact, were.) In *The Complete Barry McKenzie* (1988), I put this nineteen-thirties' joke as an epigram: an English gent says to a stranger: "I say, old chap, are you an Australian?" And the stranger says, "No, just common." All Australians are common, in a way. That's the good thing about them. They're all very, very common indeed. And any pretensions to be anything else is risible.'

'Hi.' Jane, wearing a loose grey sweatshirt which can't hide her own endowments, smiles warmly in our direction.

'Look,' says Humphries, 'we're just doing a tiny telly thing of Les talking to the Comedy Festival from London. We thought it'd be nice to have a Lesette just sitting there, you know. Or draped over the shoulder.'

'The usual thing, yeah,' says Jane, who goes off to change into something even more sensational.

'Parliament really shocked people in the way that I later tried to do,' says Humphries. 'And that was just to say: "You could be like this." Australians didn't want to face up to the fact that that is what we're like. People say to me, "I like your shows very much, but that Les Patterson. I can't stand that." And I say, "Did you hear the Prime Minister last week? Or did you hear the Federal Treasurer in Parliament talking to the Shadow Minister of the Environment? Did you hear that exchange? If you think Les Patterson is crude, has it ever occurred to you that it is impossible to exaggerate in this kind of Aristophanic climate?" '

'As Flannery O'Connor said, "To the hard of hearing you shout, to the almost blind, you make large and startling gestures." Sir Les and Edna are certainly startling gestures.'

'Yes, well, if a man has a long nose and you particularly want to remind the public about it, you have to have him wheeling it on the barrow in front of him.'

All Humphries' stage characters explore and tease aspects of Australian vernacular, of which Humphries is a theatrical pioneer. 'Clued-up readers will be quick to discern in the foregoing pages a crude and anachronistic fuckin' travesty of an Australia that never existed, thank Christ,' writes Sir Les, in his most recent literary outing, the preface to *The Complete Barry McKenzie*. 'Remember', says Humphries, whose elegant diction is in disconcerting contrast to the glorious sludge of Sir Les's argot, 'that right through the war and into the nineteen-fifties the entertainment that Australians were fed in the theatre was revivals of musical comedy; and on radio, plays performed by excellent Australian actors (some like Peter Finch went abroad and became successful) took place in an imaginary Mayfair, an imaginary Ruritania, a kind of nebulous suburb where people spoke with no accent at all. To be a successful Australian actor, you had to lose your accent, which meant effacing your origins. So in unlearning the Australian accent you also, of course, had to unlearn your background. You say in effect, "This is a place I've got to get out of as soon as possible." In a sense, my departure for England was influenced very much by the idea that you get out of it as soon as possible. I thought I could stay in Australia and become a big fish in a small pool quite

106

easily. But I knew that if I wanted to learn more about the theatre (I was becoming successful because of *Wildlife in Suburbia*), I had to leave.'

Jane appears in her brief white-fringed Lesette cowgirl costume; and Humphries immediately dons his shiny blue tuxedo jacket and the teeth. 'Where do I sit?' he says to the crew, who point him to the only comfortable chair in the ante-room. 'Here? The tannoy off? A lot of Australian comics came from Melbourne. Roy Rene. Dick Bentley. I think it might be Melbourne's respectability that tends to encourage levity and irreverence. It's always been stuffy. Light catching the seat nicely? Nice two shot, hmmm?'

The director adjusts Jane on the arm rest beside Sir Les so that her cleavage is pitched at the level of his red nose. 'Hello, Melbourne!' beams Sir Les. 'Yes, it's Les Patterson here, and I'm in London town. Doing a bit of research with my latest research assistant. You know I'd like to be in Melbourne right now because it's pissing with rain here. But I'd like to take this opportunity of wishin' all them comics the very, very best. Stick it up 'em, boys and girls! Really *stick it up 'em*! Hahahahah! They used to reckon Sydney was the tops for culture, but Melbourne is the tops for the piss-take. Are you with me? And I'd like to say all the best to Dave Allen, one of the big stars of the festival this year. You'll . . . you'll kill 'em, mate, with some of them stories. You're a beauty. And he's a fellow RC, little Dave. We've both had a papal audience. But both of us reckon the Melbourne audience beats the lot of them. Have a good time. Have a good laugh. Les Patterson wishing you all the best.'

The sound of the audience laughing at the preliminary slide-show gags fills the dressing room as Humphries touches up Sir Les's make-up before taking the stage. 'Les's vulgarity is his driving force. It's a perversion of energy, vitality, the life force,' says Humphries, checking out his eyes in the mirror and widening them until they're bright with conviviality. 'Gravity is hard to banish. People are sad.'

Then, almost as an afterthought, Humphries reaches for the bottle of Lea & Perrins and, with a quick flip, sends a dribble of Worcestershire sauce down his tuxedo shirt. 'It stains well,' he says of his little trick to keep him in Sir Les's character. 'It gives a smell as if I'm permanently at a barbecue. As the body gets hotter, the aroma of this mysterious condiment rises. If a man in a clean shirt tried to do this material, I doubt if it would work.'

'Put it to 'em, Sir Les.'

Humphries turns back to me, flashing Sir Les's priapic grin and now in Sir Les's voice: 'No worries, son,' he says and heads for the stage.

'*In recent years*', booms the announcer through the theatre as Sir Les noisily pushes through the green-room doors, '*a great deal of damage has been done to Australia's international image due to gross slanders spread abroad by those seeking to impugn the refinements and sophistication which is the Australian's natural birthright . . .*'

As the drum roll echoes through the theatre, Sir Les can be heard crossing the stage, hallooing stagehands, revving up his energy. Sir Les has been known to bolt out of the theatre and run on to the stage from the street. In Melbourne, he could be heard shouting down the passageway to the stage, 'You bastards!' But this evening only Sir Les's boozy 'Stick it up 'em!' resounds backstage. 'He's excited tonight,' says Harriet.

The announcer's voice is saying: '*It is therefore with pride that we introduce a man who has done more to promote Australian credibility overseas than any other living person . . . a man who is the monument to Australia's finest attributes . . . elder statesman, ombudsman, prototypical arts minister, wit and raconteur . . . the acceptable face of Australian socialism. Your acclaim please for Sir Leslie Colin Patterson . . .!!!*'

Highball glass in hand, Sir Les leaps from the wings into the pin spot, the Pantagruel of modern comic performers. He stops in his tracks to acknowledge the whistling and the applause that greet his entrance. 'The audience recognise the sweetness of the character that overrides his grossness,' says Humphries. 'They forgive in Les what they would not forgive in many traditional comedians.' And so it is. Sir Les tugs at his enormous encumbancy. 'Good evening, ladies and gentlemen!' he says, coming downstage and sipping his drink. 'Permit me . . .' He showers the front rows with spittle, and then strolls across the stage taking aim at another section of the stalls, '. . . permit me to introduce myself . . .', he burps loudly and with great pleasure, '. . . to you good people. My name is Les Patterson . . .'

Les Patterson was invented in 1974 to introduce Dame Edna to the St George Leagues' Club in Sydney: a travesty of grossness counterpointing Dame Edna's travesty of decency. 'Les warms up the audience, he softens them up,' Humphries explained in an interview in 1987. 'He just bombards them with a sort of super ribaldry so that even little old ladies start laughing because they can't believe their ears. And, of course, he bathes them in his copious expectorations. I must say Les has his following, including certain young women, obviously deeply disturbed young women. There was a girl the other night lying, legs open, in the front row, shouting, "Spit on me, Les! Spit on me!" I mean, the person who inhabited Les was rather dismayed.' Les began as an entertainments officer. 'I understand later that many members of the audience thought Les was genuinely a club official, which says a lot for his sincerity and charm,' wrote Humphries in his compilation of early sketches *A Nice Night's Entertainment*. 'I did not anticipate his popularity at the time of his creation.'

The rise of Les Patterson's pedigree was swift. When Humphries first took the character on the road to Hong Kong in cabaret, Patterson was elevated from entertainments officer and a figure of authority in the Plasterers' Union to Australian cultural attaché to the Far East. 'The English merchant bankers and commodity brokers and the Australian accountants in Hong Kong all recognised Les as someone they knew in the Australian diplomatic corps and took him to their hearts,' Humphries has written. And by the time the character triumphed in *Housewife/Superstar* (1976), he had become *Sir* Les and part of the newly formed Whitlam Cabinet assigned to the Court of St James, where his knowledge of show business, general culture and what he himself affectionately termed 'The Yartz' proved invaluable. Sir Les, who was awarded an honorary degree in 1983 by the Cambridge Union Society, has piquantly expressed his enthusiasm for culture in verse:

What is it I like more than tarts?
The Yartz . . .
Fillums and opera, macramé work and pomes
Hectares and tonnes of culture in all homes.
This isn't just a dream, it's come to pass.
And if you don't believe me . . . kiss my arse!

Sir Les is the antithesis of Dame Edna. 'He's from Sydney,' says Humphries. 'He could *not* have originated from Melbourne, my home town.' And also Dame Edna's. 'It's nice to have one character in the repertory who affronts another. They represent two opposing Australian classes. Edna considers Les lets the side down: most critics in Australia would agree with her. Edna represents everything that is enlightened in Australian opinion, I suppose.'

Where Sir Les is a walking slum, Dame Edna is a fashion plate; where he is a libertine, she is a tyrant; where he is all body, she is all mind; where he is indifferent to public opinion, she is a slave to it; where Sir Les's conviviality teases out hostility from the audience, Dame Edna's malice puts hostility into it; where he revels in his lewdness, Dame Edna denies her own. 'Remember when Mr Hawke had charisma?' said Dame Edna at a press conference in 1986 about the Australian Prime Minister. 'Oh, I shouldn't be laughing, it was the first time a lot of underprivileged people had ever seen the word. You've got charisma before you are elected, and after it, you're an arrogant dickhead. Isn't it funny how I can use that word and it doesn't sound yucky?' Dame Edna is the doyenne of comic denial while Sir Les lets it almost literally hang out. Sir Les is the saturnalian spirit in slapstick, a one-man fiesta submerging his audience in appetite and formlessness. In this happy breakdown of boundaries, the pure and the profane, the beautiful and the ugly, the poetic and the obscene coalesce. Faced with this priapic paradox, the audience howls.

'Pull yourself together, will you, girls?' says Sir Les, standing at the front of the stage, tugging at the lump on the inside of his trousers.

110

'I think I know what all you women are staring at anyway. I know. You're all staring at my penis, aren't ya?'

Stunned heads in the front rows snap back.

'And there she is, ladies and gentlemen . . .' Sir Les wheels around and faces the trio to the side of him '. . . There she is . . . yes, my lovely little pink pianist. Little Victy Silva . . .' The pianist, dressed in a pink organza dress to pay off the joke, moves away sharpish from the piano and takes a bow. The audience keens with laughter as Humphries guides it between danger and safety.

'It's the spirit of Aristophanes,' says Humphries, about Sir Les's special power. 'The priapic thing. Just as religious traditions become subterranean and re-emerge in other forms, the theatre has some traditions as old as religions and certain persistent themes have traditionally touched people. Perhaps Sir Les is the reincarnation of something significant. This may be fanciful, but you know what I mean. Kids who've never been to vaudeville or music hall come to my show and they *like* it. They like it not just because they like the characters. I think they even find it sexy, and I think there's a need in people for this kind of comedy.'

But talent is also sexy; and watching Humphries challenge and *win* his audience with the outrageous and the unacceptable is to be present at an exciting contest. 'If my concentration goes for a second,' Humphries told the *Independent*, 'if I suddenly start thinking about a rare book catalogue that's arrived and I've forgotten to ring the bookseller to reserve a first edition of something I want – if a thought just fleetingly crosses my mind and I hear one cough at the back of the circle, it means that the audience have sensed that my focus has gone. I'm looking at them, I'm talking the same words, the same gestures, but I'm not focused. I have to keep very concentrated.' Humphries' energy also releases something sexual in an audience which is palpable even from the wings. The paying customers wait with a kind of nervy glee to be ravished by the thrill and threat of the journey on which his characters take them.

'We've got a lovely line up for you tonight,' says Sir Les, belching loudly again. 'First cab off the rank is Barry Humphries in an artistic cameo. Barry isn't a poofdah, but he gives a pretty

111

good impression of one. He'll be followed by . . . *Dame Edna Everage*! And when the megastar from Melbourne steps athwart these boards, I want you all to give her the clap she so richly deserves. I want you to put your hands together very warmly on her opening, if you will . . .'

'You have to teach an English audience to be more uninhibited,' says Humphries, and Sir Les's leering innuendo and spectacular vulgarity performs this function. 'Tragedy', says Humphries, 'dampens the spirits; comedy dampens the upholstery.' And so it seems. Out front the paying customers are no longer under wraps but clearly *beside themselves* with laughter.

This is the professional service for which an audience pays a great clown top price: to act out its secret infantile wishes which adult society disallows. The public cannot risk taking liberties with either mankind or manners; but in the dark, with a master entertainer, it experiences the exhilarating stage-managed thrill of transgressing (and surviving) social taboos.

'No, ladies . . .', says Sir Les, picking his padded arse, as nonchalant and unknowing as a monkey. 'Oh, sorry . . . bloody weather gets you . . .' He looks up at the audience, smelling his fingers as he continues. 'I uh . . .' A finger finds its way into his nose and comes out with a 'bogey', which he tries to get rid of. He can't flick it away. 'This is a tenacious bastard, this one. I'll save him up for later . . .' And he will. Humphries, a lover of horror stories, a purveyor of theatrical grotesques, an anthologist of monstrosities in his book *Bizarre* (1965) aspires to stir the imagination beyond manners and categories.

'Yes,' says Humphries. 'That's exactly what one wants to do.' Like all grotesques, Sir Les is an invitation to disgust, an expression of Humphries' love and disdain of appearances which both recognises and resists a sense of meaning. In Sir Les's presence the audience guffaws, gasps, hides its eyes, winces, looks away, even shrinks back as Sir Les probes and pokes and picks at himself. His display of phlegm and fluids calls out of an audience an admission of its own animality which manners decoy.

Sir Les's spectacular uncleanliness announces him as an enemy of convention. An amalgam of stains which extend from his teeth, shirt, and pants to the 'Lescafé' coffee mugs on sale in the theatre lobby, Sir Les faces down an audience with a vision of its defilement. Sir Les is attacking the deepest level of the bourgeoisie's fantasy of order and purity: its acquired notions of reputable behaviour. The dissonance is both liberating and horrifying. Sir Les is a theatrical embodiment of Edgar Allan Poe's definition of the grotesque as 'much of the beautiful, much of the wanton, much of the *bizarre*, something of the terrible, and not a little of that which might have excited disgust'.

Repulsion is part of the confusion of realms that Humphries is after in Sir Les's comedy. 'The more bad taste you can dish up to the British the better,' he says. 'They don't like vulgarity. They don't like the American's freedom. Same with an Australian. The English like to know where people are. They feel very insecure if they don't. They should be disgusted with Les, but they're laughing.'

The grotesque is a celebration of contradiction: an act of dislocation and discovery. To be effectively outrageous on stage takes bravery; but to be effectively grotesque takes a kind of genius which pushes the antics beyond mayhem toward meaning. The sense of pollution in Sir Les vies with the poetry of his performance to make both finally sensational. 'If Les were merely physically repellent, he might actually alienate the audience,' says Humphries. 'But through a process of overkill he seems almost to ingratiate himself with an audience. He becomes another kind of creation, almost like a dancing bear or something. So one excuses his incontinence in the same way one turns a blind eye to the sort of scatological habits of a caged animal.'

The audience's attention is lured away from the offending bogey by the pyrotechnics of the monologue, which is interrupted as latecomers are ushered on cue into the theatre via what Humphries calls 'the scenic route'. 'I get the ushers to show latecomers to their seats the very long way, right round the front so that people who arrive late are discomfited by being seen by the largest number of people,' he told me in 1981.

'Oh,' says Sir Les, 'it looks like a couple of latecomers are sneaking in here. Hello . . . Hello.' Sir Les pads across the stage on his platform shoes as the latecomers try and fail to go unnoticed. 'Just shove past, fart in their faces. No worries, heh, heh! Serves the bastards right for being on time, eh. Les is the name. Les Patterson. Welcome aboard. We've been worried about you. We've just been filling in till you arrived. First name?'

'Philip.'

'Hi, Philip. Who's the girl?'

'Sarah.'

'Philip and Sarah, ladies and gentlemen! Let's hear it for them.'

A volley of rowdy applause greets Philip and Sarah, two turkeys who have chosen an early Christmas. Sir Les bends over the footlights and extends his hand to Phil, who takes it.

'Lovely to shake you by the hand,' says Sir Les, crossing back toward centre stage and checking out the finger of his right hand. The tenacious 'bogey' has been passed on; and the theatre rocks with laughter at the recognition of Les's little revenge.

'The moment', says Humphries, 'is kind of lyrical. It has its own rhythm, and its own pace and its own innocence.' From the wings, with the Lesettes assembling backstage in their cowgirl outfits for the production number 'Never Trust a Man Who Doesn't Drink', with Humphries doing his double-take at his finger as Phil and Sarah innocently make their way up the aisle to their seats, with the noisy audience poised for the next surprise, the delicate negotiation between comedian and public becomes the drama.

Humphries plays the audience masterfully. He guides his material carefully between disgust and delight, building up the characters of 'Phil' and 'Sarah' to raise expectations of verbal mockery and then blind-siding it with a jolt of a different kind. When the stage picture hits, the audience bends as one with a roar of laughter. In that elongated moment of hilarity, Humphries imperceptibly backs away from the audience like a prize fighter finding his corner after flooring an opponent. He's thinking, watching, waiting for the audience to come to its senses so he can pummel it again. He does not press. He does not falter. The audience is game, and so is he. Humphries feels funny tonight. 'You feel as though you're in a stream,' he says of this special state of comic grace. 'There's a kind of momentum. You're in a groove. You are treading a destined path. It's being courageous too. It's being able to throw yourself into this void and know that the audience will catch you.'

Tonight's audience catches Humphries and sends him rebounding gorgeously off in another mischievous direction. 'Sssh! Sssh!! Ssssh!!!' says Sir Les, swearing the other two thousand, two hundred and fifty-one paying customers to secrecy. 'He'll reckon he found them on the arm rest, won't he, eh? That's where I always stockpile them . . .' In one gesture, Humphries brings the audience into that essential collusion which allows Sir Les (and later Dame Edna) to whip it up into such pandemonium. The sense of delighted conspiracy unifies the audience and gets it playing. 'You do this when you throw a party,' says Humphries. 'You somehow invoke the bacchic spirit – whether it's through alcohol or the drug of humour – you unify people. They give up their individuality. They become a kind of convivial conglomerate.'

But Sir Les is not everybody's cup of pee. The character gives the phrase 'cultural cringe' a meaning all its own. Sir Les's capacity for repulsion seems unlimited. 'I can just stand Les Patterson even when he belches while dribbling on his loud tie,' admits Humphries' compatriot, the pundit Clive James, in his essay on Humphries in *Snakecharmers in Texas*. 'But to sit there with your eyes closed is sometimes to wonder at the price of the ticket.' The ferocity of Humphries' grotesque is what disturbs James. 'He is so excessive a reaction that you wonder at the provocation.' Comic exaggeration dissociates Humphries from the philistine stereotype he inhabits; but the excess is also a kind of exorcism. The grotesque makes a drama of paradox and projects Humphries' own paradoxical nature. Through the sodden Sir Les, Humphries – a recovering alcoholic – spews out both an aesthete's hatred of yobbo Australian culture and also all the spoiled bits of his past: the drinking, the family expectations, the bad nurturing, the puritan ethos of productivity, efficiency, decorum. No wonder Humphries' mother could never bring herself to watch the character.

Comedians often talk of 'being a panic', but few modern ones have succeeded as well as Sir Les in creating it. In 1985 Sir Les had the plug pulled on him in the middle of a Sydney radio interview after 'hundreds of irate listeners phoned in complaining

115

about his on-air rudeness'. In fact Les was reworking one of the lovely anecdotes with which he regales Philip and Sarah as they settle down into the crepuscular oblivion of row S. 'What do you do when a bird shits on your windscreen?' Sir Les was cut off the air before the punchline. Answer: 'Never take her out *again*!!!'

In a mock satellite interview with Michael Parkinson on his two hundredth talk show in 1978, Gloria Swanson and Dame Edna sat watching the monitors as Sir Les, behind a Sydney backdrop, extended hospitality to Parkinson, who was about to visit Australia.

'I assume, by the way, Mike,' said Sir Les drooling down his kipper tie '. . . I can't talk too intimately because we are, you know, on the satellite. But I assume your delightful lady wife won't be making this trip with you. So I've teed up, you know . . . a little bit out here for you. I needn't say any more, except let's call it Operation Golden Donut . . . I've worded up some of the hottest . . . the Qantas hosties . . . I've had a word with them. The air hostesses, of course, have read their *Emanuelle* manual . . . You can be sure, Mike, that they'll find a little room in their luggage racks for your hand baggage. No worries, son . . . Ha!!! Oh, by the way, I think the girls in Australia are going to go for you in a big way, Mike. My wife says your mouth's a bit small, but that's neither here nor there. It's a touch of the James Galways about the lips, isn't it? Probably going down to the old flute from time to time, no doubt. But there's an old aboriginal saying . . . small of mouth, big of didjeridoo.'

As Sir Les signed off, an unwitting and appalled Gloria Swanson was heard to exclaim, 'I don't believe it!'

The public are often shocked by Sir Les's unexplained media appearances. When he infiltrated the *Joan Rivers Show* in America (1986), introduced as 'Australia's ambassador and friend of the royal family', Sir Les greeted Rivers by pressing a ripe camembert into her palm. He went on to explain that, as supremo of the Australian Cheese Board, he'd sent a platter of local cheeses to the Duke and Duchess of York as a wedding gift. 'I thought perhaps as they were exploring each other romantically it would be lovely to think they could reach out in the middle of the night for a moist handful of post-coital gorgonzola,' said Sir Les.

The habitually genial American studio audience was soon booing Sir Les, who was unstoppable. 'Australia played a major role in the Second World War,' he said. 'If it hadn't been for Australia's intervention, there would be a lot more Japanese restaurants in Los Angeles.' Humphries relished the mischief. 'It is quite likely', he told the Australian press in 1987, 'that people in America think that Sir Les is our real roving ambassador. But if we are to deplore the fictitious Les, let us simultaneously raise our eyebrows at our real-life emissaries.'

Sir Les continues to be a subject of scandal and concern in Australia, where his antecedent in transcendental vulgarity Bazza McKenzie was banned from publication in his original comic book form. Many in 'the brown and pleasant land' would like to ban Sir Les, who is seen by the very politicians he mocks as a blight to national pride and to tourism. Questions about Humphries and Sir Les have been raised in Parliament and hotly debated over the years in the popular press. The power of Humphries' caricatures can be measured by the nation's fear of infection from them. He enjoys stirring it up. 'I have learned to smile when I say something vicious,' he told *The Times* in 1973. 'That way you can get away with anything.'

Sir Les, like Humphries, is a hostile sharpshooter loudly proclaiming his innocence, which earns him the final word in most of these public exchanges. When the Australian Minister of Tourism singled out Sir Les in 1987 as a 'chauvinistic, beer-swilling drunk without any sensitivity, without any feeling', who presented the wrong image to British tourists, Sir Les demanded of the press that a copy of the Minister's comments be sent to his Brisbane hotel suite. 'Ask for the honeymoon suite and if I'm not there one of my research assistants will be,' he said. 'Just ask for Sandra, Samantha, Candy, or Nikky. But dictate very slowly.'

When the Australian Government paid for the renovation of a Georgian house in London as a headquarters for improving Australia's image in Britain, citing as one of its main tasks 'overcoming the influence of Barry Humphries', Sir Les was quick to paint him-

117

self into the English PR picture. Sir Les claimed in print to have been called into action by the Prime Minister himself: 'Australia's international image needs a bit of spit and polish and you're just the man to put his mouth where Australia's money is. Let's face it, Les, London's chock-a-block with expat knockers making a fat quid selling Australia's credibility short. Smart alec galahs like Germaine Greer, Clive James and that old sheila, Dame Edna, who dresses up as a man and tips the bucket on our incomparable cultural attainments in front of the crowned heads of Europe.' Sir Les then went on to list upcoming Institute events. 'We're expecting such luminaries as Former-Sir Anthony Blunt on "Baroque Abo frescoes in the Murrimbidgee Basin", Dr Jonathan Miller's post-mortem on the first Australian convict production of *Fidelio*, and the last Abo *Aida*, Dr Pamela Stephenson on "Australian Wit and Humour in the Post-Prandial Period" and "Undressing as Satire", plus Neville Wran's sell-out lecture to the Aussie diplomatic community on "How To Be Successful *and* Common".'

The grotesque is a species of confusion, and so Sir Les registers best on stage where he can be experienced both in normal human proportion and in all his obscene, abnormal glory. 'I don't think Les belongs on television. He can't be truly Les,' says Ian Davidson, who works with Humphries on his TV shows. 'A huge penis belongs on stage, doesn't it?' But on the large screen the grotesque becomes too overbearing and too ugly to be funny, as Humphries found to his cost with his latest feature film *Les Patterson Saves the World*. 'It received the worst notices of anything I've ever done,' says Humphries, who prefers to count the film among his *débâcles d'estimes*. 'People were absolutely horrified to see Les in close-up on the wide screen. And the film was branded as treacherous. That's because, if you work in the Australian arts, you are considered officially part of the Australian PR exercise, whether you like it or not. So if you dare to represent Australians critically or even comically then you're "letting the side down". When *Saves the World* was released, there were people exclaiming in public, in print – and in Parliament – that Les was undoing "all the good work that *Crocodile Dundee* and Paul Hogan have done". I returned to England just in time to escape the lynching parties ... I've always liked to make Australia seem as inhospitable as possible. I've been known to exaggerate on occasion, but honestly if you heard just five minutes of the real Australian Minister of Tourism he would make Sir Les Patterson seem like a pale innocuous shadow. You see the yobbo is still on the throne in Australia. But it's probably a good thing ... Les is rather a likeable and intelligent man, don't you think?'

Harriet is slouched on her stool, talking to Stuart in the lighting booth on the headset. Out front Sir Les is promising to pass the names of Philip and Sarah on to Dame Edna. 'I think she'll guarantee this is a night you won't forget in a hurry,' he is saying, at once disconcerting and riveting the audience with the prospect of mayhem.

'It's a game of lateral thinking,' Harriet says, over the boom of laughter coming from Humphries' own kind of brain-teaser. 'Winner gets a bottle of champagne. "A man who lives on the fourteenth floor gets off at the tenth and walks the last four flights. Why?" '

'For his health?'

'He can't reach the button,' says Harriet.

On stage the game is more elemental, in fact it's the simplest of all child's games: show and tell. The extravagance of Sir Les's gestures is matched by the extravagance of his speech. Sir Les is saying, 'I haven't seen this show because I've been busy. I've been as busy as a Beirut bricklayer, as a matter of fact. Think it over. I've been as busy as a one-armed taxi driver with crabs. Got a mental picture of that? I've been as busy as a one-legged man in an arse-kicking competition. I've been as busy as Salman Rushdie's travel agent!'

Sir Les is a compendium of Australian slang, who puts on to the stage the half-remembered and half-invented Australian phrases which Humphries through his various characters is largely responsible for popularising. Humphries' etymological excavations and inventions both celebrate and satirise 'the dreadful language, the ladylike euphemisms outside lavatory doors' which Robin Boyd singles out in his first sentences as the distinguishing marks of the Australian ugliness.

'I was anxious to promote certain words and phrases which I thought were funny, particularly the words for chundering and the euphemisms for urination. I could use this vernacular of incontinence – all these terrible terms that I'd really been genuinely disgusted by as a prim youth when the perhaps more liberated friends of mine were experimenting with alcohol and Chinese food,' recalls Humphries about the sensational Australian slang he first put into Barry McKenzie's mouth in the mid-1960s. 'To popularise these words it was necessary for him to do it a lot. So Bazza became a servant of his own language.'

Through Bazza McKenzie and later Sir Les, the body's embarrassing needs acquire almost heroic stature as they are transformed into the high comedy of euphemism. For urination: *pointing Percy to the porcelain* or *Archie to the Armitage* or *Dennis at the Doulton, siphoning the python, draining the dragon, ringing the rattlesnake, shaking hands with the unemployed, shaking hands with the wife's best friend*. For thirst: *dry as a kookaburra's kyber, dry as a dead dingo's donger, dry as a nun's nasty*. For vomiting: *chundering, crying Ruth, Herb or Bert, playing the whale, parking a tiger, yodelling on the lawn, the liquid laugh, the Technicolor yawn*. For masturbation: *jerking the gherkin, twanging the wire, flogging the lizard*.

'Every Australian', wrote the *Times Literary Supplement* in 1974, 'should feel as proud of Humphries as of [the lexicographer] Eric Partridge – the Barry McKenzie strip and, in a diluted form the movie, has done more to introduce Australia to the world than generations of meetings of the Overseas League or the English Speaking Union.' This attitude is endorsed with a wink by Humphries himself, whose recent publication of *The Complete Barry McKenzie* has Bazza on the cover saying in the cartoon bubble, 'They say that *Pommy Bastard* Captain Cook discovered Australia – *Pig's Arse*! If it wasn't for *Me* Oz wouldn't be on the flamin' map.'

Humphries' characters have colonised not only Australia but

also its language. Many of his newly minted phrases are now part of the language. Partridge's two-volume *Dictionary of Slang* cites Humphries fifteen times. Sir Les has inherited some of Bazza McKenzie's preoccupations and has taken them off the page on to the stage. Sir Les continues to be a storehouse for rehabilitated Australian vernacular. Its poetic hilarity delights Humphries, who uses it to tease strait-laced scholarly attempts to clean up Australia's semantic act. Occasionally Sir Les even joins in academic debate about the Australian tongue, as when he reviewed the *Australian Pocket Oxford Dictionary* in 1977 for London's *Sunday Times*, wondering aloud, 'What strange minority need does this flaming book meet?'

> Cherylene, my attractive Girl Friday ... just put her green fingernail on a couple of other regrettable lacunae, as they say in the classics. Where is the wholesome folkloristic phrase *full as a Catholic school*, referring, of course, to post-prandial repletion? Where is *dingo degree*, the educational qualification of most Australian politicians? My secretary reminds me that breast-feeding is far from unknown in the Antipodes, yet I have searched this 967-page item in vain for a decent pair of *norks* ...
>
> 'I hope my little objections don't make me sound like a wowser, a kill-joy or for that matter, a French letter on the prick of Progress. Credit where credit's due, two of the words on all Australian lips, namely *elitism* and *shortfall* do get a nice little mention along with *software, hopefully, archetypal*, and *quintessential*. All of them bonzer little words and handy Down-Under epithets which any possum can use whilst boiling a billy, and kicking a few ideas around in his Creative Director's hat as he takes a second bite of the Cherry. By the by, there's a new Pom word my little secretary's creaming her gauchos over at the present period of time – 'Absolutely' – which very properly does not rate a write-up. It's Kensington for 'Yes'.

Sir Les's mission is to loosen the audience's grip on its emotions and its language. Slang, like slapstick, is a holiday from propriety and has its own raffish energy. 'She's got lips that could suck-start a Harley Davidson,' says Sir Les in one anecdote about a man, a pig, and a nubile girl washed up on a desert island who 'flashes him the vertical smile'. Spying a woman in the audience at sea with this gamey material, Sir Les observes, 'She has a face like a half-sucked mango.' Sir Les is democratic in the rough justice his slang dishes out. He does for gay bashing what Bazza did for bashing the bishop. At one point in his riff, Sir Les peels off an outrageous list of macho euphemisms for what he refers to in *The Traveller's Tool* as 'cordon bleu AIDS carriers'. Says Sir Les, recounting a meeting between Prime Minister Hawke and himself about the bicentennial celebrations, 'I said, "Bicentennial" is a shithouse name for a celebration, with respect, sir. (He's a stickler for formality, the Prime Minister.) I said, "The word 'bi' is a sullied, syllableised word. It's got connotations of poofdahism, shirt-lifting, pillow-biting, mattress-munching, Kapok-crunching, and Vegemite drilling," I said. You with me? . . .' And the audience, to their amazement, is. 'Australians are the derelicts of diction rummaging in the litter bins of left-over linguistics,' says Humphries, a man of letters, who savours the rhythms and images in Sir Les's pungent slang with obvious delectation. The grossness is neutralised by its artful use.

The mock-scholarly glossaries in the appendices of Humphries' various collections of sketches signal his own fascination with the variety in Australian speech. Humphries hoards words as he does the place names of his Melbourne. The glossaries are the attempt of an expatriate both to hold on to his culture and to criticise it. For instance, from *A Nice Night's Entertainment*:

DEAD SET (*adj.*), indubitable.

DICKERSON, ROBERT, a successful Australian painter and draughtsman.

DICKHEAD, an idiot.

DISTINGUISHED, an adjective popularly bestowed by the media upon the old, the dull and those of slender promise.

DIXON STREET, Sydney's Chinatown (Melbourne equivalent Little Bourke Street).

DUNKLING, a venerable Melbourne purveyor of wedding presents and gems.

ELITIST, an undesirable holding the dissident view that there is room for improvement in Australia.

EXACTO, pl. EXACTOS, a well-known and reliable brand of vests and night attire.

EXPATRIATE, a traitor.

FEMINIST, a woman, usually ill-favoured, inclined to chemise-lifting (*q.v.*), in whom the film-making instinct has displaced the maternal.

FLETCHER JONES, a tailoring firm famous for its indigenous trouser.

FLYTOX, a dependable insecticide.

FREAK, an Australian disc jockey who has not yet been awarded the OBE.

'By his original sure instinct, fine ear, and the formidable scholarship with which he later reinforced them, Humphries identified the pristine quality of everyday Australian English,' writes Clive James. 'A language which the self-consciousness of a literary culture had not yet dulled.'

Says Humphries, 'It was a question of listening to how a lot of Australians spoke: those rather elaborate constructions, which you hear in Sandy Stone, quite long paragraphs and recurring words and phrases. There is a refrain in Sandy Stone, you know: "Beryl and I went to bed, we had a very nice night's entertainment."' In their early years both Sandy Stone and Edna worked the same linguistic street, getting laughs not through the shock of outrageousness but the shock of recognition. 'Excuse I,' said Edna, making a 'refeened' and timid entrance with a familiar cliché, chattering on about 'maroan' and 'pavlovas'. Sandy also collapsed his audience by talking its own language about 'strife with the vehicle'. 'The effect on a Melbourne audience', writes Humphries of the birth of Sandy Stone, 'was electric and convulsive. Although the monologue was stylised and so uncomfortably close to home, they laughed as though regaled by the best joke they had ever heard. Fortunately, the word catharsis was not in current use, or I might have sententiously claimed to have induced it.'

In time Edna, like Humphries, would aspire to a dialogue beyond Australia and need an idiom that sensationally crossed cultures. But Sandy, the ex-digger turned ghost, would be permanently preserved in the realistic sludge of Aussie circumlocutions: 'the resultant consequence', 'the occasional odd glass', 'approximately in the vicinity', 'altogether it was a really nice night's entertainment for us all', 'on the occasion of my retirement'. Sandy has speech but no inner life. Silence surrounds him, and his 'grindingly prosaic' vocabulary broadcasts both the absence of experience and reflection.

'I am deceased,' began Sandy, in *Sandy Soldiers On* (1978), 'with the resultant consequence that there has been a considerable change in my lifestyle. I've never had a day's illness in my life, so this little setback came as much as a surprise to me as it did to Beryl, my good wife . . .'

Sandy's is an amalgam of slowly rendered clichés, advertising slogans, and brand names which dramatise his unexamined life. In Sandy's monologues, the phenomenal world is described with a clarity that is as uninflected as his voice. He has no point of view because his life has no point.

'Beryl had cut some delicious sandwiches. Egg and lettuce. Peanut butter. Marmite and walnut. Cheese and apricot jam. And lots of bread and butter and hundreds and thousands – and one of her own specialities – a chocolate and banana log. She'd only baked that morning and the kiddies were most intrigued. Beryl said if they promised to behave themselves at Wattle Park they could lick the beaters . . .'

'Sandy', writes Clive James of his imagist precision, 'is Ezra Pound with the power off.' Through Sandy, Humphries paints word pictures of his memories of suburban Melbourne. The character was invented as 'a way of finding out about my own background, my own life'. Humphries' affection for Sandy, his favourite among his creations, lies in his nostalgic link to his Melbourne childhood. The Latin epigraph to Humphries' collection of Sandy Stone sketches, *The Life and Death of Sandy Stone* (1990) – *Non omnis moriar* (Not everyone dies) –

admits his use of the character to recollect in tranquillity the remembered language and life of suburban Australian times gone by.

But, as Dame Edna, Humphries can be linguistically up to the minute, teasing the debasement out of the culture's buzz words. Humphries' ear for the pretentious phrase and the dead word is unerring. A great deal of Edna's fun is her satire of contemporary speech, as for instance Edna's Christmas Prayer ('for an upmarket audience'):

(*Kneel*)
Hear my prayer, O heavenly Lord
Make me viable across the board.
May my bottom line be Virtue
Lest I ever bug or hurt you.
And help me to unite the Nations
In on-going worship situations.
Up-tight and hassled though I be
Teach me to be up-front with Thee
And though my in-put be minute
When Thou my shortfall dost compute –
Pray let my daily print-out say:
Thy servant was relevant *per se*.

                                  Amen.

(*Stand*)

In her act, Edna delights in dropping into her monologue such words as 'seminal', 'abrasive', 'arguably', 'resonance'. 'Perhaps', says Humphries, 'if Edna writes a small book of poetry it will be called *Resonances*.' Edna has already titled one chapter of her autobiography 'My Ramifications'. Edna is no Mrs Malaprop. The laughter she gets out of language is not from the mistaken meanings of words, but from showing up the sloppiness in the contemporary use of them. ' "Infrastructure" is funny, isn't it?' says Humphries. 'Someone says, "We don't have the infrastructure for that," meaning "Can't do it," or "Don't know what you're talking about," or "Go away." It's a way of not thinking.'

Dame Edna, who is Humphries' way of raising hell and raising consciousness, relishes the word 'community'. In *Back with a Vengeance!*, the programme's title page is subheaded 'England's preferred community Entertainment Option'; and a note below adds, 'Ms Dame Edna Everage, Sandy Stone, Les Patterson and Barry Humphries himself are components of the Barry Humphries Community Life-Enhancement Facility'. Humphries' comic obsession with the word began, he says, 'ever since I saw that there was a disease that afflicts koala bears called "wet-bottom" – some kind of rot they get from sitting in trees too long – and there was an ad in an Australian magazine alerting people to this sad thing. The ad said: "This is afflicting more and more members of the koala community." I *hate* the idea of the world splitting up into smaller and smaller little groups. I find "gay community" hard enough to take, as though there was a kind of Lord Mayor and all that kind of stuff. I dislike the pretentiousness and exclusivity of the word. It's meaningless. The phrase "gay community" has led to the usage "heterosexual community", as though one were separate from the other. It's a very sloppy way of thinking. "I happen to be a member of the Halitosis Community." And with any luck I'm going to force you to have to belong to the "Nice-To-Be-Near Community".

'As life becomes more and more intolerable, and we become more and more anonymous, we are inventing little communities for ourselves so we can feel better. So Edna now talks about the "megastar community". In her autobiography Edna says she's a member of something called MA – Megastars Anonymous. She's very upset because her daughter Valmai has been shoplifting as well as sleeping on the steps of Parliament House with a group of aborigines protesting about cuts in Government grants to disabled lesbian aboriginal puppet film-makers. Madge says, "Why don't you raise it at your next meeting of MA?" Edna replies, "Well, the trouble is I go to these meetings, but sometimes I'm the only person there."'

Style is metabolism; and each of Humphries' characters makes word pictures in a manner unique to their personality. Sir Les lays words on with garish bold strokes; Sandy builds them sombrely from the tatty found objects around him; and Edna, the most self-conscious of the trio, is an impressionist with words whose motifs serve to call attention to her brilliance. Edna puts a fine spin on the English language. 'What an interesting person you probably are,' she sometimes says, killing a member of the audience with kindness and getting a laugh on the exact placement of the adverb. Says Humphries, 'Talking about Edna, people often say "Oh, you make it all up," but they don't realise how densely scripted it is, and tested in the presence of an audience. A word out of place can mean the difference between getting the laugh and not getting the laugh at all.'

Early in *Back with a Vengeance!* Edna breaks off in the middle of a monologue to plant in the audience's imagination the notion of someone falling out of the balcony. The setup is decoyed by her verbal panache. 'Excuse me,' she says, turning suddenly fierce. '*Paupers, stop leaning forward. I've told you a squillion times*! There was a tragedy here the other night. We've kept it out of the papers, but I have to tell you what it was. A pauper woman – a paupess actually – plummeted . . .' Having invented a word and comically reinforced it by the alliteration, Edna continues to dazzle the audience with her effortless juggling of pun, innuendo, and irony. 'She was leaning forward – it's so steep up there – she was leaning forward to get a chockie off the lap in front of her. At least that's what we *assume* she was doing. She was fumbling for a hard one, Emma, when she fell out. She wrapped her chops around the back of a seat, the toughest hard one she'd ever experienced. They had to put her in a plastic bag and take her away, Florence. I laughed . . . I laughed compassionately. I did.'

Edna's canny choice of words like 'compassion', 'caring', 'sharing', is part of the upwardly mobile game she plays with an audience. Dame Edna professes to liberalism while sending up the language of enlightenment. 'I'm not being Swissist,' she says, after bitching the humourlessness of her Swiss financial advisers. 'Don't accuse me . . . please . . . of gratuitous Swissism . . .' 'Edna', says Humphries, 'is an amalgam of "a highly artificial style but with a very strong emotional expression".' By its vivid exactness, Edna's language works the same trick as the visual grotesque: asserting both aspects of a contradiction at once. Her verbal inventions makes the ordinary strange and the strange ordinary.

'This woman', says Edna, describing a letter from a fan, 'was on prescribed medication. She was on Valium and a Sainsbury's wine box a day. She said to me, she said, she would lie naked on the kitchen floor at seven o'clock in the morning, the fridge door open, and the wine box dripping on her head. And she had Valium dust all around her mouth. She must've looked like Al Jolson. She must've. That dates me a bit, doesn't it? I mean that nicely. I don't mean that in a horrible racist way. I don't. I don't. I mean that in a caring racist way. I do. Because I'm a very liberal person, *and* I get a lot of tinted people along to see me. I do. The tinted folk *adore* me. They do. Bless their hearts. And as a matter of fact, there's a delightful little tinted chappie sitting in the second row. Hello. Hello. Huh? I thought it was an empty seat at first . . .'

The soft tattoo of dancing feet fills the wings as the Lesettes prance in place backstage waiting for Sir Les to beckon them into the white light for 'Never Trust a Man Who Doesn't Drink'. Sir Les is apologising to the audience for being too drunk to render his dead father's words of wisdom in the folk song he vainly tries to strum on an acoustic guitar. 'Please forgive me, ladies and gentlemen. Please forgive me. I'm drunk tonight. Well, I've had a drink tonight. I'm as full as a Pommy complaint box, as a matter of fact. I'm as full as a seaside shithouse on bank holiday . . . and that's chock-a-block. Ha! . . .' The trio starts up; Sir Les shouts, 'Eat your heart out, Sting!' Then, kicking up his platform shoes, he launches into his hymn to political corruption and inebriation:

'When you go out with girls let 'em know who's boss,
Make sure the sheilas come across
Before you buy them the diamonds and the mink.
He said, "You'll rise high in the public service ranks,
If you learn to accept an expression of thanks
And never trust a man who doesn't drink. . ."'

128

With his disgusting manners, his drunken toothy leer, his behemoth *schlong*, Sir Les is a genial monster bringing the house down with a demonic notion. In Sir Les and Dame Edna, Humphries has created a credible form of the monstrous. With them Humphries has ventured further than any of his comic peers into 'the possible absurd'. The term is Baudelaire's for Goya's grotesques; but Humphries' monsters are equally harmonious and viable, accomplishing on stage the grotesques' singular interplay of light and dark, joy and horror, the marvellous and the devilish. 'All those distortions, those bestial faces, those diabolic grimaces are impregnated with *humanity* . . .', Baudelaire wrote. 'The point of junction between the real and the fantastic is impossible to grasp.'

Humphries has long been interested in monsters and the monstrous. His anthology *Bizarre* (1965), dubbed 'a bestially vulgar compilation' by the *Observer* and banned by one English bookstall chain, is the literary equivalent of a freak show, collecting both the satanic fantasies of among others de Sade, Sacher-Masoch, Huysmans and scandalous images of the perverse. 'Anthologies', says Humphries, 'are generally meant to be rather nice, sweet cullings from literature or art. *Bizarre* was deliberately very dissonant.'

In his preface Humphries places his obsession in the tradition of the Decadents and the Surrealists and admits to 'a delight in folly and a profound pleasure in the presence of the marvellous and the gruesome'. 'The book', he writes, 'is addressed frankly to the jaded palate. To those who find a literary diet of steak and eggs curiously insufficient, and to whom the works of great painters are so much necessary but savourless roughage.' But from the outset, Humphries' submersion in the lewd and the demonic has been part of his dandaical attack on the banality of bourgeois life.

The first course of Humphries' menu of outrage is significantly an offering by J.K. Huysmans on the erotic work of Félicien Rops. Humphries had reinvented himself in the posture of aesthete from Huysmans' Des Esseintes; and in time his theatrical grotesques would reinvent Huysmans' account of the Spirit of Lust in Rops' fever-incited souls in order to deal with his own powerful agitations of mind. The lust of which Huysmans writes transcends the sexual: 'I am speaking of the Spirit of Lust, of isolated erotic ideas, without material correspondences . . . an impulse toward a preternatural debauchery, a plea for those convulsions which elude the flesh . . . the infamy of the soul is aggravated . . . but it is, at the same time, refined, ennobled by the thought which mingles with it, an ideal of superhuman weaknesses and of new sins to commit . . .'

Sir Les is an explosion of appetites, a version of Huysmans' 'demoniac ecstasy, gushing forth from flesh in ignition, the sorrows of fever-incited souls and the joys of warped minds'. Sir Les had already confessed his gargantuan thirst to the audience: 'Anyone who doesn't enjoy a glass or eighty of alcohol has got something radically wrong with him. In Australia we call a "teetotaller" a "wowser", which is an old aboriginal word meaning . . . a teetotaller. It's not a very difficult language really.' His delirium suddenly transforms into a song and dance. Twitching and twisting, Sir Les caterwauls:

'Never trust a man who doesn't drink
Although he may not throw up in your kitchen sink
I would rather be half-plastered
Than a blue nose wowser bastard
Never trust a man who doesn't drink.'

He pauses, glistening in sweat, and waves at the audience. 'Thank you very much, indeed. Good-night, ladies and gentlemen . . .'

The applause holds Sir Les in centre stage. 'And now,' he says, 'the Lesettes . . .'

Tassels twirling, the Lesettes strut into the white light.

'Hello, girls . . .'

'Hello, Sir Les,' they squeal in unison.

The word 'monster' has its roots in two Latin words: for something marvellous or prodigious, originally a divine portent; and also for warning. And Humphries' characters function for the audience and for himself in just this contradictory way: at once a blessing and a caution. 'As people who are inside me, if you like, the characters have certainly helped me,' Humphries has said. 'In the guise of these characters, I can syphon off all kinds of aggressions, and I can also discuss certain topics which I would find difficult to tackle in my own persona.'

Sir Les lampoons the drinking which once brought Humphries close to death. From the mid-1960s to 1970, Humphries was as legendary a boozer as any of his fictional characters. Says the comedian Peter Cook, an early and influential champion of Humphries in the 1960s, 'I remember Barry at a Boxing Day party doing something that I've never witnessed before. I think you have to reach another level of drunkenness to achieve it. I just did the normal thing by falling down drunk, but Barry upstaged me by falling upstairs. I don't know how he did it.'

When drunk, Humphries provoked worry and some wonderment among his friends. In the early 1960s, he was a frequent visitor to Oxford University's high tables, visiting his old Melbournian sidekick Ian Donaldson, who was a don first at Merton College and then at Wadham. 'He was a source of great disruption,' recalls Donaldson of a grand Wadham dinner they attended. 'Barry loved meeting the dons and finding his way into academic circles. Osbert Lancaster and Maurice Bowra were there, I remember. Barry liked to scandalise them in some way, so he'd push it a bit further. He drank them all under the table. Later on that night Barry, wearing an academic gown, appeared in the Senior Common Room. There were only a few of us there. "Look what I found," he said. He had two bottles of claret concealed in the wings of his gown. I think he went away and drank them both.'

At work, Humphries was always professional. 'He was never drunk on the set,' says John Wells, who along with the actors John Fortune, John Bird and Humphries starred in the BBC's satiric *The Late Show* (1964–5). 'I remember him coming to one rehearsal and saying, "Another strange head on the pillow this morning. A trail of hastily abandoned clothing leading from the door." He didn't know what had happened to him.' But off stage, the grog gave Humphries' exhibitionism a special, sometimes awesome dimension.

'He did stupendous things on the booze,' says Ian Davidson, who first worked with Humphries on *The Late Show*. 'He'd drop his trousers in the street. Or suddenly he wouldn't be with us, and we'd look around and there he'd be pretending to be a tramp. He was rummaging through a lamp-post bin and scattering money. He'd just been to the bank and got some money; and having the money in his pocket, he started to use it as a prop. He was pretending to be a tramp who'd just discovered a huge amount of money in the bin. He was just going "Oh, oh, oh!!!" and throwing money all over the place. He liked that idea.'

Davidson was forever being rung up by the production team with the same question: 'Where's Barry?' 'I'd have to ring the car-hire people or the taxi service to find out where they'd last taken Barry. It was like being involved with the underground in some way. People had to be traced, intercepted,' says Davidson. 'He'll keep the pot boiling, won't he? There's no sort of periods of tranquillity. He was even more energetic when pissed, certainly more difficult to follow.'

As he would do years later in the character of Sir Les, Humphries sometimes acted drunk to give him the impetus to take liberties in public, at once a mask and an admission of his aggression. *The Late Show* performers often lunched at the same restaurant on Shepherd's Bush Green. They got into the habit of ordering increasingly exotic drinks for one another and of having the waiters shuttle the cocktails between tables. On one occasion, according to John Wells, when *The Late Show*'s star, John Bird, was being interviewed by *Newsweek*, Humphries 'decided to hijack the interview. In those days, both Barry and I were getting £250 a week. John Bird was getting £1,000. He was definitely the star. Barry turned up soon after John and the reporter were seated for lunch. They hadn't begun the interview during lunch; but when they got to the point of producing a tape recorder, the waiter came over with two glasses of *crème de menthe*, which was known to be Barry's favourite drink. (He was always making jokes about *crème de menthe frappé*.) The waiter said: "With Mr Humphries' compliments." They looked over to where Barry was sitting on his own. Barry produced a pint-sized tumbler of *crème de menthe*, signalled their good health, and drained it. He banged the glass down on the table and staggered out of the restaurant. I remember the *Newsweek* man saying, "He'll destroy his brain." They got terribly worried. The interview broke up. The waiter came over to report that Barry had been seen swaying about in the middle of heavy traffic. The *Newsweek* man got nothing. John didn't give his interview. In fact, all Barry had done was put green dye in a glass of water.'

'In the sixties,' Humphries told the Sydney *Daily Mirror* in 1982, over eleven years since his last drink, 'I was so successful I never took a holiday, just worked all the time. We had a house in London, but I was hardly ever there. I never went off for holidays with Rosalind', his second wife, 'and our two children and I realise now that was a mistake. You must make time for your children, and Rosalind cared enough about me to want to see me more often and said so. But I was enjoying all the razzle dazzle of success. After leaving the theatre at night, instead of going home, I'd find myself going to a pub, then on to a club or party, I got to the stage where I hardly bothered to look at my watch.'

Finally his wife packed his suitcase and left it at the stage door. 'I don't reproach Rosalind,' he told the *Daily Mirror*. 'I reproach myself. I was deeply unhappy for a long time. I was in a nursing home, and I'd look out the window and see people going about their business and feel really isolated from the human race. I felt cut off from the joys of living.'

Sir Les is Humphries' assertion of the life force into whose grotesque of waywardness he can project and triumph over the punishing losses of his past. Delight generates forgiveness; and in that climate of affection, it is possible for Humphries through Sir Les partially to admit himself. When he talks directly about drink, Humphries is more guarded, hiding behind a patina of elegant generalisation which only hints at another story.

'I think Australians first drank enormous amounts to dull the pain of being separated, to diminish the loneliness,' he said in 1987. 'I still think that Australians feel that sense of isolation somehow, and I think they still suffer from low self-esteem. Australians still feel a long way from other people. After all, we are the only white people who have been sent so far from home. Anyone who is any good is regarded as big-headed. So we're very unsure of our worth indeed. Alcohol is then an extremely successful drug for reducing most feelings of inadequacy. So I think we suffer as a nation from a sense of collective inadequacy, and this shows in our attitude to success and achievement.'

Sir Les manages not only to banish the gravity of the audience but also to banish part of what weighs Humphries down. In Les, Humphries mocks drink and the humiliation of excess while enjoying the liberation from self-consciousness that drink confers. As a stage drunk, Humphries makes delight out of his nightmare. But, in the bad old days on the bottle, Humphries was not funny to friends like the cartoonist Nick Garland, who collaborated with him on the Barry McKenzie comic strip for *Private Eye* between 1963 and 1973. The strip began as a £7 a week panel and ended up producing two feature films, three books, and an international reputation for both authors.

'There is a central thing about Barry,' says Garland, who considers Humphries a comic genius and their collaboration 'effortless from the beginning'. 'He's very very funny. Barry always made me laugh with him and laugh in that wonderful helpless laughter. We never quarrelled. We never disagreed. But he was wayward. Drink was profoundly affecting his ability to manage life. He would miss deadlines. He would vanish. He would say he would do things and not do them. You'll hear heavy drinkers say that reformed alcoholics are boring. In every single way that is not true of Barry. He became far more interesting, far more productive, a far more amusing and generally delightful companion. Barry would say, as a number of alcoholics would, that he had a low tolerance for alcohol. He drank. It made him drunk. He didn't drink like Barry McKenzie.

'What happens is that you plan your life around alcohol. Therefore he'd carry drink. He'd have caches of drink. He'd make detours in order to get drink. He told me once, for example, that he was asked for a drink in Australia. Rather distinguished company. Because he was going for a pre-lunch drink he didn't need to carry alcohol in a bottle. He was horrified when the drinks came that they were very weak. He began to panic, thinking this was not enough. "Excuse me a moment," he said, thinking somewhere inside would be a drinks cabinet. He found one, and there was a bottle of vodka. He opened the bottle and began chugging to fill up, knowing that it was his last chance. The host walked in and saw him. The man was embarrassed, appalled, puzzled, uncertain about how to handle it; and so was Barry. He made some inane remark like "I was thirsty." But somehow behind this story, which was told as a comic story building to a climax of embarrassment, there was also a very honest description of an experience which was a nightmare to him.

'I remember many dinner parties when he didn't turn up. There'd be this phone call. A drunk – not Barry, not this intelligent, charming fellow – but a sprawling reeling drunk. Not funny at all. I can remember on more than one occasion with his second wife (he wasn't very successful in those days). You get him into the car. You drive him home. You hope he won't be sick. You get him out. You hump him up the stairs. Blind legless drunk. You throw him down on the bed. The wife says, "I can handle this now." Later he would half not refer to these incidents. They would be blurred. Drink is an important episode in his life. The determination – the absolute determination – with which he abandoned it. He's resolute. While in some ways he can come on like a holy fool, a strange sort of innocent who does outrageous things and gets away with it, he is very tough, highly intelligent, and very very ambitious. They are very resolute qualities.'

By the power of his charm and of his humour, Humphries managed to conceal much of his drunken desperation. 'I remember sitting in a taxi with a Harrods bag on my lap that had half a bottle of whisky in it and looking at the queue of heroin addicts outside Boots the Chemist in Piccadilly Circus with contempt,' he said of the time when he was 'ill and mad'. 'They were addicts and I was something else. I was, if you like, a genius out of luck. I was a sensitive person. I just drank alcohol like all the best people, like Dylan Thomas, like Scott Fitzgerald, like Malcolm Lowry, like John Barrymore, like Tony Hancock. I belonged to the aristocracy of self-destruction. And who were they? The riff-raff,

135

weren't they? They stuck needles in themselves. They didn't vomit in public lavatories like I did.'

In Melbourne in 1970 Humphries was charged with being drunk and disorderly. 'You must have had a dull day,' the papers reported Humphries saying to the police. 'Didn't you have any old ladies to arrest! Hope you have a better evening, you pathetic bastards.' (Later, the vicar who'd performed his marriage ten years before spoke successfully in his defence at the Camberwell Court: 'He has a problem with his public image and his own personal character,' said the Reverend Ian Tasker. 'His own character is different from his public image. He is a shy, retiring person, and easily hurt.')

Three days later, drinking in the area of Richmond, Humphries was pulled into an alley where he was knocked unconscious and robbed. His bloated and bruised face filled the Melbourne papers the next day. As always, Humphries sidestepped public humiliation not by hiding from it but by admitting it with laughter. 'The police are looking for two boots that fit two dents around my navel,' he told the press, adding that when he came to his senses in the mud, 'I thought I'd been dumped in a paddock. There was this need to crawl to safety.' At the opening of an art gallery which he insisted on attending the day after his mugging, Humphries read a poem about Melbourne which included the lines:

'If you want to keep your feet up
Relax and just unbend
There's a peaceful Richmond gutter
That I highly recommend . . .'

But the incident proved a turning point in his life. Recalls Garland, 'Subsequently Barry's spoken about his alcoholism a lot. He said that there came a time when he became aware that he was lying face down in an alley. It was raining. It was night and he was hurt. Something had happened. He'd fallen over, perhaps he'd been mugged. He wasn't quite sure. There he lay. This was at a time when he was successful and famous. He saw himself in this moment, and he determined to get out of it. He came to see his abuse of alcohol as a very severe handicap to his life. The way he put it to me was: "Right, here I am at the bottom. I'm going to pick myself up." '

But even Sir Les's patter owes something to Humphries' alcoholic past,' says Ian Davidson. When you're writing Les, Barry comes up with some amazing gruff macho-men-in-pub material. You think, "Where's Barry got this from going around to art galleries and auctions?" Well, he's got it from a lot of his old drinking friends.'

I've heard Sir Les's song every night for two weeks, and Humphries' joy in putting it over still makes me smile. 'He's so generous out there,' I say to Harriet, who seems more amused tonight at my pleasure than at Humphries'.

On stage Sir Les is shaking too:

'Never trust a girl who doesn't come across
It's a secretary's duty to her boss
And if your wife is understandin'
She'll know you've got to keep your hand in
It sure as hell beats tugging at your toss
(Hah! Hah! – sorry, ladies
Five six seven eight . . .'

The band picks up the rhythm. Sir Les falls back into the Lesettes' chorus line, hitch-kicking and yahooing with the rest of them.

'You have to be almost right at the end and unemployable before deciding whether you pick up the gift of life, or simply go down the tubes,' Humphries told the *Sunday Times* in 1987. 'Not to be your own man – to be enslaved by some person, or some chemical – is the only real *problem* anyone can have. Everything else is just a difficulty. I no longer have problems, although I sometimes have difficulties.'

Sir Les's riot on stage is part of Humphries' redemption off it. The fierce energy of the caricature comes from this contradiction: at once a satire and a celebration, an attack and a release.

Sir Les is bopping now. The Lesettes are bumping and grinding behind him, punching the song up for one final chorus. Sings Humphries, a teetotaller passing himself off as one of the theatre's most raucous soaks:

'Any girl who is teetotal
Is no value upstairs in your hotel
– See you later, ladies . . .'

Sir Les pinches a tight Lesette backside.

'Cause you can never trust a man
Who doesn't dr-i-i-i-n-k!!!'

'How's that!' shouts Sir Les on the song's last beat, like an elated cricketer appealing to the audience for a winning judgment. In the expanded moment between applause and exit, the audience forgives Sir Les all his trespasses. In that benediction the actor too forgives himself.

Humphries is pulled off into a corner of the stage where Katie takes his sopping gaudy costume and exchanges it for Sandy Stone's Winceyette pyjamas and faded brown plaid bathrobe. He is also ministered to by Harriet. Meanwhile in a back room just off the main stage three crew members – Moira, Andy and Nick – are at work shucking Dame Edna's gladioli, which sit in large green water-filled tubs in front of their chairs.

'Been doing it now for fourteen months,' says Andy.

'The leaves are very sharp,' says Moira, noticing my interest.

'The edges are quite sharp,' says Andy.

The production manager Nick is also stripping away the leaves. 'You could cut your hand,' he says.

'They also carry water in the stem.'

'A bit like impaling yourself on a yucca leaf.'

'An aerodynamic gladdy,' I say. 'I love it.'

'We get gladdy blindness,' says Moira. 'A bit like snow blindness.'

Harriet comes in and the talk turns to the police escort ushering Dame Edna from Drury Lane to the Palladium tonight, then to the chaos of filming the video of the show the previous week, then to a cast party in a fortnight when the limited run closes, then to the news that Humphries has just accepted an offer to play the show without set for two nights on the island of Jersey.

'You know all that whingeing about the gladioli,' says Nick, 'it wasn't that they were badly positioned. It was that we never give enough gladdies out. When we did it on the video it worked.'

'On the last night in Jersey,' says Andy, 'I'll say, "You know, Barry, it works when there's a lot more gladdies there."'

'Does Barry like to keep a limit on the gladdies?'

'He doesn't like to spend money,' says Harriet. 'So it's difficult.'

'What got into him tonight?' says Moira. 'When he came over to start Les, he came lurching up to me and said, "Give us a kiss." I just smiled nicely.'

'He was trying to make you feel uncomfortable, Moira,' says Andy.

'I just smiled. I nearly said, "Fuck off, Les." But he was about to go on.'

'He used to be quite rude to Heidi,' says Harriet. 'She wanted to say something really rude to him, but she didn't have the guts. He would have loved it.'

' "You asshole," ' says Andy.

'He would've thought it was great,' says Harriet.

Back in the dressing room, Sandy's sibilant drone crackles over the loudspeakers: 'But I didn't want to come home . . . it's a funny story. After I passed away . . . caught the ferry . . . jumped the twig . . . had my last cup of Milo, my wife – my widow – Beryl, decided to put our home on the market so she could move up to a new unit in a condominium at Surfers' Paradise . . .'

Katie goes matter-of-factly about her business, hanging up Dame Edna's £2,500 pink sequined dress specially made for tonight's

Palladium performance. There's no welcome in Katie's voice, no bounce in her step. 'You OK?'

'Fine,' she says, smiling with cold teeth.

'Is it Barry?'

Katie goes in search of Dame Edna's new shoes, and when she returns with them, she says, 'Barry forgets that other people have jobs to do as well and that they spend all day and all night doing them. We become just blots on the wall to him. Sometimes he doesn't even remember your name. Doesn't say "Hello". Sometimes I get sick of being thought of as a blob. Totally ignores me. It was all hands on deck Friday for the video. We worked fifteen hours.'

'What happened?'

'I don't want to talk about it.'

'Barry's got a lot on his plate.'

'Ask Harriet,' says Katie, scooping up Sir Les's laundry and hurrying away from more conversation.

When Harriet drifts into the dressing room to synchronise schedules for the police escort taking Dame Edna the half-mile from Drury Lane to the Palladium, I ask her about Friday's video. 'Did Katie tell you?' she says.

'No. She said you would.'

Harriet brushes her long blond hair away from her forehead and sits down. Sandy Stone has twenty minutes to recount the saga of the multi-cultural transformation of the neighbourhood around 36 Gallipoli Crescent where he lived, died and which he is now haunting. 'Barry always has to have someone to blame,' she says. 'If a problem arises, it's not like – "It's a bit of a crisis we'd better solve it" – he has to know *now*. "Whose fault is it?" Whose fault? Inevitably it's his. He hasn't told someone, and so you can't organise something. A lot of our problems stem from that.

'Sometimes a car is arranged for eleven to get him somewhere by twelve. He takes the car, goes to a bookshop on the way, so he's late. The nonsense that goes on has nothing to do with the stage management of this show. It's more like nannying. You do it all because he's very good when he gets on stage. If he needs the extra things to get him on stage, then, well, you give them to him. In Australia, it'd be around seven twenty and it's "I haven't eaten yet." So when you should be on the headset saying, "Five minutes to beginners," you're in a restaurant over the road saying, "He'd like the usual – tomato sauce with spaghetti and extra chili." He's special. He needs to know he's special, and he needs to feel special. He really feels that he's above us.

'Anyway, on Friday afternoon we had the rehearsal for the video. As I left the office Nick said, "They're expecting to see Barry." Dennis said, "No, he wasn't called." Barry won't come for rehearsal. He never comes to rehearsal. He did half a rehearsal for the first West End opening of the show at the Strand. Half-way through the rehearsal he said, "I think I'll go to the Waldorf now and have a sleep." So the men from Central and London Weekend were like, "We'd better ring him. He's coming because we spoke to him and we know he's going to be here." We know he promises anything and then just doesn't deliver.

'I rang up and said, "Barry, we're just having a rehearsal. They're expecting you." He says, "Uh . . . well . . . three o'clock's when I have my sleep . . . I have a sore throat coming on." Anyway, we had a rough afternoon. We didn't know there was going to be a tech rehearsal. There was a floor manager in the corner. There was a lighting designer in the lighting box. David Bell got to be Edna for the afternoon; but he'd seen the show maybe twice so he never stood in the right place. His director was in a producing van outside the theatre. The people in the lighting booth were like ten cues behind. It was an unusual afternoon, and we didn't know what we were walking into.

'The show was also not a normal show. A lot of talk on the headsets. Quite busy. At the final change, when Edna puts on the white frock to rise above the audience, Barry comes off stage and he's often quite tense. A cameraman crept up on the side of the stage and was filming the audience, Barry said: "The whole show's ruined. There's a cameraman on stage. *The whole show is ruined!!!*"

'It's one of his favourite lines. It happens quite often. Last

141

week a door was slammed during Sandy and it was, "The sketch is ruined. It ruined the atmosphere! Absolutely ruined!!" And I said, "Oh no, Barry. It's going really well." Anyway, he was in one of those moods. He'd finished his change, did the rest of the show and as he came off stage he said to me, "There was no heating. Why was there no heating?" I said, "Well, Barry, we've had a very busy afternoon. I'm sorry but our minds have been on other things." Sometimes I'm really good about it and say, "Sorry, Barry, it was all my fault." But sometimes it's hard to do that.

'After the show I came into his dressing room with programmes to be signed. Sometimes when I come in at the end of the show for the autographs, and he's got famous people, he likes to pretend that I'm not there. It gets quite funny. The guests can see I'm there. I go and stand next to Barry with the autographs, but he stands in front of me, like I'm not there . . .'

'It's hard to miss you. You're six feet tall.'

'There were eight people in the room. Lizzie's friends. She was making a little supper for them. She started to introduce me because she has a different set of manners from Barry's. Barry likes to know that the staff will wait till he's ready. I said, "Could you just sign the autographs and get them out of the way 'cause you're with your guests and you can look after them?"

'The other people were in the ante-room. I was in his private dressing room. We were the only people in the room. He said to me, "I don't like being spoken to in that tone of voice in front of the staff." Dennis always says that I should stand up for myself; so against my better judgment, I said, "Well, Barry, I don't like being spoken to in that way in front of them either."

'He said I didn't understand what he was going through, that I had no respect for his talent. Unless I had respect for him, I wouldn't have – none of us would have – gone out of our way for him on Friday. I said, "We worked all day for you to make sure it was right." Then he took the leather-bound clipboard with the programmes and hurled it full force across the dressing room and told me to get out.

'Lizzie was standing there with a big bowl of pasta which she almost dropped. Dennis's mouth fell open. I got my coat and left. I was in floods of tears. I didn't want to come into the theatre again. I've never heard that tone of voice from him. It was extraordinary. "Get out!!" It knocked me for six. Barry and I have arguments. I don't mind that. It was just absolute, uncontrolled anger . . .'

'What do you think you touched?'

'He always likes to be right,' says Harriet, her eyes moistening. 'He doesn't like to be criticised at all. He can't bear criticism. It's quite funny. A long time ago, in Sydney, we'd done about a hundred shows. There's a point where Edna has the guests lined up and says, "Good-night, possums!" throws the gladdies into the audience and that's the cue for the house tabs to come in. Barry didn't do it. He forgot to throw the gladdies. He just sort of smiled at the guests and was waiting for the curtain. It wasn't a long delay, I promise you. But I held it for a second and then brought the curtain in. But Barry came off saying, "I was out there for an eternity! I was out there for *ever*!! What happened to the curtain?"

'I said, "Well, Barry, when you give the cue by throwing the flowers, I'll bring it in." He said, "I never, ever, have thrown a gladiolus at the audience at that point." The next time Barry came up and said, "I think I did throw a gladdy at that time." And I said, "Well, Barry, I'll remember to bring the curtain in sooner." "Yes," he said. "Yes, you do that."

'So that's an apology from Barry. On Saturday he rang, which he never does. He called to speak to Dennis, who passed the phone to me. I didn't want to speak to him. He said, "I'm sorry, Harriet. But you don't understand the pressure I'm under. You don't really understand how difficult it is for me." '

'Do you have a picture of a wheelchair on the front door?' Dame Edna asks Leslie from Northwood, who's been lured by her into saying that her house is all brick. '(No windows at all, Leslie? What a nightmare world this woman inhabits. Must be like living in an ablutions block . . .) They're everywhere, Maude, disabled toilets. Have you noticed that, Margaret? Have you noticed how disabled toilets have cropped up a lot in recent years? They have. And what a symbol of our caring community that they have. And what a monster of bad taste I would be, incidentally, if I stood up here and criticised the disabled toilet explosion of the eighties. Except just to say . . .'

Dame Edna relishes her monstrousness and broadcasts it as part of the imperialism of her gorgeous self. Even the programme calls her a *monstre sacré*. She is big and getting bigger. That's what monsters do. They aggrandise the resources around them: people, wealth, attention. If Sir Les is a monster of appetite, Dame Edna is a monster of detachment, drawing out of an audience the admission of their own half-formed, perplexing, cruel wishes.

'Except just to say', she continues, 'I think they've slightly overdone them. I'm going out on a limb here. I think in a way it's a form of discrimination against those of us who can get about. Think about it. I mean, girls, it's always when you've had too many cups of tea, isn't it? You're in a terrible hurry. And you're *rushing*. And the only cubicle that seems to be vacant is the one with a stick figure sitting on the circular saw. Have you noticed that? I'm going to let you in on a secret. Do you know what I sometimes do, Margaret? I put on a limp and go in. I do. But if you've ever been tempted to do that, for heaven's sake, limp out. Limp out! There would be a queue of cripples waiting for you, and they could beat you to death with their frames. They could Zim you to bits. I mean this very very lovingly. I do . . .'

Dame Edna's talk of 'tinted people', her monologues about deformity attract some degree of puritan animosity as well as wild hilarity. 'Most Australians are puritanical,' Humphries has observed. 'I think I will always anger the pharisees, the puritan critics who talk about relevance. Is Edna Everage relevant? That is a puritan attitude, of course. What they mean is: we sit in the theatre, we get annoyed, we see you standing up, and we see the audience falling about laughing. And what is it underneath that makes the puritan angry? They ask: Is it just to amuse people? Is it going to edify? Are we going to get an extra pint of milk in the morning? Art is basically useless and meaningless, it will always annoy the puritan who has to find some meaning, some productivity of some kind.'

But if it annoys the puritan, it slays the rest of the audience, especially those being singled out by Dame Edna for special bigoted treatment. Says Humphries of performing this material to people in wheelchairs and people of colour, 'It seems to have a liberating effect on them. They are more uproarious than anybody else. They feel that they're part of the family. In a sense they've become non-existent. They've been pasteurised. Liberal decency has put them in some kind of rather uncomfortable ghetto. They've had their comic identity taken away from them. Everyone else has got jokes about them. People have been too *nice* to them.'

And tonight the audience is gasping as Edna sails happily into dangerous waters. Even Harriet is laughing at the routine, the excesses of Humphries' temperament forgotten in the face of the abundance of his talent. Dame Edna is saying, 'Have you ever peeked into a disabled toilet, Margaret? Have you, Maude? Have you, Joan? It's another world in there. It's like a . . . it's a little like a little gymnasium in there, isn't it? I mean you expect to see people doing aerobics when you go in there. And there's a chrome ladder going up the wall. *What do they do in there*? They spin in their chairs. They slip the door, and they shin up the wall. And they peep at us. I mean this in a caring and loving way. If there's anyone here tonight who came on wheels. Anyone with a hint of chrome about them. Anyone with a touch of Richard the Third. I'm no healer . . .'

Of course she's not. And, of course, through her laughter, she is. Dame Edna's power is in the mystery of this paradox: a mockery of monstrousness and an indulgence in it.

Dame Edna hurries away from her audience at the curtain call, with Katie bustling excitedly behind her. Dame Edna's momentum seems to catch everyone in its slipstream. The crew is galvanised into a kind of theatrical Red Alert, launching Dame Edna into her next battle with the charity audience at the Palladium.

Dennis Smith is in the Green Room explaining Dame Edna's traffic plan to the publicist Lynne Kirwin, who will place an item in tomorrow's *Evening Standard*. 'Edna is being taken off privately to a place where Prince Charles and Di will meet her. Then they are going off to a party which is invitee only. Barry is going to get changed and go to the party afterwards. Originally we were going to have limousines taking him to the Palladium. But there's a time concern with this show. So the best way to make sure Edna got there on time was to plonk her in a police car with both sirens flashing.' Humphries is a publicist's dream; and Lynne Kirwin smiles the happy smile of a press agent whose story is writing itself. Smith even has a tag line for the column item: 'Edna's opening line is going to be, "How nice it is of you to have waited for me all this time. I hope the sirens on my police escort didn't upset the rest of the concert." '

There are new faces in Humphries' dressing room tonight who chat among themselves while he freshens up in the bathroom. A chic raven-haired producer from London Weekend Television, who televised Humphries' talk show and who will be broadcasting Prince Charles's charity gala, gossips with the television make-up lady. Stephen Adnitt, the dress designer, is making a few alterations to his latest creation.

'Barry talked to me about a dress with square mirrors and subsequently sent me a brochure,' says Stephen. 'I thought it was diabolical. The dress he showed me is basically nothing like what he got. A dress like this costs between two and two and a half thousand pounds. It's made of silk jersey and completely beaded in sequins. For this occasion we wanted something that was totally over the top because Dame Edna's arriving at the end of the show, everyone else has been on and he's meeting the royals afterwards. So we wanted something that was really stunning. The flowers on the bodice were my addition. You can go over the top as far as you like, which is wonderful. For sparkle, this is the best. For outrageousness, the one he wore on TV for Valentine's Day with cherubs on the shoulder and huge hearts is the winner. Dame Edna likes to be very fashionable. When Princess Di arrived at the Cannes Film Festival wearing this black and white puff-ball dress, Barry decided it'd be nice to do something in a similar vein. So we did a black and white spotted puff-ball dress and jacket and a Windsor Castle hat. The hat had a flag that went up with little corgis and little people on the seats. He pulled a cord and he put the flag on the turret.'

'Hello,' says Humphries to the producer Claudia Rosenkrantz, seating himself in front of the dressing table. 'How are you?'

Claudia pulls up a chair next to him, huddling close like a trainer with a contender. A Fleet Street photo researcher turned Humphries' TV producer, she has the buoyancy and the quick wit that Humphries trusts. She also knows her star. 'Barry's an all-consuming personality,' she says. 'You lose your own identity if you're with him for too long. He takes up a lot of time. If there are twenty people in the room, he's got enough to keep everyone going. He once said to me, "What do you do in between me?" I've no idea.'

'I'm fine,' says Claudia. 'How are you?'

'What was it like, that show?'

'It's going very well. I've got a whole lot of ideas for you.'

'What? A lot of rock bands?'

'A lot of rock bands. A lot of equipment.'

' "I brought my own equipment . . .!" '

' "I *am* my own equipment," ' says Claudia. Humphries gives a high-pitched laugh, which signals the rewrite has been accepted.

' ". . . I don't need amplifiers. I speak the truth. And the truth is always deafening however softly it is spoken." '

Humphries and Claudia Rosenkrantz smile at each other in the mirror as the make-up lady goes to work on Dame Edna's face. 'Dame Edna is direct, but Barry has a problem being direct. He's too polite. He won't be direct,' says Claudia, who is definitely on Dame Edna's wavelength. 'There's a huge difference between Barry and Edna. Certainly the way you talk to Edna is very different from the way you talk to Barry. And the relationship you have with Edna is different from the relationship you have with Barry. I think it's very important to keep them separate. It's just something that you do. It's important to him. It's important that you believe in Edna as a separate person. He talks about Edna in the third person, which allows him to believe that Edna is completely different. Of course, Barry admits an enormous amount of himself in Edna.'

Claudia studies the clipboard full of notes in her lap. 'Now the girl who opened the show is an American singer called Debbi Gibson.'

'How did she go?'

147

'She went well. She's good. She was wearing cut-off jeans at the knee, with baseball boots, very dirty hair. I thought perhaps Dame Edna might apologise for not being around to make sure that people washed and combed their hair properly, that people weren't a bit neater . . .'

'Could I have a dressing gown, please,' says Humphries, looking vaguely in Katie's direction.

'Wet Wet Wet were in their proverbial jeans and slicked-back hair.'

Katie produces the robe. 'Take your white knickers off and pop into your pink ones.' She hands Humphries the new underwear.

'See the back of the handbag,' he says, holding up the back on which he has written the new lines to 'My Public'. 'Do you think it matters me reading the words off my handbag?'

'No,' says Claudia.

'If I make a mistake they can do it again, can't they?'

'Yes. It happens. People have fluffed a bit tonight.'

'Did they do them again?'

'Yeah.'

'Oh, that's all right. At least there's a precedent. Not that I will do, really. I don't think.'

'Now, T'Pau – the girl from T'Pau – Carol Decker – had one of the shortest skirts I think I've ever seen in my life. It was so short it looked as though she'd almost forgotten to put one on. And it was so loud that one could have heard it out in the streets. So you had a lot of loud, very raunchy bands.'

'What sort of audience? Older?'

'No, not really. Good mixture. They loved Wet Wet Wet.'

'Are they good?'

'Very good, if you like that sort of thing.'

'Sing something,' says Humphries.

'I couldn't,' says Claudia. 'I don't know any of the tunes. They're just sex symbols.'

Harriet stands on the threshold of the dressing room. 'Are you aware that there are three for the police car?'

'I wasn't,' says Claudia. 'I'm going with Barry in the police car.'

148

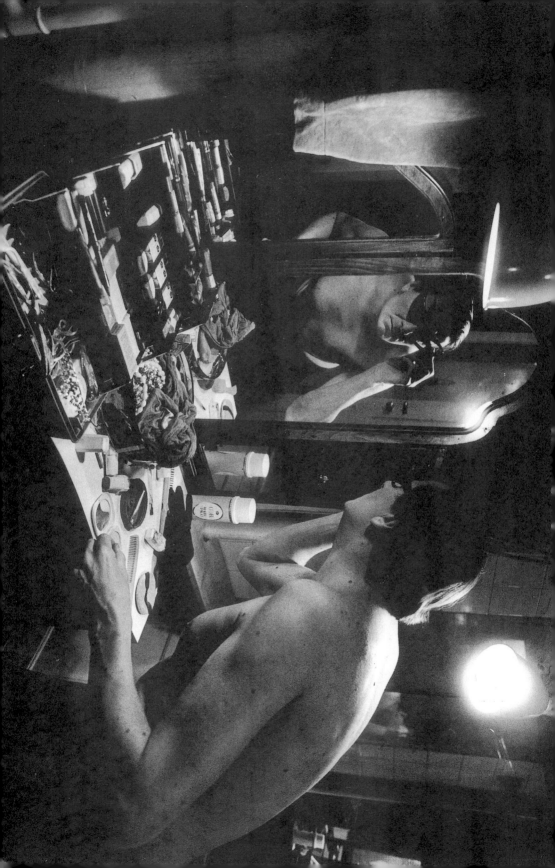

'It takes three,' says Harriet.

'We've got two other cars. We're fine,' says Claudia, turning back to Humphries. 'I want to tell you about Dame Kiri's dress. She's the only other Dame that's made an effort. She's wearing an absolutely amazing St Paul dress.'

'Won't be as amazing as mine,' says Humphries.

'Not nearly. Very very plain back with odd yellow sleeves.'

Stephen looks up from some last-minute sewing on Dame Edna's frock. 'What colour is Di in?'

'Black,' says Claudia, 'very plain dress with a sweetheart neckline. And a diamond brooch to her waist . . . Dame Kiri sang "A Place for Us." In the line up at the front of the show, the only person who got a kiss from Charles was Dame Kiri.'

'He gave her a kiss?'

'Yes,' says Claudia pressing on. 'There's this outrageous American comedienne on the bill. The hot gossip about her is she's the one who's been having a passionate affair with Madonna.'

'Madonna?' says Humphries, fixing Claudia with a glance in the mirror. 'Madonna is a woman.'

'That's right,' says Claudia. 'This is absolutely correct.'

'Perverse.'

'Horrible, isn't it?' says Claudia, laughing. 'What homes do these people come from?'

'So she's a bit of a . . . a bit of an old *chemise* lifter?'

'One of the pop stars did some very good tap dancing.'

'Yes.'

'Dame Edna doesn't have to do all that, does she? She doesn't need her equipment and her tap dancing. She wasn't around to make sure everyone looked neat and tidy.'

'Hair pins? All lacquered? Do we need a net?'

'No,' says Katie, always at the ready. 'That's only for the microphone.'

'I'll just sing the song,' says Humphries to Claudia. ' "I feel a song coming on." ' And with that, Humphries, in Edna's voice, dashes through the lyrics to 'My Public', a 33 rpm record at 78. ' "I'm everybody's swami and adviser/Next week it's . . ." ' He falters and looks at the writing on his handbag. ' ". . . Next week it's Mikhail and little Raisa . . ." ' Behind him, the room is laughing. He whips through to his updated ending: ' "Mrs Thatcher's looking gorgeous since I dressed her/Mrs Bush wears this except in polyester/There's a possum in that box . . ." ' Humphries stops to adjust his spectacles. 'These slip off,' he says to Katie, who fixes them. ' ". . . Possum in that box/Who would kill to wear my frocks . . ." ' Humphries breaks off: 'That's right, isn't it? I'll get that right. I'll just have to read it off my hand or my handbag. Do you think I should tell the audience, "I've got it written down"?'

'Yes,' says Claudia. 'But it's not *your* handbag, is it? That's the gag.'

'It's not a gag any more.'

'Oh, isn't it?'

'I think it's highly unlikely that Edna would've picked up Di's handbag.'

'Di had the words of Edna's song written on *her* handbag.'

Harriet sticks her head into the dressing room: 'There's quite a crowd gathering to wave you goodbye.'

Humphries turns back to Claudia Rosenkrantz. 'I hope I can justify this report of yours,' he says, catching sight of the writing on his hands. 'Nobody'll see all these words, will they?'

'Move your hands a lot,' says Katie.

Humphries stands and inspects himself in the mirror. 'Make-up looks all right, doesn't it? How about getting the show down at that time, eh?'

'Incredible,' says Claudia, who knows Humphries' shows can over-run up to an hour depending on his mood.

'I don't want to go straight on stage.'

'No. Relax for a second. How much did you cut of Edna?'

'You wouldn't have known anything was cut,' Humphries says, stepping into his new dress. 'That'll kill 'em. That's all I need, isn't it?'

'Absolutely,' says Claudia.

'They won't need me to say anything more. I'll say, "I don't need amplifiers because, possums, I speak the truth. And the truth is always deafening however softly it is uttered. I'm not a group,

150

well I am a group in a way. I'm a ... well, I'm a consortium. I'm a wholly owned subsidiary of the House of Edna plc." '

'Which is indeed a group.'

'I am a group in a funny way. Is the Dorchester closed at the moment, by the way?'

'Yes.'

'I normally stay at the Dorchester, but I'm staying with friends.'

'Friends?' says Claudia who knows the game and is happy to feed her star's percolating imagination.

'Friends. They don't like being mentioned.'

'No?'

'This look all right?' Humphries checks out his sequined splendour in the mirror.

'Amazing,' says Claudia.

'Will it light properly? I won't look too fat?'

'You've lost so much weight.'

Katie says, 'It's beautiful, actually.' But before Humphries can even acknowledge her compliment, Claudia is saying, 'So, what's Edna feel about those noisy dancers?'

'I'm going to say, "How wonderful of you all to wait, what a compliment you waited for me. And thank you to all those people who filled in from half-past seven until I could get here." '

'What about Dame Kiri, who at least made an effort?'

'Dame Kiri,' says Humphries, whose baritone is now giving way to Edna's falsetto, 'well, she's lovely. My other Dame. My kiwi Dame. She's the acceptable face of New Zealand talent, hm?'

'She closed the first half. You close the second. So she was just filling in for you.'

'Thank you, Claudia, for coming down. I think this is Stephen's masterpiece. I think Stephen has excelled himself, don't you?'

'You're doing fine for time, Barry,' says Katie.

'There's been a bit about someone lunging in the papers, hasn't there?'

'A man lunged at Di the other day during a royal walkabout.'

' "Madge isn't here because she tends to *lunge* whenever there's royalty around." '

Dame Edna calmly assembles her purse, her coat, her rings,

while her retinue of loyal retainers check and double-check the times, the route, the routine. Claudia, by way of nothing, says to Dame Edna, 'That's very good, thanking the groups for standing in for you. I love that.'

'Yes. I think it'll work. You're happy with the group?'

'I am a group.'

'I'm a group as well. No equipment. I'm wearing my equipment.'

Dennis appears brightly at the threshold of the dressing-room door. 'All right,' he says. 'Let's hit the road, folks.'

Before leaving the room, Humphries checks his eyes for brightness. He widens them; and, satisfied with their luminosity, heads for the door.

He strides out into the cavernous Drury Lane stage with his entourage hurrying behind. He does a little vocal bouncing in Edna's falsetto as he heads for the stage door. 'Mi, mi, mi, mi, mi . . .' He stops half-way across the stage to hitch up Dame Edna's knickers. 'You happy, Steve? You think I'll kill 'em when I go out there?'

'Especially in that garment.'

'I won't be able to read my words,' says Humphries, continuing to emit Edna's 'Mi, mi, mi's'.

'Dame Kiri sang "There's a place for us . . ."'

'There's a . . .'

'. . . place for us,' says Claudia, cutting off Edna's falsetto. 'That closed the first half. That was once again filling in.'

'Dame Kiri's a brick for filling in,' says Dame Edna, talking as he walks. 'If only all New Zealanders were like Dame Kiri. My problem bridesmaid. Of course, I support charity, there's the London Weekend Prostate Fund . . .'

Across the stage, down the cramped grey hallway, past the stage door where the woman at the desk looks up from her TV to shout 'Good luck', Dame Edna emerges into the crisp night air and the hooraying of the waiting crowd. 'Hello, possums,' she says, pushing her way toward the police car. Katie and I follow in a second car, as the blinking blue lights and sirens guide Dame Edna and her retinue to the Palladium theatre minutes away.

Dame Edna leads the phalanx of her entourage past the security guards and into the Palladium's warren of grey hallways, crammed to overflowing with entertainers. Dame Edna brushes past Michael Palin. 'How did you go? Did you enjoy it?'

'Great response,' says Palin, looking even more the *pukka* Englishman beside Dame Edna.

'Could we go somewhere a little warmer?' Humphries says to Claudia.

'Come down here,' says Claudia, descending yet another staircase.

The comedienne Maureen Lipman looms into view. 'Hello, Maureen,' says Dame Edna. 'How's that darling of yours with his hip?'

'Fine, darling,' she says, speaking of her husband the playwright Jack Rosenthal. 'You've got troubles of your own.'

'Not at all,' says Humphries, referring to a recent *Sunday Mirror* 'exclusive' with his estranged third wife Diane. ('I WAS MARRIED TO A CHAMPION MATTRESS TESTER' bannered the paper.) 'I thought it was tasteless.'

'You mean that in a caring way.'

'I'm not joking,' says Humphries, turning the conversation back to the job at hand. 'How are they out there?'

'They're all right.'

Claudia continues the descent into the depths of the Palladium. The entourage finds itself in a large, dimly lit room with all the stars huddled restlessly together behind a large mirror. 'Can't we do this somewhere *else*?' says Humphries, who suddenly finds himself the focus of attention and drops into Edna's voice like a car shifting into higher gear. He waves to this corral of celebrities: 'It's very sweet of you to fill in for me.' Towering in white tie, his back against the wall in the corner, the heavy-weight contender Frank Bruno eyes Dame Edna warily, uncertain what to make of this phallic woman.

Dennis Smith and I push past the guard and find two empty seats in row C just in time to see Palin and Jerry Hall leave the stage, and Dame Edna make her sensational entrance.

'Hello, possums!!' she bellows. Edna's dress sends spots of silver light whirling around the auditorium like a ballroom chandelier. 'I just want you to drink me in. Isn't this frock absolutely gorgeous? It is. And it's very useful. When I come home, I just throw it on the bed. I see myself from all kinds of exciting angles. It has beautiful mirrors all over it.

'And it's *so* sweet of you to wait here for me all those hours from half-past seven until I could get here. And those lovely artistes filling in until I arrived. I'm very, very proud of them. Thank you. Thank you so much, Dame Kiri, and all those little groups. I hope the sound of my police escort didn't intrude on the lovely soft music you've been listening to until now. But in a way I suppose I am a group ... for those of you who may be a bit disappointed. I am a conglomerate as a matter of fact. Yes, I'm a wholly owned subsidiary of the House of Edna, as a matter of fact. I am, plc. I didn't need to bring my own amplifiers and equipment on tonight, because I am my own amplifier. I'm wearing my equipment, possums. I am ... because I'm quite loud enough. I only speak the truth, and the truth is deafening however softly it is spoken. Isn't that a lovely thought? And one you didn't expect this evening, is it? Just a little bit of philosophy.

'Yes, I know you're looking at me, wondering if I'm real. And I *am*, darlings. I am. And I'm very proud to be here tonight because I'm heavily into charity. I am. I'm very interested in charity. And I support a very special one. I remember a long time ago I was trying to make up my mind what charity to support. And I went to one of those charity-card gift shops, and I thought I'll support the one with the prettiest Christmas card. I did! I narrowed it down to Concerned Parents Against Gingivitis and Athletes Against Athlete's Foot. One of them had a little robin red-breast in the snow and the other had a red setter with his tongue poking out. But I finally decided ... I finally decided on a beautiful card. It looked like a psychedelic Christmas pudding. And I opened it up. It was Friends of the Prostate. It was! It was an artist's impression of a prostate ... doing whatever it does ... wherever it does it. I don't know. Sorry. Call me old-fashioned, but I don't.

'And you know, ever since I've been supporting that cause ... that particular cause very specially. And I should tell you that there is a twenty-four-hour Prostathon on London Weekend Television in September. And this is a spooky coincidence because I never realised my husband Norm had a little difficulty in that area. And I had a problem prostate under my very nose for *all* those years. It's spooky, isn't it, possums? It is.

'A lot of people ask me where I stay. I used to stay at the Dorchester before it was having a face lift. But at the moment I am with friends. I can't say any more than that . . .'

Dame Edna glances up at Prince Charles and Princess Diana to the glee of the audience. 'But they are friends. I'm sorry. I'm not able to say any more. But needless to say I have every comfort there. There's mixer taps in the bathroom. There are. And even a little gold lion being sick in the bath. It's beautiful! It is! I'm not sure about that recycled embossed writing paper. I'm a Friend of the Trees, but I mean, whenever you put in a full stop it grows into a black spot about the size of a fifty-pence piece. Nor am I particularly keen on the recycled leavings of cotton wool buds. I'm sorry, but I'm not. Call me old-fashioned. But . . . I look for that little inch of grey carpet around the skirting board where they haven't reached with a Hoover. Not a trace anywhere where I'm staying . . . But I love those little boys, they're *absolutely* a treat. They are . . . playing with their Lego and trying not to build something that looks like a carbuncle . . .'

Dame Edna's reference to Prince Charles's description of the rejected plan for the National Gallery extension gets applause. 'It's not easy with Lego, is it, darlings? It's not. In fact, I'm working on a little speech I'm going to give the Royal Society of Architects about the influence of Lego on modern British architecture. I am. But . . . you know . . . I'm sorry my bridesmaid Madge Allsop can't be here. But she tends – whenever there's someone famous around . . . to *lunge*. Madge is a terrible *lunger*. And she would have *lunged* into the orchestra pit . . .'

Dame Edna looks down into the orchestra. 'Hello, boys. Bet you're relieved to see me.' Edna pretends to be aghast at the audience's laughter. 'No, please, no. I'm with my peer group tonight. I am. All sitting there peering at me. I'm used to paupers in my theatre; but there's no paupers here. There

155

might be people who are poor on paper but that's about it.

'Poor old Madge, anyway, she lunges at almost anything in the hope of getting manhandled by a bodyguard ... She's at the Theatre Royal, Drury Lane now waiting for ... Heaven's above! My audience! ... at the Theatre Royal, Drury Lane ... I've left them there. I've completely forgotten about them. I said I was popping out for a cuppa ... Oh dear, I just hope they do something useful. Talk about what I've been teaching them. Keep their hands above the desk. I hope so. But I love my public. It's very important to me. And by the way, a point of etiquette: in case you haven't read it in the small print, after I've finished, it's perfectly all right for you all to go home.

'I feel a song coming on:

'A cheering crowd at my stage door
An audience crying out for more
That's what my public means to me.
The loyal fans who queue for hours,
The cards, the telegrams, the flowers,
That's what my public means to me.
You need to have a pretty humble attitude
When you see little faces looking up grotesque with gratitude.
And from tiny tots and grannies
I love all your nooks and crannies
That's what my public means to me.

'The Queen's birthday Honours List
This lovely Cartier on my wrist
That's what my public means to me.
A limousine, a sable coat,
The lump that's rising in my throat
That's what my public means to me.
Superstars may come and go
But there's no other
That folks identify with their own mother,
To think there's people in this room
Who wish they'd sprung out of my womb
That's what my public means to me.

'The David Hockneys on my wall
The Royal visitors who call
That's what my public's done for me.
All those requests I get to stay
With famous folk in St Tropez
That's their idea of fun for me.
But they can keep Roman Polanski and Bianca
It's for the company of nobodies *like you* I hanker.
I'm everybody's swami and adviser
Next week it's Moscow with Mikhail and little Raisa,
I love to see my gladdies tremblin'
Soon they'll be tremblin' in the Kremlin
That's what my public means to me.

'And now the time has come to part
I feel a lump inside my heart
That's what my public do for me.
I feel warmer deep down knowing
That my influence is growing
And top women always take their cue from me.
Mrs Thatcher's looking gorgeous since I dressed her,
Mrs Bush wears this – except in polyester,
And there's a possum in that box
Who would *kill* to wear my frocks . . .
That's what my public do for me
That's what you do to me . . .
THANK YOU, POSSUMS!!! BYE BYE.'

The success of the famous, which Dame Edna teases in verse, is meant to be killing. But so, too, is her song. 'My Public' slays the audience and achieves that trickster's sleight-of-hand at which Humphries is master: of having it both ways. Dame Edna satirises the aggrandisement of the famous while at the same time legitimising it for herself. At the curtain call, even Dame Kiri Te Kanawa genuflects before Dame Edna and hugs her knees.

Backstage, just behind the curtained fire doors leading to the auditorium, the stars line up in the grey cramped corridor to meet

Prince Charles and Princess Diana. Dame Edna is at the head of the line, standing improbably in the midst of a bevvy of dishevelled rock acts. 'The audience were a bit taciturn tonight,' says Dame Edna.

'Sean, here!' says the lady, marshalling Sean Connery, the evening's compère, for the royal greeting. Connery dutifully gets in line. 'Mike, here!' she says and Palin follows suit. Any second now the royals will be coming through the fire doors. Dame Edna waves Dennis over from out of the shadows. They huddle together. Dennis glances over at me, and then leads me away from the scene. I understand. Celebrity is the most competitive of contests; and no rule of play is more crucial to the serious magic of a big winner like Dame Edna than this: when you're hot, you're hot; but if you're not, you're not.

5

Dame Edna's Resonances

'He plays with life, and is on perfectly good terms with the
world. He is fond of being misunderstood. It gives him a
position of vantage . . .'

Oscar Wilde, *An Ideal Husband*
(stage direction for the 'flawless dandy' Lord Goring)

April 29th, 1989. It's the last night of the Drury Lane run; and,
except for the two-day chamber version of the revue in Jersey, it
is also the end of the long and lucrative English life of *Back with
a Vengeance!*

Backstage the mood is manic and mournful. Humphries has
not yet arrived. Jane, the bubbly Lesette, wanders around with
her video camera recording the crew and the evening. Katie,
who has been at the theatre since 7.30 in the morning readying
wardrobe for the midnight 'Get Out', is packing away the framed
Honeymoon Gland in Humphries' dressing room. The paintings
on the ante-room wall are gone. The trunk-table is gone. There
is no mail awaiting Humphries' arrival. On the dressing-room
mirror Humphries has scrawled in lipstick 'RUPERT MURDOCH
W 16' and 'EDNA BELLINI OPERA'.

Harriet scurries between dressing rooms trying to get signatures
on a card for the stuntmen which reads: 'TO OUR PLUMMETING
PAUPERS'. 'I said to Barry last night, "Jazza [one of the stuntmen]
asked if there's going to be any party because otherwise he'd like
to take his boss out for supper after the show," ' Harriet says. 'So
Barry goes, "The stunt people. We haven't thought of the stunt
people. They won't be there with us in Jersey, will they, when we
have our big party?" '

Harriet smiles wanly to herself. 'The last night of a long season, there's more gladioli, snow and glitter drop at the finale and a slash curtain. So that when Edna comes downstage at the finale there's snow, balloons, glitter – special. Barry likes that. He thinks that's good. He hates pranks on the last night. He can't stand practical jokes played against him.'

'Is there anything after the show I should see?'

'No, we'll have taken everything down. Sometimes Barry comes back. Sometimes he comes back and just stands there on the stage to see that it's all gone. He needs to know it's all over. He just comes back and he just stands there. And he says, "To think the show was up an hour ago." He looks at the grid and he looks at the stage and everything being pulled apart. It's quite a poignant moment, I suppose.

'He doesn't always come back. If he's going out for supper, he might just drop back afterwards because he knows we'll all be here. It won't be to see us so much. But just, you know, to have a look at the stage. In the hat. The zebra overcoat. I remember him saying, "For me and you, Harriet, this is the real world, isn't it? Once we're in the stage door, and we're getting ready for the show." That's the real world for Barry. It's safe. He's in control. It's where he's really alive; where his true emotions come out.'

When Barry finally arrives, he strides past me in the ante-room without so much as a nod. He immediately goes to the phone and starts dialling. 'Come in when you feel like it,' he says to Lizzie Spender. 'The box is open. Catch the second act.' Jazza is summoned so that Barry can explain how sorry he is not to have organised a party. Eddy, the stuntman who falls out of the balcony every night apparently clutching on to his date only by her scarf, is summoned. Katie is summoned to listen to the comic disclaimer for the beginning of *My Gorgeous Life* which Humphries has just finished. I strain to hear, but I can only make out Katie's laughter and Humphries saying, 'Write that down.' After another few minutes it's clear that I will not be summoned. So I drift self-consciously out to the prompt corner, where Harriet is talking to Jazza and Eddy.

'It'd be nice for us all,' Jazza is saying, 'but we don't expect it because we know Barry too well.'

'Barry said he's going to have a party in May when he comes back. I said, "Best of luck." And he said, "Come have a drink afterwards," ' says Eddy, glancing at my portable tape recorder. 'You shoulda had that recorded.'

'He's such a diabolical ratbag,' says Harriet, using a term which Humphries has both claimed for himself in print and defined variously as 'an Australian crackpot' and 'a curious blend of Rasputin, Lady Godiva, Doctor Timothy Leary, the Emperor Nero, Albert Schweitzer and Yoko Ono'.

'He should be in the film business,' says Eddy, who has doubled for Christopher Lee, Clint Eastwood and Charlton Heston.

'He'd like to get it together,' says Harriet. 'He just doesn't have what it takes.'

'I'll rely on you telling us when we come to get changed if anything's happening.'

Eddy and I pass the time until curtain talking about the stunt which he devised. 'We thought it'd last only two or three weeks and that everybody'd know about the stunt and wouldn't be shocked. But it went on week after week, and everybody had a terrible surprise,' says Eddy, who invented a rig so that the ropes are disguised inside the clothes of the plummeting paupers. 'I think the best night really for something ridiculous was the first night at the Strand. We were suddenly hanging there. People screaming. Nobody knew about it at all. And suddenly I feel something on my feet. I look down at the box underneath; and somebody was doing a terrific stunt there, standing on the edge of *his* box holding my feet, trying to protect me. I mean, if I'd gone, he'd have gone with me. I kept saying, "Get off! Get off!" '

When Sir Les pushes through the green room door, Harriet is saying, 'All the weird fans have come back for the last night. Barry said to me, "Why can't I attract nice people to my show?" '

Sir Les catches sight of me standing, as I have most nights during the run, by the prompt corner. 'You gonna stand in the wings all night?' he says.

'Is that all right?'

'As long as I don't see you. It's just very awkward.'

'All right,' I say, my mouth suddenly tasting like brass. 'OK.'

Sir Les follows the path of Katie's flashlight around to his entrance.

'The first and last nights are always strange,' says Harriet. 'Always the longest. It's as if it was a drug for Barry. He doesn't want to let the audience go.'

'When he said he didn't want me in the wings, he didn't mean it, did he?'

'No, John,' she says. 'He just wants you under his control.'

None the less, Sir Les's jolt makes me uneasy in the wings, so I drift back to his dressing room, which resounds with the tinny relay of Sir Les's voice and the rumble of laughter. Caterers are setting out glasses in the ante-room for the post-show gathering. Over the loudspeakers, Sir Les is saying, 'Barry isn't a poofdah, but he gives a pretty good impression of one. He'll be followed by ... *DAME EDNA EVERAGE*! ladies and gentlemen ...' The dressing room fills with the echo of applause at the mention of Dame Edna's name.

The dictated disclaimer to Dame Edna's autobiography is taped to the dressing-room mirror. A few days before Humphries had been talking about the fun of such a note. 'In other words, saying, you may play a part in my life if you want to, to be involved and drawn in; but for those few who feel reproached by the truth, I'm giving them other names which will effectively *expunge* them from being a footnote in history,' he said. 'I wonder if there are any other examples of this? With Edna people delightedly *choose* to suspend disbelief.' Over the three weeks' Drury Lane run Humphries has savoured the idea of the disclaimer and its vindictive triumph, made all the sweeter because of the considerable difficulties both Humphries and his character had in breaking into the English scene. And now the audience over the loudspeakers are cheering when Sir Les says to the unfortunate latecomers, 'I'm going to pass your name on to Dame Edna ...' Dame Edna renovates life, not only for the audience but for the people whose real life she touches. The disclaimer on the mirror reads, 'Most people would be proud to be mentioned in this book but I have changed the names of those few misguided folk who wouldn't.'

*

Edna was damed spontaneously, on camera, by the Socialist Australian Prime Minister Gough Whitlam. Happy to hitch his then popular public image to Edna's rising star, Whitlam made a guest appearance in the final scene of *Barry McKenzie Holds His Own* (1974), the second successful film collaboration by Humphries with the director Bruce Beresford. 'Did you know that the Prime Minister and I once slept together?' Edna says to her cousin Barry McKenzie, as they approach Sydney airport and a hero's welcome at the end of their adventures in Central Europe. 'It was at the Opera House during the second act of *War and Peace*.' The joke is cribbed from Ronald Firbank's play *The Princess Zoubaroff*; but the finale was wholly original, a surprise even to Humphries. Edna came out of the plane and fell into the Prime Minister's arms. Whitlam said, '*Dame* Edna. Arise Dame Edna.'

For once Edna was overcome with emotion. '*Dame* Edna,' she said, none the less having the film's last word. 'Ohhhh!'

'Thereafter, she was Dame Edna,' says Humphries. 'In a sense, Edna takes directions from herself, not me. If the character seems to be developing that way, I generally go with it. I don't allow the puritan conscience to arise in me and say, "What is she doing being a famous person when she should be back in Melbourne telling them what's wrong with their bathroom fittings?"' And he adds, 'The other night at the charity function, Prince Charles said, "How are you, Dame Edna?" So she's accepted at her own evaluation of herself.'

Dame Edna's evaluation of herself has even been codified into educational material. '*Question*,' it says after the chapter on Dame Edna in an Australian student volume, *The Humour of Barry Humphries*, 'Why do you think Dame Edna has come to be one of the best known, if not the most famous, women in Australia?' Edna didn't become a Dame until nearly twenty years after her invention, but over the years she's gotten progressively grander and more imperious. Even before Edna went abroad, Humphries was inching her up the social ladder from Moonee Ponds, which was 'too old and too working-class a district of Melbourne to have produced the genteel Edna', to the Melbourne suburb of Highett. In *Wild Life in Suburbia: Volume Two* (1959), Edna sang in waltz tempo:

Don't think I'm disloyal to my Moonee Ponds soil,
I adore it – but let me confess
When I'm back from abroad, I'd love to afford
To change my historic address . . .

The best Highett homes have hundreds of gnomes
All scattered about on the grass
There's wrought iron too, in a pale duck-egg blue
And *acres* of sand-blasted glass . . .

On Edna's return to Australia from England in 1962 in *A Nice Night's Entertainment*, she sang of 'Australian Vitality'. Her enthusiasm for all things royal was reflected in her voice, which occasionally slipped into the intonations of Her Majesty. But the imperialism of Edna's self did not dawn quickly on Humphries, perhaps because the progress of his career and those of his characters was woefully slow to take hold in England. 'A number of people prophesied success for me who saw me on my home ground where I *knew* I was funny,' says Humphries. 'There's nothing better than seeing a comic who thinks he's funny. If he's not entirely sure that what he's saying is amusing, or if his anxiety gets the better of him, he's not doing himself justice.'

In the early anxious years in England, Humphries didn't always feel funny. He arrived in June 1959 on the eve of an appearance as Sandy Stone on a TV talk show. 'I don't think anyone made anything of it,' recalls Humphries. 'After that, I was pretty consistently out of work.' It wasn't until November 1959 that he landed a small part as the madhouse keeper in *The Demon Barber*, a musical about Sweeney Todd at the Lyric, Hammersmith – far from the West End. Humphries lived in a basement flat in Notting Hill Gate with his second wife, Rosalind, a dancer who worked at a greengrocer's by day and danced for good money at a strip club at night, while Humphries briefly worked at a Walls' ice-cream factory by night in order to audition by day.

'I didn't work there very long,' he says. 'I've tended to exaggerate that episode in the factory. But it was my only experience of factory work. It was a hellish experience and sort of Dadaist as well. I was working on a conveyor belt. It was Chaplinesque. Because of my maladroitness on the conveyor belt, I was put with the morons. I wasn't *allowed* to work on the conveyor belt because I kept dropping the ice creams. I was put in a room where a group of us sat around an enormous plastic drum throwing damaged ice creams into it. But I got paid, and I also had this anecdote. I felt I smelled rather of raspberry ripple when I went to an audition.'

When Humphries talks of this period, his conversation returns to the phrase 'people who were kind to me'. Changing cultures is always a shock to the system, especially one as highly-strung as Humphries'. The sense of solace and support was life-giving to him because it was in such short supply. The revue writers Peter Myers and Ronnie Kass were kind. John Betjeman was kind. Eric Maschwitz, the director of BBC Light Entertainment, was kind. The Australian comedian Dick Bentley, to whom Humphries would later return the favour, was kind. 'But', says Humphries, 'it's one thing to feel benevolently towards a struggling young actor, it's another to immediately offer him work.'

And Humphries struggled to get a theatrical foothold in Britain. His Testimonial Performance in Melbourne had raised the fare to England; but once ensconced in the louche atmosphere of Notting Hill Gate, Humphries was skint. 'Barry was absolutely broke. On one occasion, Barry told me that he and Rosalind were down to threepence, that was all they had in the world. It cost fourpence to make a phone call so they couldn't even go out and ring their friends for a loan,' says his compatriot Ian Donaldson, who hung out during the early insecure years in Humphries' basement along with other artistic Aussie expats, like the painters Arthur Boyd, Sidney Nolan, and Francis Limburner. 'He said he'd just discovered the concept of the overdraft. He'd never known about this before. He said, "You go along to your bank manager and say I'd like a trillion pounds please, and he hands it over in paper bags. That's right, you can survive on that forever." As long as the overdraft existed, Barry thought there was no need to work. He did want to buy paintings and books.'

'You'll see it in *My Gorgeous Life*, the slow progress,' says Humphries. Finding work within five months might seem good luck to a journeyman actor, but Humphries had a high regard for his talent and even higher ambitions for it. If his career seemed stalled, his intellectual life took on a new amperage. He seized on his London days with manic energy. His appetite for England and all things English filled his unemployed hours. 'He was extraordinary,' says Donaldson. 'He fitted in immediately. He knew London. He knew about various writers and artists who we thought were dead. He knew the right pubs to drink in, the right people to talk to. He established this extraordinary network – still not getting employment – but becoming known and being seen as someone of extraordinary knowledge who was also entertaining.'

Humphries paints a much more lacklustre picture of himself. 'I was very much on the social periphery,' he says. ' I didn't know anyone in particular. I never lion-hunted as fellow Australians had done. I couldn't bring myself to descend on people. Although, of course, I knew the poems of all the Sitwells by heart, and they were there to be met and would have probably been pleased – I never contacted them. (In later life I got to know Sacheverell Sitwell.) And then in the distance at the Royal Academy I saw Augustus John. I knew about all these people, probably more than many of the people in England. I knew their books, their pictures, their writings, but I didn't track them down out of a kind of reticence. I rather regret it now because, if I'd been a little *bolder*, it would have been interesting.'

But living on the edge made life interesting enough for Humphries and kept him in high, sometimes manic spirits. 'I remember laughing all night till it hurt and being exhilarated by his humour and our discovery of London, and the feeling of getting away from Melbourne,' recalls Ian Donaldson, who joined Humphries on his reconnaissance missions in his adopted city. 'And I remember him trying out all his scripts and jokes. We always thought they were funny, even if they weren't in the theatre.'

Bolstered with Pevsner's *The Buildings of England*, *The Blue Guide*, and the invaluable *London Night and Day*, Humphries absorbed his new home as he had his Melbourne. 'Whenever I was with Barry, they tended to be all-night sessions,' says Donaldson. 'He had a lot of time and loved to sit and gossip. He was still not known, and so he could do outrageous things. One night about 2 a.m. he said, "Let's look up *London Night and Day* and see what we should be doing." The book told you what was going on every hour of the day. It said, "2 a.m. – go to the Turkish Baths on Jermyn Street." So we did. We had this whole ritual of going through the Turkish Baths, all the various steam houses. Then, there were little sleeping booths you went through. You steamed up, you had a swim, you slept.

'We woke up at about six. And Barry said, "Let's see what the book says to do at six." It listed a pub in Covent Garden. So we went off to the pub where all the market workers drank. We started drinking at six a.m., and then travelled home in the rush-hour tube at nine with all the business men going to work in their suits.'

In Easter 1959 Humphries was sighted wearing a CND badge on the famous Aldermaston March. His hair was unfashionably long; his clothes not a dandy's fine threads but an impoverished actor's blue jeans and dark turtleneck. Friends from those days remember Humphries singing Victorian music-hall songs in pubs in Highgate; reciting A.E. Housman and Henry Vaughan in Welsh pubs; taking over a Penzance tea room to rally the spirits of a cancelled wedding party with 'Highett Fidelity'. 'It was Barry at his most considerate and brilliant,' says Donaldson, who witnessed the tea room emptying of bemused regulars and Humphries at his most hilarious. 'Barry knew that the only way to save the situation was through theatre. So he told stories.'

Humphries also listened to stories, especially those of the ex-patriate Australian community that lived around London's Earls Court, dubbed 'Kangaroo Valley' for the high density of Aussies. 'His memory sharpened by absence and new experience,' writes Clive James of Humphries in the early 1960s, 'he became more conscious than ever of the all-pervading oddness into which he had been born. On every voyage home his ears were tuned more keenly, his eyes skinned another layer. If he had not had his Europe, he would never have completed his rediscovery of Australia.'

London gave Humphries the detachment to see Australia more clearly; and Edna returned the favour in *A Nice Night's Entertainment*, by showing Australians her London. Humphries concocted a slide show of Edna in her red overcoat, posed against the backdrop of the city's sights, among them – the Horse Guards, Piccadilly, and what she called 'the statue of Trafalgar'. Humphries' characters were percolating in his imagination even if they fell flat on English ears. 'In London it was a question of finding a voice that people could actually hear and wish to listen to,' Humphries says. London seemed like the Big Table at which he was not allowed to sit. 'People are talking, and you're outside,' explains Humphries. 'You sort of tune in. You think, "I want to come in on this, but I have to wait until the moment." '

While he bided his time, Humphries diligently kept refining his characters. 'Barry was writing scripts all the time. He was working on his characters. He was thinking of Australia a lot,' says Donaldson, who acted as a sounding board for the material. 'He went to this awful place – the Down Under Club – you can imagine what that was like. You could see expatriate Australians there. He was horrified and enthralled by the place. He'd go there to talk to the people. He'd tell me he'd met so-and-so who'd just arrived. He'd dwell on a phrase and think about it. Maybe later in the night, he'd come back with the phrase the person had said and say, "How can he use a phrase like that!?" The phrase would be incorporated into the script and become a sort of leitmotif.

'It was built up out of amusement, exasperation, indignation, and a measure of affection about all this. Barry was hypnotised by Australia, but really appalled by the Australians who kept passing through. There's great Australian life going on in Earls Court. There were parties always going on there. He'd go to the parties. He'd meet Old Melbournian boys who still regarded him as a long-haired, non-sports-playing poofdah. They'd have a few beers and be abusive to him. He'd treasure various things they'd say and go right home and scribble it down. He'd have something clever to say back to these guys, who were usually pretty thick.

'They were very interesting encounters to observe. Barry'd approach them with a mixture of amiability, which drew them out, and contempt. Edna has that, doesn't she? She's so amiable and so welcoming and so nice; and then the dagger goes in. Barry was able to use that Australian agreeableness to get people off their guard. But the smile goes on again, and you don't quite know what's happened.'

'I've suddenly discovered that England is really a province of Australia,' says Humphries. 'And so I needn't have been frightened all those years ago. If I'd gone straight in. But I wasn't ready.' Although he soon got work on the West End, appearing as Sowerberry in Lionel Bart's *Oliver!* (1960) and, later, in his *Maggie May* (1964), parts too small to earn him a biography in the programmes, Humphries did not get much satisfaction. 'I think Barry's mood in London when I met him was bad,' says Peter Cook, a comedian's comedian who was then at the height of his celebrity both as an entertainer in *Beyond the Fringe* and as an impresario of outrageousness, who owned substantial shares in the satirical magazine *Private Eye* and was the proprietor of the Soho comedy club, The Establishment. 'I feel sure that he was certain he was very talented. I don't think he liked being in a minor part in *Oliver!* Why it took Barry so long to become established – and, indeed, adored – over here I don't quite know. I think in those early years, he was feeling a bit embittered.'

The envy that Dame Edna would later put back into the audience as vindictive triumph was felt fiercely in those days by Humphries. 'I thought, "Here I am in a musical comedy playing a small part, when I'm really better than most people. While I'm doing this, they're out there having a good time doing what *I'm* good at." I felt some resentment.' Cook, who was a fan of Humphries' records – and especially Sandy Stone – but who had never seen him perform, generously threw Humphries a life-line and asked him to do a three-week season at The Establishment for £100 a week.

'Big money,' recalls Humphries of his Establishment gig in 1962, in which Sandy Stone and a timid Edna made their theatrical debuts in England. 'Very big money. As soon as I got there, though, I felt a little uneasy. The shape of the room was long and narrow. The audience weren't close to me, and they weren't an experienced cabaret audience either. The huge success of satire and *That Was the Week That Was* had led them to expect a certain kind of humour. Very topical and often very witty and very irreverent about British institutions. My kind of rambling regional monologues, which depended for their effect not on jokes or on impersonations of political figures, were really unsuitable for that kind of place. They wanted Harold Macmillan. They didn't want Glen Iris, Melbourne.

'Furthermore, in the close proximity of that club, Edna, who didn't wear pantyhose in those days, was a kind of thin young man in rather unconvincing female attire talking about her family, for chrissake, and interior decoration. She talked also about London and coming to London. I can't remember any of the material at all. I was so nervous I don't think I did justice to whatever material I had, anyway. I didn't *feel* funny. When you don't trust the audience, it doesn't trust you. So in a sense it was nobody's fault. It was courageous of Peter to put me there. I don't think I did as well as I could've. I mystified people. Not many turned up. A few barracking Australians, a kind of claque, who did me more harm than good. It was the wrong time and the wrong place. What was to be a three-week season ended up a ten-performance season.' Says Cook, 'If nobody comes in at all, there's not much point.'

In the annals of The Establishment, according to Peter Cook, no turn went down worse. 'The stoniest of stony silences,' says Cook. '*Nobody* found Barry remotely amusing. It was dreadful. Must have been dreadful for him. There were about three or four people who thought this is very, very funny. Mainly John Betjeman, John Osborne, and me. I felt ashamed of my fellow-Londoners for not appreciating him.'

In *My Gorgeous Life* Dame Edna turns the punishing memory of humiliation into hilarity by blaming her actor-manager Humphries for the disaster. *He*, she claims, went on *before* her and emptied the room.

'I had a bit of a weep afterwards [Dame Edna writes]. Barry had gone home in a huff, the worse for a few sherries I'm afraid . . . This was the lowest ebb in my career, but I have described it honestly and courageously. I was hurt at the time and my confidence was badly shaken, but I decided to have a few tough new clauses written into my contract with Mr H. I also vowed that if I ever found success outside my native land, I would remember this incident . . .'

And Dame Edna has remembered it. Both Edna and Humphries have long memories. 'If Barry feels wronged or betrayed, he will not forget,' says Nick Garland. 'He will continue to keep them on a kind of hit list. He goes after them with humour and contempt, putting them down with little asides.' Humphries' flop at The Establishment inevitably is a target for the psychic ju-jitsu of Edna's put-downs. Memories of public humiliation leave deep wounds in any artist, especially one as notoriously sensitive as Humphries. And through Edna, Humphries can at once hide the wound and keep it open, feeding both his anger and his delight in getting even.

As the title of the present show admits, Dame Edna embraces her celebrity with a vengeance. And, like Humphries, Edna deals with her corrosive sense of envy by becoming the envied. She revels in her distinction in the same way and for the same reason that all the programmes of Humphries' one-man shows contain encomiums about his genius and photos of him with the cultural icons of his era. 'Barry Humphries is the first Australian satirist, he is also one of the funniest men in the world. If you don't think so, then it's your fault,' wrote Spike Milligan for Humphries' second one-man show *Excuse I* (1965), adding under his scrawled name, '(being of sound mind)'. On the same page is a photo of the young Humphries with another licensed trickster, Salvador Dali. Humphries' insistence on his comic and intellectual pedigree belies his long, sometimes hurtful struggle to have it validated.

'Barry first came to my attention at The Establishment,' recalls Garland. 'The act was a failure. But the people who were there – John Bird, John Fortune, Peter Cook, myself – we were all *enormously impressed* by Barry. We all immediately began talking in this preposterous parody of Australian to each other. He became somebody whom you reckoned. He was instantly subsumed into our culture, into our vocabulary, into the way we spoke.' And when Garland came to Cook to write Barry McKenzie with him, Cook immediately suggested Humphries. Peter Cook never doubted Humphries' excellence. 'I thought Barry would go on to be a big turn,' says Cook. 'I didn't particularly pick out Edna. I thought Barry would eventually be enormously successful because he was so bright and so observant. We British would eventually catch up.'

Cook encouraged Humphries to join a group of revue satirists he was organising for his club: among them John Bird, Eleanor Bron, John Fortune. 'They were kind of early jeans wearers,' says Humphries of the group. 'It was very difficult to break into that. They belonged to the English Club. They belonged to the same university. I thought, "Well, I'm a university wit, but I went to the *wrong* university. And I'm not going to be able to join this club." I even went to rehearsals. No one gave me a script. I was just sitting around. I didn't quite have the nerve or courage to go up to whoever was in charge and say, "Look, I've been coming to rehearsals for three weeks and no one's actually given me a part. I go out to lunch with these people, and I'm beginning to feel as though I'm making a mistake. I'm misunderstood." I was frightened they'd say, "Yes, you are misunderstood." So I never went up to the boss. I was really very sorry for myself, and puzzled. In the end, I did my own act.'

But Humphries was soon playing with the big boys. Says Garland, 'The people who had the power, who were on the make – Jonathan Miller, Alan Bennett, Eleanor Bron, John Wells, Richard Ingrams – those were the people we were moving among. It was a struggle for Barry. The English have plenty of eccentrics, plenty of people pretending to be Oscar Wilde and wearing their hair long. Thousands of them. It took Barry a little time to get the measure of this.' With a leg up from Peter Cook, Humphries crashed the cliquish Shrewsbury set who ran *Private Eye*, appearing in the magazine's columns both in the Barry McKenzie cartoon and as its astrologer 'Madame Barry'. He was cutting comedy records like 'Old Pacific Sea', 'Chunder

Down Under', and 'The Earls Court Blues', and doing character work for Joan Littlewood's Theatre Workshop at Stratford East as well as in the West End. (He would appear in seventeen shows in the West End over the subsequent decade including *The Bedsitting Room* with Spike Milligan, a memorable Captain Hook – 'I'm going to take a peep round the poop' – in a Christmas pantomime of *Peter Pan* and Fagin in the revival of *Oliver!*) He was also tapped to join BBC-TV's *Late Show* wits in 1964–5.

'The odd thing was that his comedy didn't go down well with the audience,' says John Wells, who along with John Bird, John Fortune and Humphries were vying with each other for air time for their material. 'The whole show was live. I remember once watching Barry's act, which was about the Duke of Edinburgh being greeted by a man kangaroo on the occasion of the royal visit to Australia, which I thought was hilarious at rehearsal, and being amazed when it went out at the cut-aways to the audience looking completely bewildered. Edna, also, didn't go over. I think it was the references. You have to live with the character a bit. There was definitely some feeling that Barry wasn't *persona grata* with the director. I think that's when the relationship with Ian Davidson began to take off. Ian was a very junior director, but he was prepared to film some of Barry's most fantastic fantasies. Barry almost made his own department inside the programme.'

Humphries' star, like his subsequent home addresses in Maida Vale and Highgate, was on the way up. He was becoming something of a fixture on the vivacious London scene. England was in radical transition from being top dog to America's poodle, from the discipline of wartime scarcity to the ease of new abundance, from thirteen years of Conservative Government to Labour, from the Old Boy network of established power to the New Boy power of pop culture. Youth was asserting itself and calling the old meanings and manners into question. It was a bumptious flamboyant time and Humphries' bumptious flamboyant behaviour was a match for it.

Humphries was well positioned and well equipped to ride the new wave to glory. The vectors of his life went out in all directions over the English scene, generating a momentum which, at a certain speed, led to his inevitable disintegration by the late 1960s. Humphries wanted to be everywhere at once. In time, the character of Dame Edna would allow him to act out this fantasy of omnipotence. With her 'super-stardom', Dame Edna could claim (and have) access to almost anybody. The teeming social tableaux of the mid-1960s to early 1970s which the Barry McKenzie cartoon lampooned – the flower people, TV producers, avant-garde film-makers, folk-singers, psychotherapeutic phonies, and hangers-on – was a caricature of Humphries' own social delirium. He was on stage, on record, on TV and on the bottle. He was doing book reviews for the *Spectator* as well as a cult cartoon for *Private Eye*. He was photographed as a totem of the changing times by Lewis Morley, lying on his chaise-longue with his beloved framed Charles Conder fans on the wall, nibbling his pinky, looking pale and strange: an opaque glass of fashion but still a mould of form. John Lennon liked Humphries' long hair and changed his accordingly. Yoko Ono, inspired by the photos of buttocks in Humphries' *Bizarre*, made her avant-garde film *Bottoms*. Humphries was promising but not established. His frustration was beginning to show both in the drink and in the occasional chink in his dandy's sang-froid. John Wells was present when Humphries paid off a taxi bearing his colleagues from *The Late Show* who were beginning to make their names in television. 'Five shillings?' said Humphries, *sotto voce* to the driver. 'Ten bob, if you say, "Thank you, Barry."'

Harriet reports back after huddling with Humphries in the scene change for Sandy Stone. 'I went over, and he said, "You know it's very difficult when someone is in the wings watching me."'
    'So he wants me not to be there?'
    'No, I think you're fine, John,' says Harriet, bringing the lights up on a drab room in the process of renovation, where Sandy sits in his old armchair, 'invisible' under a dustsheet. 'I said to him, "It must be very hard because it's distracting." I was very sympathetic because I usually am in that situation. I remember there was a time when he used to have Lizzie in the wings, and the crew was asking what was wrong with Barry because instead of facing the front of

the stage he'd do the whole show to the prompt corner where she was. Lizzie was looking adoringly at Barry, and he was moving farther and farther to the side.'

After the new Greek occupiers of 36 Gallipoli Crescent remove the dustsheet and make their exit, Sandy Stone is alone with his thoughts and his audience. Harriet steps back with me into a dark corner of the stage. 'Barry gets a bit sensitive about last nights because it's the last night he can do it,' says Harriet. 'He gets a bit . . . like a child. Petulant. Often Barry has to look for something to criticise. It gives him some perverse satisfaction to know someone else is wrong. Closing night he's nervous. He gets a sensitive tone in his voice, like when he's sick. He just needs looking after. He said, "Why is John in the wings?" And I said, "It just helps me because you change from night to night." And he said, "Yes, I do, don't I?" '

Later, at the intermission, with our maps of the stall seats hidden behind our programmes, Harriet and I go down into the stalls to choose Dame Edna's victims. 'Sometimes', says Harriet, 'Dennis and I go up in the boxes and look down. Dennis usually has a clipboard which he thinks nobody notices; but it's quite obvious what he's doing.'

We manoeuvre ourselves down front where an usherette is selling ice cream. Our backs to the stage, we scan the milling crowd. 'Every now and then you feel obliged to look up so they're not aware that you're always choosing the stalls. It's the first six rows or so. If he wants to, he can see farther back than six rows. Sometimes it's eight or ten.' She glances over my shoulder, and I slowly turn around. 'This woman in the second row is what we're looking for: middle-aged or older and slightly frumpy. Preferably fat, dowdy looking. Nice kind faces, generally. Never anyone grouchy. If they look really offended, as if they've had a bad time with Les.' She marks the Dowdy Woman's seat in the map plan and whispers, 'Second row. A possible senior, though a little bit young.'

'Is *she* good?' I point to a beefy matron with a bouffant that wouldn't budge in a cyclone. Harriet is happy with the find. 'The older women are much more willing to be obliging on stage,' she says. 'They're not as nervous.'

Humphries, like any inspired comedian, is very conscious of his comic silhouette. The antic spirit should never be at a loss and looks all the more glorious set against people on whom loss is stamped, whose ordinariness is temporarily banished by being included in Dame Edna's extraordinary game. Dame Edna even calls attention to this stage-managed redemption when she asks her last guest to bow her head. 'Isn't it pathetic that this is the highlight of her life?' says Dame Edna before waving a gladiolus over the head of the guest in one final blessing and sending her back into the workaday world:

'Lucky possum that you are
You are now a mini-star,
A big fish in a tiny pond
Thanks to my magic wand.
Timid once now you are bolder
Since Edna's gladdy touched your shoulder.'

'I like people of a certain age on stage,' says Humphries. 'They're more interesting. They look better when they're close to being contemporaries of Edna's. A nice little line-up of lovely-looking people wouldn't look so funny. As people get older, they get more staid, more dignified. They also have their own little performance. Even the most unconscious, humble person has some persona, some performance to go through.'

'Does Barry really count the map?'

'He counts it,' says Harriet. 'He says, "Where are they? Where are they? Six back four in." I don't know how he remembers their names.'

'That's his skill. He's professionally polite. Do you think that one in the black dress is too young?'

Harriet slowly pans right to the middle of aisle four. 'Yeah,' she says. 'Too young.'

'There's Jonathan Miller's wife,' I say, pointing out Rachel Miller. 'She's fun. She's a doctor.'

'Too intelligent,' says Harriet. 'I'm going to look on the other side of the aisle, OK?'

'She's got a good sense of humour.'

'Barry likes to laugh at everybody else,' says Harriet, 'but he can't stand people laughing at him. If he says something that's funny which he doesn't mean as a joke, you have to leave the room and laugh. He's so hurt if you laugh at him.'

Dame Edna likes to disconcert her audience. In previous shows, she's asked for, and received, shoes from the audience for her inspection. She's coaxed four people on stage to cook a barbecue and then left the paying customers alone in front of two thousand people while, with consummate daring, she made her exit for a costume change. She's insisted that her audience sit still for a Polaroid picture to remember it by. 'You could feel the audience posing,' says Ian Davidson, weeping with amusement at the preposterousness of someone trying to photograph an entire audience and imitating its communal smile. 'A little picture would come out, and Edna would say, "It's not very good of *you*."' Dame Edna has also pulled a flashlight from her purse and trained it on the critics, trying to make them identify themselves – a job made easier by a sign saying 'Critic' which dropped down over their assigned seats.

Dame Edna's stage hijinx mirrors Humphries' off-stage habit of wrong-footing the world around him. 'Barry is a rather eccentric man. He's not like other people. He likes to show off and be disconcerting,' says Garland, whose cartoon character Barry McKenzie unwittingly created turbulence around him while the creator, Barry Humphries, does it out of a knowing subversive mischievousness. 'There is a purpose behind these pranks: to do the least expected thing and by doing so to create this curious fractured world where he is king because he is calling the shots.'

Garland tells of the time in 1967 when he was cartoonist for the *Daily Telegraph*, and Humphries met him in Fleet Street for lunch. They had agreed to meet outside the newspaper. When Garland arrived, Humphries was doubled up in laughter at the newspaper's display window which had a Garland cartoon in it. Says Garland, 'Barry was standing in front of the window apparently helpless with laughter, laughing so hard he was leaning against the wall gasping for air and gesturing to people walking by saying, "Look at these incredibly funny jokes in this window."

'What he was doing was partly creating a huge disturbance on the pavement (nobody recognised him in those days) and also having a go at me since the sort of political cartoons I was doing were not intended to bring about helpless laughter. He was sending me up. He continued the joke for a while. I said, "C'mon, cut it out," laughing and pulling him away. And, still, he would return to the window, holding his side. He snapped out of it and said, "Where should we go?" By that time, I was already feeling amused and disconcerted in this mixture that Barry so likes to create. He said, "Well, let's go to Simpson's."

'We walked down Fleet Street and down the Strand to Simpson's. All the way he'd be stopping people in the street, in a particularly vacant and vacuous way. "Hello. What's your name? Hello. What's your name?" He was pretending to be an idiot, a severely retarded man out with his keeper who was behaving normally. Smiling. Affable. Friendly. Vacant. And people responded to him kindly. People said hello back to him, completely believing that this was a retarded man. They'd smile at me too as if to say, "It's OK, I don't mind." There was something in his persistence in doing this and in the strange kindness with which the people responded and the odd atmosphere. I remonstrated with him to "Cut it out", meaning, "Why do this to those people?" We got to the restaurant, had a perfectly good meal, plenty of talk, and, when we were leaving, he went to the loo.

'In the lavatory, Barry went to one of the urinals and said in a very very loud voice, "I'm not really urinating. I'm only pretending to. Because I can't urinate with a room full of people." There were a number of men in the urinal. The atmosphere became absolutely electric. He was speaking at the top of his voice so that everybody would hear. He said, "It's quite difficult actually not being able to pee in a lavatory full of other people because you want to but you can't. In fact, once I went through this ridiculous situation and went back to the table and was so confused I peed on the table . . ."

'Barry told this long story because it was very funny. I was

178

also terribly embarrassed, wishing somehow that the earth would open up and I would somehow vanish. At the same time, I was half-amused by the embarrassment on everybody else's faces. I was also thinking they'd done nothing to offend him, yet everybody was disturbed. Nobody knows quite what's going to happen or how to behave. Barry had created *exactly* the atmosphere he wanted to create. And that's what he does on stage in a huge sense.'

Dame Edna embodies Humphries' comic genius for turning his desire to be unusual into something creative. 'It's like fireworks,' says Garland, 'it's pyrotechnic.' In life as on stage, the power to disconcert gives Humphries the power to be a rule unto himself. It's a game which puts Humphries in control of his moment. What is awesome to those who have witnessed Dame Edna on stage or Humphries off it is the special kind of wild fearlessness with which he gets laughs by breaking the rules. 'Barry's very brave,' says Garland. 'He's *really* courageous. He has something of the foolhardy courage of somebody who doesn't even seem to feel a certain sort of fear. I'm not sure there's not even a funny sort of bravery in the auto-destruct side of him, the high risk with his life and his career. He's an addictive character. Perhaps fame and money and power are now drugs for him. It's not alcohol any more. It's another high.'

From the outset Humphries' appetite for misrule was a means of mastering fear by creating it. 'One had to impersonate a brazen person,' he says. 'One had to act as if one were courageous. In performing, one still has to act as if one is confident. If what you're doing is urged, hurried, apologetic, the audience will smell fear a mile off. So you have to put up a smokescreen. You have to act as if you have no fear.'

Faced with hostility, Humphries' impulse is always to attack and to reverse it: controlling rather than being controlled by others. 'Whenever enough people were looking at him and looking rather hostile,' says Ian Donaldson, recalling nights on the town with Humphries dressed disreputably in his dusty cassock from *The Demon Barber* and with his hair still floured from the show, 'he'd adopt a limp. He'd become a cripple and shame them for having laughed. On one occasion, I remember drinking at a pub called the Grenadier, down a long cobbled mews. There were a lot of young chaps outside the pub. They were Sloanies wearing cavalry twills and tweed jackets. They saw this extraordinary character coming down the lane. They began to jeer at him. Barry immediately went into his spastic limp. He limped the whole length of the cobbles, and the laughter stopped immediately. They were really rather horrified at this cripple coming right down toward them and then coming into their pub. They made way for him. There was a clear path to the bar. He bought his drinks and then started talking to them. They backed off. Barry regarded London as his theatre. It was a stage on which to perform.' And Humphries has said as much. 'I wanted to bring life into the theatre, and theatre into life.'

'Barry played out his fantasies in the way that very few of us do,' says John Wells, recalling Humphries in a manic phase during a trip to Blackpool with the *Late Show* team to do a satire on the Tory party election programme. 'Perhaps that's what I admired and envied him for. There are dangers in doing what he did. I remember an incident with a costume man. Barry'd already done something outrageous like pull the tablecloth off in the restaurant. We were already in trouble. The costume designer was very much on the margin and certainly hadn't come out of the closet. He was very sensitive about it. After we'd ordered, Barry suddenly lent across the table and kissed him smack on the mouth. He didn't do it because he fancied the man. He did it because it was the most terrible thing he could do under the circumstances. We were all completely chilled. He did it merely to dramatise the situation. It was in the air, so he did it. But otherwise, almost everything he did was very amusing.'

The sense of danger in Humphries' behaviour took life out of the ordinary and thrilled his friends as it now does Dame Edna's audiences. 'He was certainly frightening to be with but therefore very exciting,' says John Wells. 'He was slightly like a mad child. He was certain to make a scene in every restaurant. I used to be sitting there in some anxiety for the moment when he'd do something outrageous. He was always taking the piss out of waiters or making overtures to people at other tables. There was quite a lot of girl chasing. I felt very inhibited, and he just seemed completely uninhibited. He's an unbelievably life-enhancing man. He really does have completely crazy ideas which are terribly funny. I'd read French and German literature at Oxford but had never actually met anyone who appeared to me to carry on like a writer. Barry seemed to me to carry on like a real, proper artist. He broke all the rules. He said things you remembered. He behaved like a genius. He did carry on like Salvador Dali.'

Wells got involved in abetting Humphries in some of his capers. 'I socialised a lot with Barry, very happily,' he says. 'Once he decided he wanted to go to Paris. He hadn't got an updated passport. So I said rather pathetically and helpfully, "I think we should see if there's an emergency service at the Foreign Office." We went down to the Foreign Office, which was naturally closed. Barry walked under the gateway into the yard. There was some Foreign Office man who was just driving his girlfriend home and had got out of his car to talk to the porter. Barry went up to him and asked in a rather odd way if he could direct him to where he could get a passport. While the man was pointing to some remote corner, Barry got into the car and started making advances to the girl. The man was furious. So we were chased out of there. We were then told that Barry could get a temporary passport if he had a photograph of himself. We went to some all-night photography place in Piccadilly. Barry got into a booth upstairs, took his own photograph, and went downstairs to collect the photo where it was being developed. It wasn't a machine, it was an actual laboratory. A hatch went up. It was a West Indian man behind the counter who was about to produce the photograph. And Barry said, "Now I understand why it's called the dark room." He finally got to Paris by saying his mother was dying of cancer in a Paris hospital and bursting into tears at the barrier. They let him through.'

The tumult that Humphries created around himself was excused by the laughter it generated. Wells recalls watching Humphries, sporting his long hair and his unlit electric bow tie purchased at a local joke shop, lurch up to a couple who had just come through the swing doors of their Blackpool hotel. 'I wonder if you could direct me to the nearest public library,' said Humphries. 'I'm particularly interested in . . . *biography*.' At the mention of 'biography', Humphries made his tie light up.

Dame Edna is the distillation of the off-stage spectacle Humphries used to make of himself. She creates in the audience that tension Humphries formerly put into the world around him – an atmosphere of anxiety at just how far he would go, how deep he would draw the spectator into a collusion whose laughter was strangely uncomfortable. Humphries now lets Dame Edna sound the notes of outrage, egotism, contempt, and ambivalence. Humphries himself remains politely mum. The split can be confusing. 'We were working at the Traverse Theatre in Edinburgh, and Clive James was in the show,' Wells remembers. 'Barry strode in and cut Clive completely dead. Walked past him, changed into Edna, came out and said, "Hello, Clive." She sat on his lap, sang Australian folk songs with him, ruffled what was left of his hair, was extremely affable, went back and changed into Barry, walked out, and cut him dead. That has happened a great deal.'

'I've never come across a comic who so completely held you in thrall by his ability to make you laugh; and, having got you, screw you up somehow and make you feel something peculiar has happened,' says Nick Garland. The mixture of terror and elation translates as joy in the theatre; and off stage, more often than not, the exhibitionist's love of surprise is received by Humphries' friends as a form of generosity. 'Once we did a show in Edinburgh and stayed in this squalid hotel,' says Wells, recalling its stench of beer and piss. 'In the morning, over breakfast, Barry said, "I'm going to a bookshop. Would you like to come along?" A limousine with a chauffeur with white gloves arrived. Barry'd ordered this car at a time in his life when he couldn't afford it just to pick us up from this awful hotel. He drove us to a bookshop run by the most crusty and frightening of old booksellers to whom I'd have had to clear my throat three times before speaking. The bookseller was full of erudite menace and aggressive gentility. Barry stopped him dead with booming theatrical confidence. "Have you got any Lafcadio Hearn at all?" he said.'

'Lesettes, Lesettes,' whispers Harriet into the prompt corner microphone. 'Call for your last chat show on the West End.'

On stage, Dame Edna has extracted from her victims the remaining tidbits of their interior decorating secrets, letting *them* do the shopping-list humour that *she* once did. Emma from Hornchurch's pink wallpaper. Florence from Dublin's fawn bedspread. Sarah from the East End's semi-detached house without an *en suite* bathroom. 'No?' says Edna, 'In a semi, everything's *en suite* really, isn't it? An *en suite* kitchen. *En suite* neighbours. You're a lovely person. And I love that little Senior Citizen with you too. He is adorable.'

Dame Edna is manoeuvring the audience to join her on stage as extras in her epic. 'Did you ever see my wonderful show *The Dame Edna Experience?*' she says. 'Linda, did you see it? It was marvellous, wasn't it, Linda? Linda's getting a bit more animated by the minute there. Did you see it at all, my TV series? Did you, Florence? Lovely. I tell you what I started doing. I was just talking to friends like Charlton Heston, Larry Hagman. And then it proved too popular. They said they wanted me to do another series this year. I said, *I will*. But I said I want *real people*. I said this time actually I want non-entities. I want . . . I want women like you, Florence, as a matter of fact. Whose chances of becoming a celebrity are – ha, ha – let's face it darling, *nil* . . .'

Edna declared herself a superstar in the mid-1970s. It was a smart career move. 'Now that she has grotesquely elevated herself, she imagines she is a superstar,' Humphries told me backstage in 1981. 'But as we know, many people are labelled as superstars by the press just because the press have accepted their private fantasies. "Superstar" really means money. In fact, Edna's more provincial than ever. The more she speaks of her global popularity, the more she really sounds like someone from the suburbs of Melbourne or Toronto or anywhere beyond the metropolis. The character increasingly feels at liberty, liberated by total ignorance, to speak on anything whatsoever.'

The mutation in Edna's character occurred in the mid-1970s, by which time the West was used to parody display and celebrity rule. 'I noticed', says Humphries, of Edna's evolution into a superstar, which gave her a universal focus and turned her quickly into a piece of cross-cultural folklore, 'that Barbra Streisand was starting to make pronouncements on things. They were views on poetry and art. These people who were traditionally philistine were not meant to excel in intellectual pursuits or matters of alternative religions. But not only did they have opinions, but their opinions were published. MacLaine, Fonda, Streisand and women far less intelligent. So Edna caught the wave her countrywoman Germaine Greer had helped to generate and started doing a little fancy surfing. It was originally a conscious parody of what these other people were saying. For instance, Streisand came out and said that her favourite picture was Edvard Munch's *The Scream*. That played right into Edna's hands. She said it was her favourite picture, and she'd had it made into dinner mats. Also when these stars started to talk about being "very private people" – remember when that phrase was about? – Edna leapt on that. It was only people who were *fiends* for publicity who ever said it. As she became more famous, she adopted the postures of modesty. So she became a kind of cipher and also a megaphone for the styles and affectations of the period which changed very rapidly. You had to be very up to date.'

Edna's protean adaptations are both part of the trickster's pattern and part of the style of the times. In the programme to *Back with a Vengeance!* she identifies herself as Housewife, Megastar, Investigative Journalist, Social Anthropologist, Children's Book Illustrator, Film Script Assesser, Diseuse, Swami, Polymath and hard-nosed Literary Agent specialising in radical women's issues. (Her bio photograph shows Dame Edna posed with the book *Sexual Harassment: A Pictorial History*). 'More and more, I find with Edna that you can throw anything into the cauldron,' he says. 'And somehow it's just Edna's new shape. That's how she's developing today.'

The boundaries of her personality have extended to the highest reaches of public office. 'Mrs Thatcher seems to be becoming more like Edna,' says Humphries, of the spookiest of Dame Edna's resonances. 'First she was a kind of housewife, then the politician, then finally she became the star. And now she likes to show that she's still a bit of a housewife.' So does Dame Edna, who was quick to remind reporters before the opening of her show, *Back with a Vengeance: The Second Coming*, that she was the only star who got to the theatre early so as to vacuum it. She also spells out her influence on the Iron Lady to politicos, like Mrs Thatcher's arch enemy, the former Tory Prime Minister Ted Heath.

'I get a lot of calls from the Prime Minister at all hours of the day and night, asking for advice,' she told Heath in 1990, whose gravity and intelligence made him one of her best TV interviews. 'Does she ring you?'

'Not in thirteen years,' laughed Heath.

'The other night she rang at three in the morning, driving me mad,' confided Dame Edna. ' "Where is Hong Kong?" she said. She said, "Edna, Edna . . .", she was crying . . ., she said, "How do I pronounce *Ich Bin ein Berliner*?" She said, "How do I *pretend* to like the environment?" '

'Bring on my Talk Show hostesses, please,' says Dame Edna, suddenly Lady Bountiful dishing out compliments to the Lesettes and promises of BMWs and world trips to the audience.

This is the moment that the audience has feared and been thrilling for, the moment in which Humphries, in a sense, recapitulates in the audience his childhood terror of being wiped out. Such is the power of Humphries' control of an audience and Dame Edna's tyrannical charisma that, no matter how far away they sit, everyone in the theatre feels a *frisson* of terror that Dame Edna might choose *them*. Says Humphries, 'I've taken to holding out these bribes – "Now my next big major prize winner is . . ." if there looks to be a difficult, recalcitrant member of the audience. I prefer the doubtful ones.'

'So,' Dame Edna says, 'without any further ado, I feel the excitement mounting. And so I would like to invite to your ovation a very special person that I noticed, ha, almost as soon as I stepped on the stage tonight. Let's hear it please for Florence, all the way from Dublin . . .'

With the entire audience straining to see her and the boom of two thousand deeply relieved people clapping at the sound of her name, Florence finally is coaxed up out of her seat and up the stairs at the side of the stage into Dame Edna's waiting arms. 'Hello, darling. Hello, Florence. How nice to see you,' says Dame Edna, giving her a big hug and a big smile. 'You delightful woman. You are absolutely delightful. And what lovely, lovely happiness you radiate too. You do. Hairdresser's, this morning, Florence?'

'No,' says Florence, her brogue discernible even in the monosyllable.

'I didn't think so for a moment ... However ... never mind ...!'

In the moment between the uplift of Edna's compliment and the sting of her putdown, Humphries winks at Florence to disown the laugh and relax her fear. 'Barry has got the audience so well drilled that they're all laughing at the same time. They're a solid mass. And they all turn to their partner to seek confirmation. You can see this. I've sat in the box and watched the audience,' says Ian Davidson. 'Between the moment of laughter and when they turn for corroboration, there is a moment of audience blindness. The audience isn't looking at the stage. You can do things in that moment. Barry usually smiles and winks at his victim.'

Florence is ushered, laughing, off stage to be dolled up for the Talk Show. Dame Edna turns back to her audience. 'And now my Yorkshire pilgrim, *LINDA*!! Here she is.'

But Linda isn't budging.

'Come on, Linda. Come on. Wait a minute. What's the matter, Linda darling?'

'I would prefer not to come,' says Linda.

'What? Mmn.'

'I would prefer not to come.'

'No?' says Dame Edna, no more Mr Nice Girl. 'But the audience would love you to come. And to be branded as a spoilsport would be horrible, Linda. Wouldn't it be ghastly? Leaving the theatre people spitting on you. I mean ... I think the little bank manager next to you is trying to discourage you, isn't he, darling? Is he? He's having an inhibitory effect on you. You're the first woman – and this is my last night in this theatre ...'

'Ah!' says the audience *en masse*.

'... who's ever rejected my offer, Linda. Isn't that sad? I hope

186

it doesn't bring you *terrible luck* for the rest of your life. What is Linda's seat number, Lisa? Ah yes, yes. You would have . . . you would have won the BMW. Ha, ha . . . I'm so sorry. Never mind. Some people are killjoys, aren't they? It's a lovely opportunity to meet an understudy. A woman who we've spoken to before and she's longing to come and join me. And what an ovation she'll get when she does. It's the lovely SARAH!! . . .'

Sarah, tonight's erstwhile nude cartwheelist, gets a big hand and is greeted by Edna with fulsome praise for her 'little outfit'. Says Dame Edna, 'I think you've paid me the greatest compliment coming straight from work to my show.'

The audience creases up. Humphries gives Sarah the wink and rounds on the uproarious crowd. *'Please! Don't be so rude! Have your manners just flown out the window?'* To which the answer, happily, is yes.

'Now let's hear it for Dame Edna's seminal, pivotal, mould-breaking, and revolutionary TALK SHOW!'

On stage Dame Edna's joke is to make non-entities seem like celebrities; on television the game is to make celebrities seem like non-entities. This reversal of viewer expectation has made Dame Edna not just a star of the London stage, but a household word in every nook and cranny of the British Isles. 'The badge, Madge!' says Dame Edna to her silent bridesmaid, the butt of the Dame's malice who sits lugubriously beside her and who hands over the name tags which Dame Edna pins to her guests. Charlton Heston is 'Chuck'. Tony Curtis is 'Tone'. Dusty Springfield is 'Dust'. Ted Heath is 'Ed'. Douglas Fairbanks Junior is 'Jnr'. Germaine Greer is 'G.G.', by chance the Cockney slang for horse. Zsa Zsa Gabor, whose name is ludicrous enough, gets three badges.

As a TV host, Dame Edna is like no other. In the most recent edition of the show, Dame Edna entertained her guests in her 'penthouse'. Her interviewees were 'house guests', satirising at a stroke the first principle of fame's imperialism – that in the aristocracy of success there are no strangers. Peering at Jane Fonda over the video intercom to her 'lobby', Dame Edna refused to let her up to the thirty-fourth floor to plug *The Old Gringo* because she wasn't properly dressed. The former Prime Minister Ted Heath was treated with equal imperiousness. Said Dame Edna, 'Well, look, I'm not quite ready for you, darling. I'm sorry. Just hang around there for a minute, darling. Bye.'

Dame Edna sends up not only the habitual sycophancy of talk-show hosts, but also their impoverished vocabulary. If no TV host has ever behaved so badly, none has ever used the English language with so much panache. When Douglas Fairbanks Junior appeared on the show, TV viewers saw Douglas Fairbanks Junior's face come up on the video intercom and Dame Edna crouched near his raffish image saying, 'Did you get the shopping, Douggie?'

'Yes, I did. But I got cutlets,' said Fairbanks Junior explaining that the lift was broken.

'What's wrong with the stairs, Douglas?' she said, adding brusquely, 'I've seen you in the films. Shooting up the rigging like a rat up a drain. I've seen you jumping off stuccoed balconies and clinging to live lianas with a cutlass in your mouth, too, darling. Put your shopping bag between your teeth and pretend the cutlets are a cutlass.' Then, aside to the camera, she added, 'The exercise will be good for him.'

Dame Edna exists most gloriously with an audience; and if TV detaches her somewhat from both her audience and her anarchy, it compounds her confusing reality. In close-up, with the technology of illusion making her seem actual, Dame Edna can play games not only with the viewer's imagination but with history. Humphries' original concept for the show was to have Dame Edna interview people like Klaus Barbie, Leni Riefenstahl, and Kurt Waldheim. But even Gore Vidal, who was mooted, couldn't pass muster with the ratings' obsessed panjandrums of London Weekend Television who were dubious about non-showbiz personalities.

'Edna in trivial conversation with a heavyweight person is amusing,' says Humphries, mentioning Jackie Onassis, Paloma Picasso, Mother Teresa as ideal guests. 'It seems to me that it doesn't matter if nobody's heard of them. Edna hasn't heard of them either, really. She knows they're high-powered. They'd come on to the show with a kind of aura about them. It's better that they're not all show biz and not all featherweight veterans of Terry Wogan and Johnny Carson.' When Dame Edna goes up against lightweights, their fear is palpable and the contest can seem unwittingly unpleasant. But when she's matched with people as secure in their accomplishments as Humphries, then Dame Edna, her guests, and the audience have a ball.

'The spontaneous thoughts are just wonderful,' says Claudia Rosenkrantz, the producer of the second *Dame Edna Experience*, who tries to maximise Humphries' wit by encouraging detours from the script. 'I sometimes hide the autocue when things are really going well. I don't want his attention distracted or for him to go back to the easy option of what's up there. I'll always put it back to rescue him, but Barry's at his best when he's challenged, when he's really concentrating, when he goes with what's happening.'

And so too are the guests. Although always well briefed, Dame Edna's questions are at once hilariously near the knuckle and off the wall. 'You old swashbuckler,' said Dame Edna to Douglas Fairbanks Junior, wiping her 'lippie' off his cheek from her welcoming hello. 'Your swashing days are over. You're starting to buckle a bit . . .' From that outrageous beginning, the interview took off into the scintillating Humphries shell game of mixing historical fact with her often lewd fiction.

'You escaped from your family into a very early marriage, didn't you, Douglas?'

'I did indeed. I defied the wishes of my family and went and got married when I was nineteen for the first time.'

'And who was the lucky girl?'

'I don't know how lucky she was. Joan Crawford.'

'Oh, you old name dropper.'

'Wife dropper.'

'My son Kenny is the president of the Joan Crawford Fan Club. And you're the founder member, aren't you? With the emphasis on member, I would say . . . I think I can say this without fear of successful contradiction, Joan became a bit of a ratbag, didn't she? I mean this very nicely. I do. She had some funny little ways.'

'Oh yes. She was a nice, hard-working, dedicated girl. But she always liked to use substitute words for things.'

'What, for example?' said Dame Edna, sending up her salacious appetite by couching the question with a most *faux naive* tilt of her head.

'She used to call a kiss a "goober"!'

'A "goober"?' said Dame Edna, grimacing so that the wattles under her chin fan out. 'Sounds yukkie, doesn't it? Sounds like something you have trouble getting out of a chenille bedspread, doesn't it? I'd have to write "goober" on a piece of paper and give it to the dry cleaner. What other little phrases?'

'I don't think I should repeat them on the air.'

'Did she have a funny word for making love?'

'Uh . . . Only you would think of something like that.'

'I'm a romantic person.'

'I keep forgetting that, yes.'

'Did she have a funny word for her *front bottie* . . . I'm using the medical word.'

Dame Edna pretends to the gentilities of the conventional talk-show host while getting away with murder. At the end of the Douglas Fairbanks Junior interview, she drew his attention to the dour Madge Allsop. 'She's an older woman,' said Dame Edna. 'I'm not going to say anything about this, but does she turn you on? You're an older man now, it must be harder to find older women. Where do you . . . *cruise*? Twilight Homes?' When she traded girl talk with the much-married Zsa Zsa Gabor, Dame Edna asked, 'Did any of these husbands of yours have anything in common at all? I mean, like a mole in the same place. I personally like a man with something in the same place. I do. I like it in the same place every time.' Said Zsa Zsa, 'Me, too.'

In conventional talk shows, the host listens while the guests talk, but with Dame Edna, who assumes the guests are there for her amusement, the formula is reversed. They have to listen hard while *she* talks. Rarely is she bested. Dame Edna probed Ted Heath about his homes and the names of his Spanish staff. 'I have a cleaning lady called *Purificación*,' said Dame Edna. 'And I have another Spanish helper called *Contracepción*.' Said Mr Heath, sharpish, 'How do you get the two to work together?' TV viewers had the unusual sight of Dame Edna laughing out loud at repartee that beat even her to the draw.

In close-up, Dame Edna's vividness is such that even the guests are confused by the blurring of gender boundaries. Says Humphries of filming with Douglas Fairbanks Junior, 'He turned to Ian Davidson on the set and said, "Isn't it funny that the stagehands keep referring to 'Dame Edna' and never say 'Barry'. Why do you think that is?" Ian said: "It's more comfortable for them." And Fairbanks replied, "That's funny because they never called Barrymore 'Hamlet'!" Which was an elegant way of saying that Edna is a real enough person that they don't think of it as a performance. It is *Hamlet*. They're in it.' But the show tries to exploit confusion of reality and the credulity of the viewing public still further. 'Most upmarket London penthouses have very highly trained Filipino staff,' said Dame Edna. 'Mine is no exception. Except the little woman who Vims my vanitory unit is my next guest. She's the former First Lady of all Filipinos. Yes. IMELDA MARCOS!!!'

'Imelda Marcos' entered to applause, took a bow, and began walking down the stairs towards Edna. 'She's wearing my shoes!' said Dame Edna, in horror, blowing a whistle she had taken from her purse. A barking mastiff bounded across the set and chased the stand-in off stage. Humphries has introduced other surreal pranks into the Talk Show's illusion of actuality.

In Dame Edna's first series of shows, Charlton Heston appeared at the top of a steep and dangerous staircase in a wheelchair.

'It's just a bad sprain, Dame Edna,' he said.

'Charlie, my darling, I thought you were giving an Ironside impersonation . . . Don't move. Please. Please. We've got a trained nurse here, Chuck. Up you go and please help Mr Heston, sister. Help is coming, darling. She'll help you. Now gently, gently. Take it very gently, the stairs are very steep.'

'Heston' and the nurse proceeded to tumble down the stairs. Humphries' other guests, who could only see 'Heston' on the monitors, were terror-stricken. Heston subsequently received thousands of get-well letters until he appeared the following week in one handsome piece. Other public figures have met similar disastrous fates. 'Kurt Waldheim' appeared at the top of Dame Edna's stairway only to be dropped through a trap-door. And the 'Duchess of Kent', on her entrance, was snared in a booby trap and swung from her heels as Dame Edna signalled for a commercial break.

Tonight, it's Katie who is doing the signalling. She pulls a strand of her hair straight up so that Lisa, the Lesette introducing Florence from Dublin, can see it. The sign means that Florence, who has to change into a wig for the Talk Show, is wearing her own hairpiece. Florence comes out from behind a changing booth decked out like a show girl. Andy takes a Polaroid picture of her. 'I only came to see the show,' she laughs. 'I didn't come for this.'

Behind Florence is the rack of clothes into which the other guests will change: a punk rocker's leathers and Mohawk wig, an Edna look-alike outfit, a nun's habit.

'Well, Lisa,' comes Dame Edna's disembodied voice backstage, 'who's our first non-celebrity guest?'

'Your first guest, Dame Edna, is Florence from Dublin . . .'

'Don't worry,' says Katie, guiding Florence to the edge of the wings, where a Lesette pulls her into the full glare of the stage and a barrage of applause.

While Edna proffers champagne and taramasalata to Florence, commenting on her skull cap with yellow ostrich feathers, 'Nice clothes suit you,' Katie hurries back to the others. 'I once had a woman come back saying "I'm not going to do it," ' says Katie. 'Usually you can talk them into it. You promise that they'll have a good time and that the worst part is over. Actually coming up on stage is the worst part. If they're difficult backstage, I leave them till last and rely on the other people to jolly them along.' But what out front seems to the audience as a potentially sadistic game is no sweat to the off-stage amateurs who never have anything to fear from Dame Edna.

As the other victims line up for their Polaroid memento, waves of laughter resound backstage. 'I'm the senior partner's wife,' says Emma from Hornchurch, dressed as an Edna look-alike. 'They're gonna love this. It's going to make their week.'

192

'Next is Emma from Hornchurch,' coos Lisa.

'I've never been on stage before,' Emma says as she steps lively past me into Dame Edna's setup. Says Dame Edna, 'Look at you, darling. Talk about "Send in the Clones" . . .'

Sarah from the East End can't stop laughing. She's wearing the nun's habit. 'I think it's extremely funny,' she says, 'because I'm Jewish, just recently converted. I've always wanted to go on stage. What more could I ask?'

Once on stage, the guests cram on to Dame Edna's post-modern sofa like so many dummies on a ventriloquist's knee. Dame Edna gets them to nod and respond while she pretends to ask for some collective wisdom about her wayward daughter Valmai. 'She shoplifts now, she does,' says Dame Edna, keeping her guests captive with the cod intensity of her eye contact. 'She goes into some of those Bond Street shops. She steals things. Puts them in her pantyhose. Particularly frozen chickens when she's in a supermarket. Of course, the store detectives can smell those barbecued chickens when she goes out. Because she's a human microwave. She thinks she's an art collector. She thinks she's Peggy Guggenheim. That name ring a bell? She collects primitive art. New Guinea sculpture. Do you know much about New Guinea sculpture, Sarah?'

'No,' says Sarah, running the gamut of her dialogue for the evening.

'You've missed nothing, darling. It is grotesque. It's mostly wooden willies . . .'

And with the notion of penises firmly planted in the audience's mind, it's a quick segue to the Gladdydämmerung which has been Edna's traditional spectacle of mayhem since the mid-1960s. Humphries himself is not fond of the flower with which Dame Edna has poked, pelted, and pleasured the world. 'There's nothing more holy', said Dame Edna in *An Evening's Intercourse with the widely liked Barry Humphries*, 'than massed gladioli.' And from the audience's delight, so it would seem. 'The mood of those last ten minutes cannot be produced in words, where the audience becomes truly happy,' wrote one critic as early as *Just a Show* of the joy the gladdy bonanza inspires. John Osborne was also at the show. 'I watched Humphries throw his gladdies to the audience and persuade them to wave them back at him,' Osborne wrote. 'It was like throwing your past at the world and saying "Catch!".' A courageous and beautiful act if ever I saw one.'

'It's gladdy time,' says Dame Edna, frogmarching her accomplices downstage to the footlights. 'There's some glads. I want you to throw one at a time *gently* into the audience. Don't forget to let go. The Flinging Nun. It's gladdy time, a very beautiful moment in my famous show. Gladdy time. I mean what other show . . . Could you imagine Barry Manilow doing this? . . .' Dame Edna throws a gladdy over her shoulder: 'Or Stevie Wonder? . . . *Not in a million years! Not in a million years . . .!*'

Edna likes to say that she's into things beginning with G. She's got a lot of G-spots: ginseng, gynaecology, gravity, giving, gladioli. The *gladiolus gandavensis* or gladdy has been the symbol of Dame Edna's suburban swank and her anarchy since the mid-1960s when she first grabbed a bunch of them out of a vase off her accompanist's piano and gave them to a woman in the front row during *Excuse I*.

'I saw the woman looking at them enviously,' recalls Humphries. 'I decided to give them to her. But she passed them along the front row to everyone. The sight of these people holding the glads gave me the idea of persuading them to wave them to music, which was the very first time I involved the audience in some kind of participation with the character. They waved them in time to the tune of "Home Sweet Home". Our own diva Joan Sutherland had recently concluded an operatic recital with the song, much to everyone's relief because they had to pretend to enjoy the operatic excerpts. Then, suddenly, here was a sentimental song they all knew. At that point her damehood was assured. Edna decided on what she called her "Joan Sutherland Ending", that is to sing "Home Sweet Home" and persuade the audience to sing it.

'A little later in the season, when the gladdies came in, they waved them in time with "Home Sweet Home". Gladdies were the flowers of special occasions: weddings and hospitals. They would ornament a hallway or a church, very desirable things to have around. To me they symbolised the overblown comforts of suburban life – optimistic, insensitive, colourful, sturdy and phallic. I suppose. Oddly enough, their phallic properties didn't occur to me until I saw the audience brandishing them.'

'Two things save the show,' wrote Irving Wardle in *The Times* about Humphries' *Just a Show* (1968). 'The fact that, ultimately, Mr Humphries is not sending up Australia so much as building a suburban never-never land, and an ability to get beyond satire into a vein of sheer craziness which comes out most strongly in his appearance as a patriotic matron bombarding the house with gladioli and leading them into a frankly phallic finale.'

A decade later in *Housewife/Superstar*, when the critical response to Dame Edna had shifted from the tepid to the triumphant, her phallic fun had taken on gigantic, aggressive proportions. Having flicked, lobbed, and flung gladioli over the footlights for a decade, Dame Edna tried turning the high-tech cylinders of her set into anti-aircraft guns and shooting the flowers into the balcony.

In the next show, *An Evening's Intercourse with the widely liked Barry Humphries*, having exploited the phallic fantasy of the flower, Dame Edna probed the facts of the gladdy's sex life. 'Little did I ever dream that some flowers, MY PRECIOUS GLAD INCLUDED, did it to *themselves*,' she wrote in the programme, including photos of the flower's reproductive process. 'It's a jolt and a half when you learn that something you've loved and lived with for a lifetime is a, well . . . a hermaphrodite.'

'It's gladdy time!' shouts Dame Edna. 'Gladdy time! There we are. And still more to come!! Gladdy time. Close your eyes, catch them with your teeth.' Gladdies shower the stalls.

From the stage-right wings, Jane is laughing as she trains her video camera on Dame Edna tossing the flowers into the audience. Dame Edna has mastered a backhand flip, propelling each gladdy higher, until the audience is watching gladioli fly up to boxes three tiers high.

'What about me, Dame Edna?' says a woman from a fourth-tier box.

There's a drum roll. Dame Edna backhands the gladdy up

to her. It falls short of its target. Another drum roll. Another try. The gladdy arches up past the follow spot. The woman reaches for it, and, with an ear-piercing scream, topples out of the box.

People beneath her shriek and scatter as she holds on and clambers up.

'Has anyone got a blanket?' shouts Dame Edna, and then passes down a blanket from the stage. There is a moment of pandemonium. Panicked playgoers are cowering by the exit door. Four stalwart members of the audience hold the grey blanket beneath the woman, bracing themselves to catch her.

'Heaven be praised! There was a rope ladder in that box!' says Dame Edna. 'Oh, wouldn't it be ghastly if that happened every night!!!'

Harriet turns to me: 'He'll probably be in a good mood for the rest of the show. He enjoyed it. They look silly.'

'Up, up, up! Hold your gladdy by the end of the stem for maximum gladdy thrust. And when I give the word – there we are, darling – up, up. What a beautiful sight.'

The audience sings 'The Gladdy Song' with Dame Edna, and, at her command, stands and trembles the gladdies. The evening is almost over, but not before the proper benedictions. The guests are applauded and sent back to their seats with appropriate gifts: Camembert, Nivea cream, Steradent, a jar of Vaseline, a pair of Norm's Y-fronts along with flowers and bottles of champagne. Before Dame Edna's Assumption, there remains the blessing of her disciples. Florence and Sarah bow their heads as Dame Edna sends them back into the real world:

'Go forth now, be kind and true
Like Dame Edna was to you.
May Love and Laughter always blossom,
Now little Florence and Sarah are life-long *possums*.'

Soon the dry ice is filling the stage with smoke, and Dame Edna's apotheosis is in its full magnificent swing. She has saved the most spectacular stage picture for last as she rises on the hydraulic lift high above the audience singing about her shyness. No one in the audience wants Dame Edna shy. They want her loud and vulgar and daring as she always is. They want her filling their life with the articulate energy of great clowning:

'Yet, I must confess that I've felt slightly better since
You've helped me sublimate my grief-stricken reticence.
So . . . now . . . g——oooooooodbye . . .
I got my act together and my head held high so high
I'm a merry widow with a roving cye
Yet I get so terribly shy
When the time finally comes for me to say
Was it good for you too, possums?!
And goood——bye . . . Good-night. Darlings . . .'

The cherry picker deposits Edna back on stage, and the din of applause and bravos continues over her bows. But she can't sit still for an audience even in its adulation. Dame Edna is twisting to a samba beat, blowing her carnival whistle, waving to her paupers. Her need for attention is no smaller than the audience's need for joy. Dame Edna doesn't want to leave the stage, and the audience don't want her to leave it. Even when the curtain falls, Dame Edna is still a presence. A spotlight lingers on her hand, which plays near the floor in front of the curtain. Behind the curtain Dame Edna is on her stomach gesturing into the noisy void. She begins by giving the audience a wave – 'almost a caress', says Humphries – and ends by almost giving it two fingers.

'Good, wasn't it?' says Humphries, breathless and thrilled as he walks past me toward his dressing room. 'It was wonderful! When we started throwing blankets to the audience. You see . . . How extraordinary. We've played – how many performances? – and we're just learning how to do it.'

Outside, after the show, people linger under the dark blue columns of the Drury Lane's portico. Sarah from the East End is exiting with her armful of gladioli. A young man within earshot says, 'There's Sarah. There's the star of the show.'

She nods in his direction and walks slowly down the marble steps into the chill of the London night.

Humphries wheels his baggage toward Heathrow's Gate 12 for the two o'clock flight to Jersey. The hound's-tooth coat, the tilted fedora, the black and white wing-tipped shoes matching his black polka dot tie announce to the world that this is a theatrical. Heads turn as Humphries passes; and if they meet his eye, Humphries smiles politely. We've arranged to fly together and to take these two days for an expanded talk. Dame Edna's autobiography is finished. The show, after these remaining two performances, is finished. Dame Edna herself, at least until after Humphries' holidays, is finished. And in forty-eight hours this month-long game of hide and seek called 'getting the story' will also be finished. But, as always with Humphries, the route, while fascinating, is never straight. At the gate, he goes immediately to the pay phone, dialling through the numbers in his black Filofax until the flight is called. Once in his seat, Humphries confesses that he's exhausted and needs sleep.

So conversation doesn't really begin until the company manager Jack Hylton hands Humphries a memo in the back seat of the limousine taking us to Fort Regent, the entertainment complex for the island, where the crew is even now setting up. The memo reads:

LOCAL INFORMATION
Wine Bar: The Bagot
Local Personality: As busy as Dick Shenton's Press Agent *or*
                      As Busy as Derek Carter's Press Agent
Low Suburb: Grands Vaux
Up Suburb: St Brelades

There is a large and low-paid Portuguese population who come in to work in hotels for the season (30 weeks) . . .

The locals call themselves Jersey beans. Residents of Guernsey call residents of Jersey crappos. Residents of Jersey call residents of Guernsey donkeys. There is a strong rivalry between the two islands . . .

There is a bailiff of Jersey named Sir Peter Crill. He is very strait-laced. Last year he banned a Shakespearean play because it had a nude scene. A wowser . . .

Le Masurier's wine or a crate of Mary Ann is local equivalent of a Sainsbury's Wine Box.

Humphries peruses the memo. 'How's the stage?' he asks, putting the typed sheet carefully in his briefcase.

'Something like seventy seats wide,' says Hylton, who'd flown at dawn with the £100 of fresh gladioli for the two shows.

'Very wide stage?'

'It's desperate, in fact.'

'Too high? Too far?'

'Holds 2,000. It's one of those.'

'Paupers?'

'Up at the back.'

'So is it not much fun to see a show there?' says Humphries.

'It's what they're used to. If you don't know differently, I suppose, it's fine to see a show there.'

'Is everyone rich here?'

'Yes, it's a very wealthy island.'

'How do they live, in sort of little . . . like in a market garden?'

'I was just talking to the driver. A maximum of fifteen new residents a year are allowed on to the island. The residence requirement is serious money.'

'No paupers, then,' says Humphries. He stares glumly out the window at the sea. 'Is the hotel close to the theatre?'

'It's a cab ride,' says Hylton with a perkiness that seems to send Humphries into a more ominous mood. 'I have to say it's not a theatre. It's a small stadium. It's got a proper stage with a proscenium arch. There's lighting there, but you're talking about a multi-purpose hall. If you look up to your right, you'll be able to see the venue in a moment. It'll be a place at the top of a hill with a dome on it.'

'What's it called?' says Humphries, as the hill looms up through the driver's windscreen.

'Fort Regent. It's right on the top of the hill to the left of that tower.'

'The Germans were here, weren't they?'

'That's right,' says Hylton.

'Are we sold out?'

'Still two hundred and fifty seats left. We've got half a dozen radio people in tonight. They'll get on the radio tomorrow, and I should think sell whatever is left.'

'If the show's any good, that is,' says Humphries, who promptly changes the subject, lightening his mood by considering Edna's future plans. 'I've been talking with my agent about the book cover. I think we prefer a photographic cover, don't you?' Humphries reaches in his briefcase and produces the proposed book jacket, a caricature of Edna with gold comic lettering that spells out *My Gorgeous Life*.

'My instinct would be for a formal, regal cover. Not giving the joke away. This says funny.'

'Says funny.' Humphries mulls it over. 'This is just a rough, mind you. The idea is wrong. The designer is intransigent.'

'It should be solid. Very sedate. Like Harold Macmillan's biography. Or Churchill's. Or Noël Coward's. Marbled endpapers. Piss elegant. Unpromising in a way.'

'Yes,' says Humphries. 'Exactly.'

'Very monumental.'

'Almost boring.'

'You're expecting something very polite, and what you get under this sedate façade is something off the wall.'

'Yes,' says Humphries. 'That's exactly what I want. I really think this drawing's wrong.'

'It should be a famous portrait artist doing a portrait of a famous personage.'

'That's exactly it,' says Humphries. 'There's a Terry O'Neill photograph on the back and that looks good. I think the cover has to be a famous photographer.'

'I'd love to read it.'

Humphries gropes inside his briefcase and produces the first four chapters. 'You're welcome.'

200

'Do you spoof autobiography?'

'No,' says Humphries, more alert now. 'I just tell a story. I may unconsciously parody all kinds of things, but there's no conscious parody of *anything*. It's Edna creating her own form.'

Humphries' publishers are printing about 40,000 copies. They're expecting a bestseller; and, as an indication of their eagerness, Humphries' pages will be in proof within two weeks of his handing in the manuscript. I suggest Richard Avedon for the cover, an idea which Humphries takes to like a bass to a top-water lure. The notion succeeds in distracting him from the grim prospects of tonight's performance. Leni Riefenstahl is also mooted. 'She's still around,' says Humphries. 'I think still working. She's always been interested in anthropology. Her film, whatever was it called?'

'*Triumph of the Will*. That'd be right for Edna. You could've called your book *Triumph of the Will*. I wonder if they'd get that?'

'They probably wouldn't,' says Humphries, who has continued fantasising about photographers and is momentarily contemplating the surrealist Man Ray and his solarisation technique. 'How weird,' Humphries smiles. 'With Edna doing something with an egg.'

The limousine winds up the steep hill to the Fort. 'It's really extraordinary this,' says Humphries. 'Like Alcatraz.' A gate has to be unlocked, credentials checked, and then we're waved through. The limousine pulls up to the entrance; and as the driver opens the door for Humphries, he asks for his autograph. 'Two shows you're doin', is it?' says the driver as Humphries makes his mark on a receipt pad. 'Tonight and tomorrow night?'

'I think I am,' says Humphries. 'I don't feel as though I'm going to. I'm sure I'll be doing something. It feels quite unlikely.'

The Fort is cavernous and disconcerting. So when the auditorium is finally reached through the labyrinth of passageways and esplanades, the sight of the crew's familiar faces is especially welcome and reassuring. The pianist Victy Silva and the drummer are improvising on stage. Jane, along with the rest of the Lesettes, is lounging around in a T-shirt and blue jeans behind what amounts to no more than a large platform. Jane's full of news about her video and the copy of the closing night's stunt which she's making for Humphries. Andrew is rigging the lights. Harriet is setting up a makeshift prompt corner in what little backstage space there is.

'Hello,' Barry says brightly to one and all, walking out on to the stage. He bounces on the massive platform boards. 'Well, this is nice,' he says. 'It's all right.'

'What would you like to do?' says Harriet.

'I'll just go to the dressing room for a second. Put the microphone on. Try the sound. Whatever you want me to do. Then I want to go back to the hotel and lie down.' But since the dressing room is nearly fifty yards from the stage, it takes Humphries fifteen minutes before he's back on the boards, staring up at the sound box. 'You there? All right?'

There's no feedback, so the sound man has to shout OK from the box. 'Ready now, girls,' says Humphries, who has put on Sir Les's blue jacket over his own. He runs through 'Never Trust a Man Who Doesn't Drink'.

'You think the public will absorb the sound?' he says in the direction of the sound box. And when no answer is forthcoming, he turns to Harriet. 'Where's my exit? Up?'

'Downstage, Barry,' says Harriet.

'All right, downstage.'

Humphries runs through the finale. At the conclusion he calls out to the sound booth. 'Alan, it's nicer now. I think a lot of that will be absorbed by the public.'

'The boominess will be absorbed,' says Alan from the booth.

'Is the sound quite good?' says Humphries.

'Yes. You're not hearing anything back, Barry, because of the drapes all around the building.'

'So long as it's not a dead sound. I like one with a bit of life.' Humphries breaks off and goes into Edna's voice. 'Hello, possums.' He looks down at the front of the stage. 'We gonna have stairs here?' he says to Harriet in his normal register. 'There should be stairs, but there aren't.'

'Oh,' laughs Harriet at her large oversight.

Humphries stands by the piano working lines for 'Shyness', since Edna will be merely 'standing before' her audience not 'rising above' it tonight. Then there's one last sound check for

Sir Les. 'Have I got a show for you!' says Humphries in character. 'It's a mainland show. You lucky bastards! Direct from the West End . . .'

'OK?' shouts Alan.

'Showing signs of fatigue,' says Humphries.

On the way to the taxi taking us to our hotel, Humphries stops to watch a vaudeville act in an open-air theatre at the Fort. Three singers, in costume, are belting out 'Maybe It's Because I'm a Londoner' to an audience of six. Children play tag in the aisles.

'Do they have to do that all the time?' says Humphries to Jack Hylton.

'That's been going on since quarter to twelve. They just get fifteen-minute breaks.'

'Quarter to twelve?' says Humphries. 'They must be bored to death. On till when?'

'Six thirty. You've got your mornings and evenings free. It's thirty weeks' work.'

'How demoralising to see all those kids running in the aisles,' says Humphries.

'You're working to six people, aren't you?'

'Yes,' says Humphries, turning away. 'It's terrifying.'

When Humphries arrives back at the Fort for the show, Katie is there to meet him at the entrance and hurry him to his dressing room. 'It's bizarre,' she says.

'Hopeless,' says Humphries who can't believe his dressing room is half a football field from the stage. To make matters worse, once inside his dressing room, Humphries can't make the phone work. He slumps down at his dressing table and studies Jack Hylton's memo. 'I'm as busy as Dick Shenton's press agent,' he says, testing the suggestion in Sir Les's voice and breaking off. 'Do you know what I sometimes find? If I make a reference, quite an acute reference, to a local person in a provincial city, people are so shocked to hear that real life so rapidly percolates into the world of make-believe that it's all silence rather than making appreciative noises. In a big city, when local scandal or personality is mentioned, there's generally a big laugh. But in places like Tasmania or Jersey, it is so unexpected and so *mysterious*, you see, that a local councillor could find his way into Les Patterson's monologue, that it kind of short-circuits the audience's brain. You don't get a laugh. They think it must be some other Dick Shenton.'

One of Hylton's notes is that the British TV star John Nettles lives in Jersey. 'I can't think of quite how to incorporate him,' says Humphries, getting into his bathrobe. 'The main thing is to get ready and comfortable. I'm in someone's bathroom, aren't I?'

'It's so strange, Barry,' says Katie. 'The wardobe is actually in the men's changing room. I left the door open to lug things through, walked in, and there were four naked men. They all sort of leapt and screamed.'

'What's the place look like?' says Humphries, a question to which he knows the answer and which signals a polite retreat of his imagination into his world.

'It's a barn,' says Katie.

'It's like a kind of swimming pool,' says Humphries. 'I just hope I don't slip into old euphemisms like "you lovely London people". You forget. I can't say "you old tax-avoiders", can I? You think they'll mind just getting Les and Edna? It's very short.'

A letter has been handed backstage for Humphries. He asks Katie to open it while he starts Sir Les's impressionistic make-up. 'There's a lady in her fifties. The way this guy describes her she looks older than her age,' says Katie.

'Suffering from Alzheimer's, probably,' says Humphries.

'He says she has a friend that looks like Les.'

'Heavens. What is the kindness this person is asking us to do?'

' "This woman is in desperate need of your loving touch and analysis. She needs probing. It's spooky that you've decided to perform on the birthday of your greatest Jersey fan, Mrs Jenny Johnson. We shall be in row H8. Kathy Greer, her other friend, is a bit like Madge really and just needs a good old-fashioned talking-to. I'm a perfectly healthy male who just fancies more mature women like yourself. I hope you enjoy yourself during the two days. Don't spare us from your megastar largesse." '

Alan, the sound man, comes in.

'How do they look out there, Alan? Cold, are they?'

'All right,' says Alan. 'OK.'

' "I'm as busy as Dick Shenton ... " They would have heard of Ken Dodd's tax problems. They'd be very tuned into tax here. Anything to do with tax. Edna's come over here to look at her structure, you think? Edna might even own Jersey.'

Humphries tapes Jack Hylton's memo to the dressing-table mirror and glances at it as he completes Sir Les's face. 'Sir Peter Crill,' he says. 'That's a wonderful name. "Crill." I'll say, "In Australia we call a non-drinker a wowser. I suppose you'd call it a crill. There'd be a thrill for old Sir Peter Crill. Over-crill. We call a strait-laced person a wowser. I know what you call him here. A crill, I reckon." There'll be a puzzled silence then, I should think.'

'You never know,' says Katie.

'What's happening now,' says Humphries, all dressed. 'What's the time?'

'It's three minutes to eight.'

'The lighting will be such on stage that I won't be able to read what's written on the back of my hand,' he says. 'I went to Sissinghurst yesterday. I'd never been there before. And I went to Vita Sackville-West's study. I thought Edna could do a one-woman show called "Vita". What American could she do? Of course, Madge is Toklas to her Stein. Eleanor Roosevelt she could do. I wonder what Senator McCarthy's wife was called? I think he was a shirt lifter.' And with that, Humphries strides out to try and find the stage.

'Oh,' says Humphries, flanked like a prize fighter by his attendants and making his way to the distant arena, 'it doesn't feel like a show. There's no music.'

'Wait another fifty yards, you'll get music.'

'You're not having to push your way past chorus girls in narrow corridors,' says Humphries as he passes a man doing bench presses.

'What's a weight lifter doing here?' he asks.

Katie introduces Humphries to an usher called Alison, who'll guide us the rest of the way. 'You look great, Alison,' says Sir Les. 'I've had a drink tonight. Peter Crill. I've got him sedated and tied up to a chair backstage. I could say that. I bumped into him earlier on. He was trying to stop me going on stage. We fixed him. He's got a sock in his mouth, and he's trussed to a chair in my dressing room.'

'And you're playing him Lou Reed tapes,' I chip in.

Humphries' eyes twinkle at the thought. 'I'm playing him a lot of old Derek and Clive. Are there Lou Reed tapes as well? What are the songs?'

'Walk on the Wild Side.'

The Lesettes are just coming out of their dressing room. 'Hello, girls,' says Humphries. 'I can't believe this. It doesn't feel like a show, does it, eh? Awful. Look at this. Listen to them out there. Is there any of my material that is of a regional nature that I should change? On this lovely night on Jersey island. Hmm?'

Humphries passes behind a barricade into the backstage area. 'They get a lot of good shows here?' he asks the usher.

'Mostly musicals.'

'But not lovely artistes. They don't come here. Max Bygraves probably comes here.'

Humphries motions Jack Hylton over. 'Don't you think we should have a little feed tonight? Tomorrow night everybody's going to be busy packing up. You'd have to commandeer a joint.'

'I'll check it all out,' says Hylton.

'Something decent.'

'Oh yes,' says Hylton.

Humphries turns to me. 'I'll say, "You're a tax exile, and I'm a sex exile." I'll say, "I'm a sex exile, you know. I've been getting too much lately. I'm prepared to give the sheilas . . ."' – Humphries opens his arms wide – ' ". . . to give the sheilas about ten per cent of it. Eh?"'

Humphries climbs up the stairs to the cramped backstage area and peeks through the curtain at the audience. 'I don't feel theatrical here,' he says. 'No excitement. I don't feel like I'm in the wings. I like to creep up on an audience.'

To watch inspired laughter register with an audience is to be present at a great and violent mystery. Faces convulse, tears stream, bodies collapse not in agony but in rapture. By the poetic power of one performer's personality, people are literally forced 'beside themselves', pushed beyond despairs and repressions to a zone of delight that begins in recognition and ends in momentary ecstasy. Gut-wrenching, side-splitting, belly-aching laughter is more than gaiety as its convulsiveness displays. What is released in the explosion of laughter is a deep contradictory thing that is both joy *and* pain, mischief *and* madness, pleasure *and* panic. Jokes can hit the psyche like punches, and the audience receives them as body blows. We've all felt it. We know the exhaustion and the hurt. I have seen a man jackknife into the aisle, pounding the floor with laughter at the curtain call of Spike Milligan's *The Bedsitting Room* (1963) when Milligan played 'God Save the Queen' on a kazoo from the wings and then appeared in front of the standing audience saying, 'If you'll stand for that, you'll stand for anything.' The audience had to step over the laughing man to make an exit.

At the opening night of S.J. Perelman's *The Beauty Part*, I sat next to a man who laughed so hard at Bert Lahr's impersonation of a red-baiting tycoon that he had to stuff a handkerchief in his mouth so the show could go on. And on this Tuesday night in Jersey, in an uncomfortable hall, without benefit of any but the most essential props, Barry Humphries joined my pantheon of great moments, those sweet high-water marks by which one measures one's life and times. Humphries accomplished that rare and gorgeous thing called 'knocking them dead'.

In fact, he did more than knock dead the 1,700 entertainment-hungry Jersey beans. He slaughtered them. Bodies heaved hypnotically back and forth in their seats like seaweed in a turbulent sea. Each line, especially those about Sir Peter Crill, seemed to jazz the audience and drive it still crazier with pleasure. Backstage, as Humphries came off with his face sweating and with his thumbs up. 'What fun,' he said. 'They were great! I say, that Crill joke worked a treat! No worries!'

Dame Edna certainly wasn't worried. As she waited for her cue behind the curtain at the side of the auditorium, Dame Edna chatted up the mulatto usherette. 'Hello, pet,' said Dame Edna.

'What a nice little island you live in. Is there inter-breeding? Are you married to a close relation? What do they call people from Jersey?'

'Beans,' said the usherette, laughing.

'Jersey beans. Give me a pen,' she said, taking the usherette's ballpoint and writing on her hand. 'A bean.'

Later that night the whole company is sitting around the table of an Italian restaurant that has agreed to stay open for the players. It's late, and Katie nods off at the end of the table. Humphries is seated in the middle of his troupe, an elated if exhausted host. As the wine and antipasto make the rounds of the table, Humphries sips his San Pellegrino and talks about the Jersey matron called Betty whom he'd asked up on the stage. 'She was a bit grand,' he says. 'She whispered to me, "Oh, Barry, you *are* a card."'

'That ain't right,' says the buoyant Jane. 'To me, Edna's Edna, and you're you. They're two different people.'

'Yeah,' says Chris Wyles, the drummer and Jane's boyfriend. 'Les is vulgar and mean; and you're not like that, Barry.'

'Certainly not,' Barry says with a smile. His eyes have a bright, startled look: his performing face.

Humphries and I walk back to the hotel together. It's a starry night. The side streets are empty and, after such a raucous evening, the quiet is startling. This is the romance of vaudeville life: the strange town, a quick recce of the hall, giving the audience something extraordinary, the gossipy contentment of a communal meal with the troupe, then moving on, leaving behind the memory of some wonderful excitement.

Vaudeville life has all but vanished from late-twentieth-century entertainment. On the old American vaudeville circuits, like the ones my father used to play, the tour was forty-eight weeks, three towns a week, five shows a day. It was an exhausting schedule. Then, vaudeville was so prevalent that greasepaint could be purchased in any drugstore. Now those theatres are movie houses; and few performers have the luck or the prowess to get their education in front of a live audience. Humphries is one of the few. The romance of vaudeville and its great goodwill still lives on in him.

'We'd been as far north as Aberdeen and as far south as Southampton and east to Leeds and Newcastle and west to Belfast and Dublin,' Jack Hylton told me tonight. 'There was nowhere on the mainland we hadn't touched. So I thought of Jersey.'

Humphries strolls silently beside me in his white socks and sandals.

'I've only seen one man have power over an audience like that,' I say as we enter the hotel. 'My father.'

'That's a compliment,' Humphries says. He turns back toward me at the elevator. 'I'll give you a bell around ten thirty–eleven. We'll talk all day.'

'Barry here,' the clear, hard voice says down the phone at 11.30 the next day. 'Sorry, I had a few telephone calls. I've got to change my tickets to leave for my holiday from Gatwick, if that's OK.' So it's an absolute maybe, which is the Humphries style.

But the talk does take place. In blue jeans and his beloved sandals, Humphries clambers with me over the breakwaters at St Helier's Bay in the hot glare of the midday.

'Edna is an extraordinary mixture of reprehensible traits – maybe all reprehensible traits – she hardly exhibits a good quality to the audience. Even family feeling is derided and debased. None the less the audience is somehow persuaded that this collection of reprehensible qualities makes up a warm and fundamentally nice person who seems to be expressing a form of love to them. They are actually conscious of love.'

'You really think so?'

'Yes, I think so. It's the Pavlovian Pavlova. She reveals herself. It's an evening of honest self-revelation. She holds nothing back. She's extraordinarily naked before the audience. They see all her prejudices as well as all her virtues. After having insulted a woman in the audience, she says, "Aren't we getting on well?" The woman agrees. In a sense this woman is getting the kind of going over she hasn't had since perhaps she was a child. A lot of it being quite unjust. She may be wearing a very nice dress which Edna doesn't happen to like. But there on stage is someone who is saying: I'm not an actress. This isn't a show. I'm just sharing with you.'

'But it is a show. And you're an outstanding character actor, and the character's partly you.'

'Yes,' says Humphries.

'The character allows you to liberate a lot of feeling which is as unacceptable to you as to members of the audience.'

'It's a kind of benediction in the end,' he says.

Humphries buys an ice cream which begins to melt as he expounds on Edna's finale. 'The end of the show is like the end of a pantomime where the Dame becomes rich. The Dame becomes resplendent having gone through the pantomime in boots and sensible skirt. Edna, too, has to appear resplendent and there's a kind of Assumption . . .'

'Rising toward her immortality.'

'Rising up. Even in her book, Edna says "*If* I die", not "*When* I die . . ."'

'What I love about the show is, as you say to the "mutes", the colour and light. It's a feast.'

'You have to appeal to the audience on that level alone,' he says. 'What they are seeing is what they are getting: colour and movement. In a way that should delight them. That should be sufficient. Then you give them all these other things as well so that they can choose what wavelength they want to tune in on. Whether it's just a capering comic figure or something else. It's quite nice to hear that people who don't speak English have enjoyed the show because they are literally responding to colour and movement, of which there is enough.

'A funny person is a funny person, isn't he? There's a difference between a comic and a comic actor. A comic actor is a serious actor who can create a comic figure; but a comic is a person who is *intrinsically* funny, who somehow, whatever the guise, has an antic spirit. It doesn't worry me much any more – since I consider myself possessed in some measure of this quality – that people who don't even know me are generally amused when I get on the bus . . .'

'Because you're the bringer of pleasure?'

'Yes,' he says, 'yes. I've got a funny way of doing things in my

210

own life. I notice people smiling when I'm walking along. Actually when I was younger I noticed it. I thought it might be handy. It might keep me out of trouble. I had a way of playing sport which was comic. I just did it in a different way. I didn't like doing it so my reluctance was considered to be risible. I've later rationalised that and tried to understand it by thinking about other comedians. They are actually physically funny. You just had to look at Tommy Cooper. He was funny without saying anything.'

The talk turns to Ronald Firbank, whose novels Humphries owns in Firbank's own special edition he had printed for his mother. 'I got the message of Firbank even though I was an Australian schoolboy,' he says. 'It was just the angle. I got what was funny about it without having the cultural background.'

'The collision of artifice and vulgarity.'

'It was that. You've hit the nail on the head. The highly risqué, the rather robust ribaldry of the books. Also Firbank's artificiality disguised a seriousness, perhaps even from himself.'

So, of course, does Dame Edna disabuse Humphries of his own gravity. After a while, Humphries says, 'In Edna's book, there's a lot about her parents, as there seems to be in Germaine Greer's book. I'm interested in books by children about their parents. Edmund Gosse's *Father and Son* is a great book. I like Michael Arlen Junior's book about his father. And yours is in the same category. I've got them all in a group at home. I even liked Susan Cheever's book about her father. There aren't many books which describe the parent realistically and lovingly as well. That element of love has to be there somehow. It's impossible to write truthfully about any human being without love. Of course not. How can you? You have to accept them. That means you're accepting your own dullness, inadequacy, stupidity, hypocrisy.'

'Do your parents come into the dialogue your characters have with an audience?'

'No,' he says, 'not yet.'

But scratch an exhibitionist, and you'll find poor parental attending. Dame Edna is a caricature of bad nurturing and an indictment of it. Dame Edna can't mask Humphries' own ancient wound from obliquely expressing itself, albeit with a comic spin. To Edward Heath, who talked on television about his 88-year-old father still wishing he'd taken up a respectable occupation, Dame Edna replied: 'It's funny, isn't it, because my mother still can't adjust to the fact that I'm a megastar. It's extraordinary that our parents have some sort of fantasy ambition for us. It's nice to please them. I sometimes think that my parents were unpleasable, Mr Heath.' In her autobiography, Edna asks her mother, 'Mummy, were you proud of me as a little girl? Was I always saying clever things?' A doctor's injection knocks Edna's mother out before she can answer.

Dame Edna ensures that Humphries' presence is always felt. She exists best, as Humphries does, with an audience whose attention can be carefully controlled. ('When Barry spots an audience, he's off,' Ian Davidson told me about Humphries' compulsion to perform. 'It's very difficult to keep a meeting going because Barry can treat us as an audience. It works. It's hilarious. And it is constructive in the end. But it is not a meeting in the proper sense.')

'In the theatre I'm at home,' Humphries says. 'It's where I find some kind of metaphor for all these conflicts and these mysterious contradictions. The joke is the perfect resolution. If I stood up and tried to talk about how I felt living in England as opposed to Australia, I could make up quite an interesting piece about it, a sort of essay which I would read aloud to the audience. Edna can do it so much more lightly. She can actually do it in a more sophisticated way because she can make the audience *feel* the difference. When she suddenly says after a very long time that she has a number of houses – "Don't be jealous" – and then she adds: "I'm an Australian, incidentally," it says a lot really. It says: You probably think I'm one of you. It also gives the audience the chance to think, "We knew all along." She thinks we didn't pick it up.'

'It empowers the audience in some way.'

'It's a way of inventing a conversation with that person who's not nearly as interesting as oneself – the audience. Who are silent out there.'

*

212

'This is important!' Humphries says at one point, discussing Edna's autobiography. 'Edna describes her inability to feel the appropriate emotion at the big moments in her life. Her marriage. Her wedding. She's hoping for a transcendental experience, and it doesn't happen for Edna, I think.'

The subject of feelings leads finally to our own new relationships. 'Sometimes you're so unused to receiving generous healthy responses that you misread them,' he says. 'The other day Lizzie and I were talking about holidays. I said, "There's this hotel in Italy. It's quite a way out. Sounds very nice." Lizzie said, "The weather isn't very good in that part of the world. If it rains, it might get boring."

'I immediately bridled and thought, "What does she mean?" I said sarcastically, "Well, I wasn't planning to go there on my own. I don't think it's going to be all that boring." But I didn't smile as I said it. So there was an awful misunderstanding. I was offended. She suddenly mentioned the world "boring", and I thought, "How could I be boring?" I mentioned this to my doctor, and he said, "Does it occur to you that she might have been concerned for you? That *you* would be in this place, and you might just get a little bit bored in the middle of nowhere. Does it occur to you that a woman could be interested in your welfare? Because that's more than likely what she meant." And, indeed, it was what she meant.'

'It doesn't always have to be a struggle.'

'I was so much into pleasing,' he says of his previous marriage. 'I thought I was entertaining this person. Isn't that my role? After all, if I can't please them in depth, at least I can *amuse* them. There's a great deal of unlearning to do.'

As Humphries leaves the hotel on his way to the second and final performance of *Back with a Vengeance: The Second Coming*, he sees a copy of the *Jersey Evening Post* on the bar. 'Was there a review?' he asks Jack Hylton, opening the paper. They read in silence. 'Very enthusiastic,' says Humphries.

'Especially the second paragraph.'

I pocket the newspaper and follow them to the waiting taxi.

'How did I bring Crill into it last night?' says Humphries.

'You said you tied him up and gagged him in the dressing room . . .' says Jack.

'Yes, but I led into it . . .'

'You followed it on from a wowser.'

'Yeah. What's a wowser? I spoilt the wowser line.'

'You said, "I suppose over here you'd call it a crill."'

'What if I say, "A wowser is an aboriginal word . . . but it's also a word for kill-joy. I don't know if you have a slang word for it over here. Crill, I suppose."' Satisfied, Humphries leans back in his seat and enjoys the view of the calm sea at twilight.

I glance at the local paper. 'We were reminded', it says, 'on more than one occasion that we were privileged to be there. But it is unlikely that these shores have ever witnessed such a talent as that of the brilliant Barry Humphries.'

'You can't believe how good the Jersey audiences were,' Humphries is saying to Dennis Smith in Australia on the phone in the executive lounge of the Jersey airport. 'Tumultuous. The best I've ever had.'

I make him a cup of tea and leave him to the telephone. It's going to be a long call. Humphries has a fistful of faxes to deal with, including news of his former wife's £6,500 excess baggage bill for her noisy decampment from Hampstead to Sydney. Humphries admits he works hard to keep morbid thoughts from overwhelming him. But there's no point in him reading today's *Daily Mail*, whose page three story is about a speech his ex-wife has given to Sydney businesswomen on her 'radical celibacy'. LIFE WITHOUT EDNA — HESSIAN UNDERWEAR AND NO MARTINIS says the headline. I spirit the paper off the high-tech lounge table and into my overnight bag. 'Made London seem like a lot of sissies,' Humphries is saying. 'They were also uninhibited, intelligent, and vociferous.'

Humphries is wedded to the telephone. In a burst of enthusiasm over a newly bought LP, he's been known to call an old Australian chum from England to play the entire record. Ian Donaldson recalls being awakened at 4 am in Oxford by Humphries. ' "It's Barry

214

calling from Australia – did I wake you? I'm sorry. What time is it? Is it the middle of the night? Did I get my times wrong?" And so on until, after about twenty minutes, I realised he was in London.'

The portable telephone gave Humphries a whole new arena for clowning and for mystification. 'He once was coming around to my house and telephoned me three times to say where he was,' says Nick Garland. 'He had his little walkie-talkie phone. At one call he was at Swiss Cottage. "I'm just coming across the road. I'm not sure it's wise because there's a car coming. AAAAAAAHHH!!" Then the phone went dead. It was clearly a joke and very funny. Later he rang again to say he was closer and on Haverstock Hill. Eventually the doorbell rang. The phone began ringing as I answered the door. Barry was standing there dialling to say, "I have arrived." '

But the telephone is the bugbear in everyone's relationship with Humphries. 'Whenever you've got Barry,' says Claudia Rosenkrantz, 'you haven't really got him. He'll come in sometimes for a production meeting, and I've got fifteen things to talk to him about, and I can't get him off the telephone. Suddenly, he'll get up and say, "I have to go." He likes everything to be vague. He doesn't really like people knowing where he is.' Humphries uses the phone to interrupt himself in the same way that Dame Edna consciously changes course in the middle of a monologue. His style of playing is also a style of being. He is always interrupting himself to get to the phone. 'I've just got to make a phone call' is a catch phrase in his daily life which gives him a sense of momentum but confounds those around him. 'It's a great technique in writing comedy,' says Ian Davidson. 'If you've got three good jokes but no tag, you just interrupt it. You change course. Barry interrupts himself constantly. It's sort of a technique in life he has. He uses the phone. He's always on to something new, something different. Nothing ever gets finished. It's always interrupted. You get a tremendous feeling of pace when you write or live like that.'

Humphries doesn't get off the phone until our flight is called, but, once in the plane and airborne, he seems eager to talk about Edna, which is as much his antidote for anxiety as it is the public's. 'When I get to Gatwick, I'm going to pick up the phone and ring the person at Macmillan who's doing the copy-editing,' he says. 'There's a woman there who's been putting in commas. I don't like too many commas. I said, "You might think it needs a comma, but I want a kind of headlong vocal feel to it. I want it breathless." It's important there are commas to articulate meaning and emphasise rhythm, but not commas for the sake of grammar. So that every now and then there's a rather artfully constructed paragraph. Then we get back to Ednaese. It should be like a letter, a gush, occasionally hanging on to the banister of a punctuation mark. But otherwise, it's pretty much a headlong, up and downstairs monologue.'

Humphries starts to fantasise about Edna returning to New York, where his hit *Housewife/Superstar* died an ignominious death in 1977. 'My producer Michael White got a rather lugubrious man called Arthur Cantor to produce the show in New York,' he says. 'He had one serious disadvantage. He'd never seen my work. He recommended Theatre Four, which is as off-Broadway as you can get and not near any other theatres.' In a letter to me in 1983, Humphries characterised the theatre as 'a small auditorium which could only be entered by stepping over the slumbering forms of derelicts, each in their miniature lake of vomit. They, and their more ambient companions, represented the only "passing trade" Theatre Four seemed to attract.' The reason Arthur Cantor selected it, according to Humphries, 'was that *The Boys in the Band* had been there. To use his own words, he thought "another fag show might do well here". He used that expression to my face.'

The previews, Humphries wrote, 'were a sensational success, and it seemed we were a hit. The novelty of the entertainment appealed to all who saw it and the major problem of "man dressed up as woman" in a tradition alien to the American theatre didn't worry anyone because most thought Edna *was* a woman – proto Tootsie. With Ian Davidson's help I carefully adapted my London and Australian material, formerly addressed to a middle-class, Anglo-Saxon audience and soon to be exposed

216

to an English-speaking public with an alien cultural background, Jewish Puerto Ricans, Danish Eskimos, Negroid Corsicans, etc . . .' Sir Les opened the New York version by explaining to the audience that Australia was the New America, a continent so sophisticated and fast moving that its inhabitants loved coming to New York for peace and quiet. 'The show exploited this simple inversion very effectively since most comedians visiting America make jokes about its dehumanised urban life – its noise and its muggings,' wrote Humphries. 'I, on the contrary, described New York as a peaceful haven compared with Australia. Les introduced Edna, in her denim outfit, who patronised the audience and had long extemporary conversations with adoring fans and look-alikes from Brooklyn Heights. It occurred to me at the time that Edna looked quite Jewish, and this seemed to work in her favour. What seemed semantically foreign was genetically familiar. "A lot of people think I'm a Red Sea pedestrian," she confided proudly to the audience. Optimism ran so high that the producers decided on a Sardi's party which I felt to be an ominous choice. Death-wish Cantor drove the *New York Times* critic, Richard Eder, from the theatre to his office after the first night so that he could meet his copy deadline, and it was that review which killed the show within a couple of weeks.'

Humphries gazes out the airplane window lost for anything more to say about the New York débâcle. And then he adds, 'Michael bravely kept the show running as long as he could. We ran a couple of weeks. By that time, the *Times* had done its damage. I think I said some rather cruel things about Eder, a club-footed father of five who had been transferred from their Madrid desk to drama critic.'

In Andy Warhol's *Interview* magazine the writer had asked Humphries if it was time to forgive and forget the *Times* critique. 'Of course,' he replied. 'However, the next time I'm in Madrid I'll do a little research. And Edna will be quite busy. She was talking for a while about getting a bull and having a short bullfight in the show so that it would appeal to those critics with a sort of Iberian cultural background. She wanted to use an incapacitated Catholic bullfighter and a club-footed bull.'

And, when asked in conclusion for any advice to pass on to less seasoned performers, Humphries said, 'One must never resent the unfavourable review one might receive. And no matter how disappointed or wounded the artist really feels, he should never display any feelings of animosity or verbalise them to members of the press. This is very bad for the image and may be considered crude or tasteless. I've always had the odd stinking review – everywhere. I'm no exception. But I've never let an unfavourable notice affect me. I read them and forget them. Put them out of my mind forever. Remember, it's just bad luck if the person who doesn't get you happens to be an influential journalist with five children and a club foot.'

Humphries' failure in New York can be explained away by the notorious obtuseness of the *New York Times* to quality foreign products, by the position of the theatre, by the nature of American entertainment, which has no pantomime tradition and generally not much appetite for irony. But, whatever the reason, North America still remains an elusive challenge to Humphries. 'We did wonderfully successful previews,' he says. 'All sorts of people came and enjoyed the show. While I was in New York, I did some television. I did a talk show with a man called Bill Boggs, a lunchtime thing. I was beginning to feel funny on that programme. I think the way to go is television. I think if I'd done a few television shows, got confident and done the show, things would have gone better. There was some pressure after I closed off-Broadway to go down to the Village and continue the show down there. Perhaps it would have worked. *But* my confidence had been bruised. I felt at the time rather as I did in London in the mid-1960s when I first presented some of my Aristophanic Australian creatures in late-night satirical cabaret. The time wasn't ripe, and somehow I lacked confidence or effrontery to put them across. So I went to L.A. and stayed for a couple of months at the Château Marmont, wrote a new stage show which I then presented in Australia called *Isn't It Pathetic at His Age?*'

Humphries says his next show is going to be called *A Delightful Show*. His mind wanders to an anthology of poems he's doing. He talks about Philip Larkin, Henry Vaughan, Gavin Ewart,

William Plomer, and a writer called Dorothy Nimmo, whom he's discovered in the *Spectator*. 'I wrote to her,' he said. 'She sent me a privately printed book of poems. She's only published a few private editions.' After a while, Humphries turns to me saying, 'Who was that woman photographer who died?'

'Diane Arbus.'

'Edna's toying with an idea of doing a one-woman show in America called *ARBUS*. "Edna Is Arbus." It's really the life of this woman. It's a big challenge for Edna. I mean that would offend quite a few people, that idea. She's been vaguely canonised, hasn't she? Certainly in the woman's movement.'

'Why Arbus?'

'Because she's not very interesting to start with. She's a photographer . . .'

'Who photographs monsters.'

'She did, eh?' says Humphries, laughing. If Humphries knows Arbus, surely he knows her subject matter. Is he putting me on? With Humphries you're never quite sure. 'It'd be such an awful show, wouldn't it?' he says. 'There'd be blow-ups of her photographs and Edna . . .' He giggles to himself, 'Edna would take perhaps a few snaps of people in the audience who are as close to monsters as she could find.'

'Couldn't she turn the camera on herself?'

'In other words, if I were well enough known in America then I'd make the joke. I'd say my next project is a one-woman show based on Diane Arbus. I am Arbus. Perhaps there should be a wing of the Twilight Home in Edna's autobiography called the Diane Arbus Wing for the American readers. We can just add one.'

'What? Dark room?'

'X-Ray unit. Eh? Eh?'

'Edna would like it because she photographs the "Richard the Thirds", the "Lord Byrons".'

'The club-footed ones,' says Humphries. 'The Dudley Moores.'

'A friend of mine once wrote a musical on Byron called *Funny Foot*.'

Humphries gives the high-pitched laugh of genuine amusement.

'Very good,' he says. 'Zelda too. Edna has often talked about Zelda Fitzgerald.'

'What qualifies her for the role?'

'Nothing at all,' says Humphries. 'It's just that it's funny that Edna knows about Zelda and feels she can absorb her, can annex Zelda in the way Barbra Streisand tried to annex *The Scream*. Edna could say, "You thought, you who are just learning about the Western culture, you who have just a smattering of culture, you who went to *Travesties* by Tom Stoppard and who nodded knowingly because you knew it all before Tom Stoppard even told you, you who have just started to read *Save Me the Waltz*," guess what? Edna's got there first. She's redecorated the Zelda Fitzgerald wing. You can't be high-minded any more. It's been spoiled. She's spoiling the fun for the intelligentsia.'

'What about the Joan Didion Cryonic Unit?'

'Who's Joan Didion? I've never read her.'

'New Journalist. Always describing her own feelings. Migraines. Neurasthenia.'

'So it would be the Joan Didion Anaesthesia Unit,' he says. 'I can think of a lot of jokes when I get to America. It'll be funny. Do you know Jean Toomer? Slightly tinted. His wife, whose books are forgotten, Marjorie Lattimer, is wonderfully good. Of course, I like that writer Ellen Gilchrist. Isn't she wonderful?'

'Of the Southern writers my favourite is Flannery O'Connor.'

'I've only read *Wise Blood*,' he says. 'If you could point me in the direction of some others.'

'I like Zora Neale Hurston. *Their Eyes Were Watching God*.' Humphries takes out a pad and writes down the name. 'She also wrote essays and short stories. One of her short stories is called "Spunk". Edna uses the word "spunky", but of course spunk has a sexual connotation.'

'It's a sort of schoolboy phrase for semen. I used it for a song that Edna sang on the BBC.'

The pilot's voice tells us that the aircraft is approaching Gatwick Airport, where it's windy and overcast. Humphries begins to sing to me as the plane descends.

220

'The English have a quality
I'd like to sing about
It's not the sort of quality
Bestowed on wog or Kraut
When things are on the sticky side
You never throw a tizz
A special something sees you through
I'll tell you what it is –
Spunk, spunk, spunk
You're so full of British spunk
You're never in a panic
You're never in a funk
So in a time of crisis
There's nothing quite so nice as
Singing spunkspunkspunkspunkspunkspunkspunk . . .'

'It's a scream.'

'Edna sang it in one of her earliest appearances in a series called *The Barry Humphries Scandals* back in 1968. It was filmed in full colour with an elaborate decor of Union Jacks and a chorus of thirty extras, a full orchestra and the George Mitchell Choir. That programme was taken off the air largely because of "Spunk". The idea was that the people *knew* what the word meant, but they were meant to pretend that they didn't because the song was all about courage and fortitude, which is, after all, what the word also means. Fortitude. So it was a song about fortitude. Someone at the BBC, with a sort of Mannikin Piss smile on his face, said, "Well it does have another connotation in England." "Well," I lied, "I've never heard of it." I really wanted to sing about spunk and phlegm. Because phlegm is another important thing that people should have. I have yet to write "Spunk and Phlegm".'

'How does the rest of it go?'

'I can't remember all the verses,' he says. 'This is getting quite wobbly, isn't it? We're wobbling, aren't we?'

'You're fine.'

Humphries face relaxes as he starts to sing:

221

'The dissolution of the monasteries
Was a very bad affair
It was so iconoclastic
There was stained glass *everywhere*
The poor old abbots in the habits
Said, "My God what's hit us?"
So each of them slipped
Down into his crypt
And sang this *spunk dimittis* –
Spunk spunk spunk
We're so full of British spunk
It's diabolical to be
A poor redundant monk
So in this time of crisis
There's nothing quite so nice as
Singing spunkspunkspunkspunkspunkspunkspunk . . .'

'I always see Edna through a phallic lens. You slough it off.
The point is – I don't believe you.'
Humphries laughs.
'Did anybody else ever say anything about it?'
'They don't say it. They get it,' he says, looking around the
cabin. 'It's getting very wobbly in here, John.'
'It's steady, Barry.'
'Look at the visibility. It's very bad. Think of all the other
planes taking off.'
'Is the joy in a song like that forcing people to hear the
word?'
'To rub the audience's nose in the ambiguity of the word.'
'It's a great song for Edna to sing.'
Humphries has both hands on the armrests. 'I remember another
verse,' he says, looking nervously out the window.
'We're going to be down very soon.'

'A chappie who saw
The Second World War
Has somewhere wisely written

"If it wasn't for a handful
Of ex-public schoolboys
Who bravely made the Spitfires
We'd-never-won-the-Battle-of-Britain"
But up spoke Winston Churchill
Above the battle's din
"You poor little Poms
Will be safe from the bombs
If you sing with Vera Lynn" –
Spunk spunk spunk
We're so full of British spunk
Though the place is full of foreigners
And the pound has done a bunk . . .'

'Oh dear,' says Humphries as the plane's wheels lock with a
thud into place.
   'It's been lovely, Barry. Thanks for your generosity.'
   'I've enjoyed your company, John.'
   'And I yours.'
As the plane touches down on British soil, Humphries is singing
to himself:

'But in this time of crisis
There's nothing quite so nice as
Singing spunk spunk spunk
We're so full of English spunk.'

Coda

Dame Edna Works the Room

'To become a spectator at one's own life is to escape the suffering of life.'

Oscar Wilde

I saw Dame Edna once again in October. A publicity release from Macmillan about *My Gorgeous Life*, couched as a letter 'From the desk of Dame Edna' with her name embossed in red on the letterhead, brought with it a pink cardboard cut-out pair of her harlequin glasses. It was an invitation to a special Audience that Dame Edna was holding for photographers and journalists to honour the publication of her autobiography. 'Dress informal,' it read. 'And PLEASE no genuflecting.' The glasses were also the ticket of admission. 'Pop-out your own personal Dame Edna Everage facsimile spectacles', it said on the side, 'and wear during the audience'. This was going to be the damndest publishing party I'd ever been to.

The book launch began with a photo call on the Thames Embankment behind the London Weekend Television office where the second season of *The Dame Edna Experience* would soon be recorded. London Weekend had provided the rather bedraggled bouquet of gladioli awaiting Dame Edna at the reception desk and also the white Rolls-Royce with a gold-plated bird on its hood which was parked in the walkway to the river where, in due course, Dame Edna would appear. Humphries had arrived late and was changing. The photographers milled around in reception while a PR girl passed among them handing out press releases. 'Possums, it is my duty to return,' Dame Edna was quoted as saying about her TV show. 'Millions of people have been suffering from PEDS – Post Edna Depression Syndrome – and I have to come back to rid them of their withdrawal symptoms.' For Humphries the difficulty was in keeping Dame Edna away. After the book launch and the photo call, she would have to lie doggo for a while with the press and with the public for fear of over-exposure. So today would be something of a temporary swan song for Dame Edna, one of her last chances in the next year to make a proper public spectacle of herself.

'She's not known as "Barry",' says the PR lady, guiding the photographers to the location beside the Thames. 'Don't call her "Barry". Call her Dame Edna. You can also have her sitting on chairs if you ask her politely.'

A skateboarder wheelies along the Embankment flagstone. Two bobbies, hands behind their backs and shoes squeaking, stroll indifferently past the equally nonchalant photographers, who set up their tripods and take light readings of the windy grey morning. Two punk lovers lean against the Embankment railings gazing out at the barges, their hands thrust into each other's torn back pockets. It's an ordinary London morning until Dame Edna walks into it or, more accurately, drives into it.

As the Rolls-Royce circles the photography area, the PR lady thrusts a copy of *My Gorgeous Life* through the window to Dame Edna, who huddles regally in the shadowy left corner of the Rolls.

'Over here,' says an LWT official, beckoning photographers to shift position to the rear of the Rolls. 'You'll understand why I say you're better off in a minute.'

'Dame Edna!!' the photographers start calling as her tapered leg sticks out of the car. Dame Edna is a study in pink: pink skirt, pink pillbox hat, pink purse, pink book jacket.

'This way, Barry!'

'Good morning, everybody,' says Dame Edna. 'I have a little surprise for you.' She walks to the rear of the Rolls-Royce. 'I mustn't forget this,' she says, and opens the boot. Madge Allsop is in it.

'Anyone want a shot of Madge coming out of the boot?' says Dame Edna, who knows a good image when she invents one.

Madge is as lacklustre as the morning: tan shoes, grey jumper, grey coat, and black bag. After she is snapped emerging forlornly from the boot, Dame Edna immediately seizes on Madge as a prop to help strut her stuff.

'Can we bring the nose of the car behind you?' demands a photographer.

'I think that's a wonderful idea,' says Dame Edna Everage. 'Having a Rolls image. This must be the first shot in history of a celebrity posing next to a Rolls-Royce.'

If the setup is a journalistic cliché, Dame Edna's posing with Madge isn't. The price which the famous pay for their celebrity is other people; and Madge is the browbeaten symbol of Dame Edna's tyrannical aggrandisement. The spectacle of Dame Edna's vindictive triumph includes the comforting reminder in Madge of the ordinariness she's left behind. Madge is the ghost of emptiness past. Edna is forever beaming, Madge forever po-faced. Edna is dynamic, Madge affectless. Edna is all talk, Madge all silence. The invidious comparison by which stars measure the distance between themselves and others is built into the joke of Dame Edna's imagery. Madge is posed on top of the hood, under the hood, at Edna's feet, against Edna. There is a slur of camera shutters, the pop of flashbulbs, the chorus of photographers yapping to their subjects as they stare through their viewfinders: 'That's the idea. Nice shot. Lovely. Just rest her head on the bonnet. That's lovely. Just pat her on the head.' Dame Edna gets Madge to lie in front of the Rolls aping her position on top of it. 'Don't smile,' says Dame Edna *sotto voce* to Madge as the cameras clatter.

'Now let's think of something original,' says Dame Edna, posing on the hood with her finger on her dimple, laughing and waving at the cluster of photographers.

'One more minute,' commands the PR lady. 'You've got to set up quickly.'

Dame Edna perches on the hood. 'I'm going to try and favour everyone. I'm going to do a pan.' And with that, she slowly draws her head in a semi-circle offering up her face to the avid cameras with a new pose for each one.

'Huge smile!' bawls a photographer. Dame Edna does as she's told.

'Thank you,' she says at the conclusion of her photo opportunity, moving among the photographers and joking with them. 'Make sure it's on the right-hand side.' Dame Edna spots me in the crowd. 'Lovely piece in *Vogue*,' she says, about my review of the book, and then is peremptorily trundled by Claudia Rosenkrantz back into the Rolls-Royce for the quick ride across Waterloo Bridge to the Waldorf Hotel in the Strand for the book launch.

Dame Edna stands in front of a blow-up of the Terry O'Neill photo which is now the cover of her autobiography. Pink organza is draped around the photograph. On either side of the daïs on which she talks to the crowded room are two vases of gladioli on pedestals. As I push my way past the maze of cocktail tables and waiters with trays of champagne, I notice Lynne Kirwin and Lizzie Spender and Humphries' agent Ed Victor and, of course, Claudia Rosenkrantz. The room is happy, so happy in fact, that even the table at which my overcoat accidentally knocks over a drink hardly looks up. They are listening to Dame Edna. None of the guests are wearing their cardboard glasses; their rapt attention signifies that they are already at play. This is going to be not so much a book party, more a nightclub act.

Dame Edna is talking about going to L.A. and being spotted by a reporter in a luxury hotel. 'He said, "What are you doing here, Dame Edna?" I said I'm *trawling* for celebrities. I can say now that Barry Manilow is going to be one of my guests. Liza Minnelli, Tom Jones, Douglas Fairbanks Junior. I'm surprised that some of these people are still alive; *but* they are. And they're thrilled to be appearing. As more people sign on the dotted line, you will be kept posted. Suffice it to say that I said to London Weekend that I don't want to sit in a yukky studio this time. I want to be in something comfortable. I want to really do this programme from my own home.

'Which home, they said, Malibu, Montreux, Mustique or Melbourne? I said, "Mayfair will do because I'm into M's. The public will be getting a rare glimpse of how I live, how we in the megastardom community live. Meanwhile, of course, it's a dual celebration because I've also performed an act of exorcism. You didn't know that I was an exorcist, but I am. I've done a bit of exercise, not that I can swivel my head around the wrong way like the kid in *The Exorcist* and that yukky green chunder. Wouldn't look very nice, would it, on this pretty suit of mine? Designed, incidentally, by my talented son Kenneth. "Kenneth Everage Modes – Melbourne and Malibu."

'However . . . I've let it all hang out in this new . . . Macmillan. I chose them because they begin with an "M". And because Lord Macmillan is a very old personal friend. I've spent many an exciting time in the lift with him. But, be that as it may, darling old cuddly whispering thing that he is . . . since my husband passed away, I'm smiling because I'm in therapy . . . since my husband passed away, I've been performing this act of exorcism. It's nice therapy too. To write it all down as it was.

'There aren't many show business personalities – (and what a pathetic description of me that is, isn't it? could you really call me a show business personality?) – I decided not just to tell the story everyone knows. But to tell the story nobody knows. Not even me. My first words. I had to interview my mother in a maximum security Twilight Home. Had to give her that drug they used in *The Guns of Navarone*. Scopolamine, or something. She spilt the beans on my early life as a bubba. And how she felt when I was born with mauve hair. The first child in Australia to be born with wisteria locks . . .' Dame Edna pauses to spell it for the reporters. 'W-i-s-t-e-r-i-a l-o-x.'

'I'm Jewish, by the way. I discovered that. I am,' Dame Edna continues. 'I'm a Red Sea pedestrian. This book is going to sell a squillion in north London. My reincarnations are interesting. I'm not superstitious, but I do believe now that reincarnation has been scientifically proved. I've been Boadicea, Mary Queen of Scots, Ethel Merman, and Cinderella. Isn't that exciting? As a matter of fact, I was Anne Hathaway, who wrote most of Shakespeare's material. And funnily enough, when I went to Anne Hathaway's cottage for the first time, I walked in the door, I went straight to the kitchen and made myself a cup of tea. I knew exactly where the power point was. Now if that doesn't prove something very very spooky . . . It's question time. I'm going to mingle. I'm meant to do a little mingling. Any little questions? Any little exclusives . . .?'

And with that Dame Edna steps down off the podium and goes among the faithful. The original plan was for Dame Edna to table hop among the journalists; but such is the power of her presence that the journalists rush forward and surround Dame Edna like moths to light.

'Any thought of you marrying again?' says Tony Pinell of the *Daily Mirror*.

'I've toyed with the idea,' says Dame Edna, towering above the throng of tape recorders and steno pads held up to her. 'Isn't that a terrible thing? I did while Norm was alive, as a matter of fact. One of the last things I said to him was, "Norm, if I tied the knot with someone else . . ." It was difficult to communicate with him because he was on this prostate machine, and you could only hold his hand by putting yours through an air lock on the side of the machine. So I had my hand in this orifice, and I was squeezing his hand and I said, "How would you feel, Norm, if I got married?" His hand suddenly relaxed. Or something relaxed. I wasn't quite sure what I was squeezing in there as a matter of fact.

'Now I've had a few offers. Klaus von Bulow. But I'm allergic to coffee. And I'd drink such a lot of black coffee if I lived with him. But, uh, people get a bit dozy when they're with Klaus. Who else have I considered, Claudia? Other eligibles . . .?'

'There's Patrick Lichfield, of course,' says Claudia Rosenkrantz, who has positioned herself ten feet away but directly in Dame Edna's line of vision. 'And Prince Rainier.'

'Could you imagine me Your Serene Highness Queen Edna of Monaco?' says Dame Edna. 'Isn't that beautiful? I'd have to be careful not to adjust my lipstick in the rear-view mirror of the car, driving along those steep old roads. The palace is pink. I'd change the colour.'

'Did you have to turn down many stars for your show in America?'

'There were people wanting very much to get on the show,' says Dame Edna. 'And unfortunately it's very hard to tell these people that they're a little bit yesterday's news. It wouldn't be kind.

There are people from my childhood that I adore and idolized that London Weekend are resisting. Van Johnson. They said no one will know him. I said, "Never mind. People will get to know and love Van Johnson." The freckles are still there. They are. The lovely twinkling eyes. Unfortunately Esther Williams declined. I wanted to interview her in a tank, underwater. She wouldn't. Poor little Esther.'

'I hear Zsa Zsa Gabor threw a party for you,' says Stuart Gilles from the *Manchester Evening News*.

'Yes, while I was there Zsa Zsa threw a big party for me. There were a lot of her generation. Vincent Price and Kathryn Grayson were there. You remember Kathryn Grayson. She sang a little ditty unaccompanied . . .'

'Would you have handled the Zsa Zsa incident a little differently?'

'Certainly,' says Dame Edna. 'I'm always polite to the law. I think it's a mistake to seek publicity in that way. I think it was a very miscalculated incident. Also very uncalled-for expressions were exchanged between them, weren't they? I was asked to give evidence at the trial. I was going to be giving evidence as an expert on the English language. The policeman said something beginning with "f" to her, didn't he? Ending with "off". "If someone says that to you in English, what does it mean?" I said, "Go back to Australia as quickly as possible." She said that's how she'd interpreted it . . .'

'Are you well known in other countries?'

'Now I am,' says Dame Edna, enjoying herself. 'Thanks to London Weekend's policy of giving the show to other networks. Isn't that a good idea, though, because it gets me known? I'm a household name in Sweden. They've forgotten about Volvo. Bang & Olufsen are in the shade now. I always thought Bang & Olufsen was a massage parlour. I did. Until I realised they made gramophones. No subtitles. My body says it all. It's Access Edna. I'm a hands-on megastar. Could you imagine Paul Daniels, charming person that he is and instantly likeable, giving a little presentation, standing as close as this? Not in a million years. He wouldn't, would he? Oh, I'm worried though. My hair. It's wisteria. It stays the same. Look at Michael Parkinson the other night. Did you see his hair? What colour would you call that? I think he's been using Grecian Two Thousand. And Cilla [Black] is going bald. What is happening since I've been away? Apart from Emma [Thompson] getting married, just to publicise *Henry the Fifth*. Kenneth Branagh wanted me to play whatever it is she plays – what is it, Catherine, the Queen? – I said if it means marrying Kenneth, no. I tower over that little talented tot.'

'You enjoy Shakespeare though?' asks Arne Wilson of the *Sunday Correspondent*.

'I do because I *was* Lady Macbeth in a previous life. She's a much-maligned woman. She's just a woman coping with a husband in mid-life crisis.'

'Do you sing with Liza Minnelli on your show?'

'Oh, I'll be singing with them, or should I say, they'll be singing with me,' says Dame Edna. 'One of my special guests is Chubby Checker. He's back in the news. I'll be teaching him the "Edna Twist". Did you know the twist is back? Which is just as well for you because that was all you could ever do.

'What I try to do is bring out the best in people. Sometimes that's difficult. In Germaine Greer's case it was impossible. By the way, she wrote a talented book about her parents, didn't she? And yet it didn't show them in a nice light. Whereas in my book, possums, I mention Germaine because she came as a little girl to my kitchen for grooming. She did. And one morning she came in, Norm was scrubbing the kitchen floor as usual. She looked down and said, "They do it so much better than we do, don't they, Edna?" That was the germ of her philosophy. Everything more or less was based on that observation. She was a sallow type of a girl. But very talented.'

'Did you ever attempt to burn your bra?'

'No, I never did,' says Dame Edna staunchly. 'As a matter of fact, I never wore a bra. I was always sort of flat-chested. And I never felt self-conscious about it either because my legs are my good point. I think there are very few women who are physically perfect all over. Mentally they're generally deficient, aren't they? I think it's my tongue which is my most active organ. And my brain.

231

Finally that's what men find attractive about me, and women can identify with. And I think the book and the TV series are going to help people. It's hope. It's the message of hope.

'There are such a lot of people who are locked into a life in which they see no means of escape, vicariously, if not in actuality, they themselves can feel that they are up there in my penthouse chatting away to guests. Some of my guests are actually staying with me. Dusty Springfield is going to be on the show. Which will be very good news to my son Kenny's friends. It was at Kenny's request that I invited Dusty. She's over there in Amsterdam, of course. I don't know much about Holland except the story about the kiddie with his finger in the dyke. I'll be asking Dusty if she knows that story . . .'

'Dame Edna, I understand you're going to do a crusade into the provinces. What will be your message to the millions?'

'I'm going to do book signings,' says Dame Edna. 'Harrods tomorrow. I'm nipping along to that little multi-coloured store in Knightsbridge. Little P.D. James sold about four hundred books yesterday at Harrods. So that's a record I have to break almost within the first five minutes. I'm hoping the book will be banned in New Zealand because there's a lot about my bridesmaid Madge in it. It's not difficult to get banned in New Zealand by the way. I did a show a few years ago in New Zealand called *An Evening's Intercourse with the widely liked Barry Humphries*. "An Evening's Intercourse" is a very good name for a show. And it had been at the Drury Lane no less. I decided to do a New Zealand tour; but they wouldn't put the advertisements in the paper. That's *true*, because of the word "intercourse". I cancelled.'

'You were recently in Australia and Melbourne housewives said you don't resemble Melbourne housewives any more . . .'

Dame Edna swivels around to the questioner who is a handsome woman in her mid-thirties from an Australian radio broadcasting company. 'Who? Which ones? Which housewife in particular?' says Dame Edna, sharpish. She shoots a quick glance to Claudia Rosenkrantz.

'I get looks that say, "Is this OK?" "Am I all right here?" ' says Rosenkrantz about her collaboration with Dame Edna. 'It's just a look. The eyes go up a bit. There are other looks. I know when Edna's not pleased. I know when she's angry. There's a tightening of the face and lips. It's not nearly as pronounced as when she's pretending to be angry. She was angry with the journalist. That's Edna angry. "Which housewives? Where do they come from?" That was Edna cross. Barry cross is not pleasant either. Edna's more direct cross than Barry. Barry will always skirt an issue. Edna will come right out with it. Barry has this terrible problem about being polite. I wish sometimes that when he has a problem – and if I've done something to offend him – that he'd just say it. But he won't do that. He's too polite. That's a big problem. Edna just levels with you. Barry will never give you a direct answer.'

The lady from Australian radio is persistent. 'Thirty years ago you were a soul sister,' she says, 'but things have moved on.'

'What's that accent, darling?' says Dame Edna.

'A bit of Australian,' she laughs.

'Where originally?'

'America.'

'American,' says Dame Edna. 'An insight into Australian housewives. So which one are you quoting?'

'Several,' she says. 'The rumours are . . .'

'When did you last go to one of my shows in Australia?'

'I haven't.'

'You haven't, no. Well, they're mostly women *weeping* with identification,' says Dame Edna.

'So do you feel that the bond is still there?'

'The fact that they don't have these clothes, these jewels, this car, this bridesmaid . . .'

'Or these friends,' smiles the Australian woman, indicating the claque of reporters.

'I've heard rumours', says Dame Edna, 'that you're no longer like a typical American investigative journalist.'

At this jolt, Dame Edna's interrogator changes course. 'I understand,' she says, 'that your friend Barry Humphries had a nanny named Edna.'

'You did! Many years ago.'

233

'Tell me about her.'

'Well, she was a very nice person according to Barry. Her name was Edna, and she looked after him when he was a bubba. And I think, when he and I first got together, as you'll read in the pages of this book . . .' Dame Edna catches the eye of the Macmillan publicity lady '. . . Charge this woman for a copy of the book. (I'm just teasing.) When Barry and I got together, I think my name was the appeal. I think he wouldn't be aware it had connected, like little "Rosebud" in *Citizen Kane*. I think there was a little connection there when he found Edna. Felt a *rapport*. Alas, we're not the close friends we should be. A bit sad.'

'But you still feel a bit of an identification with the old nanny?'

'*I* feel identification?' says Dame Edna. 'No, I never met her. She must have been a nice person. There's something quite nice about Barry, but will we ever know him? Will we . . .?'

'If you are somebody who makes your own life a work of art, which you are publicly doing,' Nick Garland told me about Humphries, 'it becomes even more important than to most people to protect your privacy. Because you've invested so much in making a certain sort of impression.' As Humphries spins out for the reporters the longest shaggy-dog story in theatre history called Edna's Life, I can now, after all these months, decipher in Dame Edna's conversation some of Humphries' actual prejudices; and decode some of the facts from his own life that are woven into Dame Edna's fiction. But it's a mug's game. What's important is the impact of this brilliant comic shadow play.

'The life of a comedian', Humphries told me, 'is an instinctive expression. It's an instinctual, unconscious expression of something which is not carefully thought out even though it may coalesce with quite reasoned strains of intelligence.' Dame Edna taunts and teases the public with the conundrum both of personality and of comedy. Humphries knows that the media abhor a secret; and Dame Edna flaunts the mystery of herself to captivate the press. It works a treat. Dame Edna has the reporters spellbound. They will not move from this spot on the polished parquet floor for the best part of an hour. Even the waitress with her tray of canapés leans into the crowd of reporters to hear Edna's monologue.

Dame Edna's method, like Humphries', is to create an atmosphere of collusion. 'He takes *you* into his confidence and talks aside about others,' says Nick Garland, correctly identifying the Humphries style but in no way diminishing its power to charm. 'You and he are in collusion. It's only subsequently that you realise that it's the same with everybody. Everybody has a sense that they have been taken behind the screen, behind the act. And in a way you have; but in a way, you haven't. The inviting of this confidence is quite an important part of him.'

'Dame Edna, do you ever get tired?'

'I do get a bit tired,' says Dame Edna, showing no signs of it. 'But I have immense stamina and physical health. You can tell that close up, can't you? You feel the vibrations. You feel there are cosmic rays here. I did interview the old nurse who was there when I was born, and she spoke of a strange light in the maternity ward. I mean the woman was pretty senile, but it's possible. It was a special event.'

'Where were you born?' says a timorous woman reporter from the *Melbourne Sun*.

'In Melbourne.'

'Where exactly?'

'In a hospital. "Where exactly?" You want to go there, don't you, darling? I came to Melbourne as a young girl. I was born in a private hospital in Wagga Wagga. And then I came to Melbourne. It's all here. I'm not concealing anything, for heaven's sake. I tell the story of Lois, in this book. My daughter Lois who was stolen away by a koala bear. It's a terrible story. It's more than a problem, it was a tragedy. We were in the country; and I went out and she was gone. There were koala there, and she was gone. I'm wondering who's going to play me in the film of this book.'

'Who would you like?'

'Meryl Streep has too strong a New Zealand accent. Wonderful, but a New Zealand accent. Mel Gibson could be Norm.'

'Lester Pigott,' chimes in Claudia Rosenkrantz.

'Lester Pigott could play Norm. Thank you,' says Dame Edna. 'He wants to play Norm. Who could play me? Who do you think? Kylie Minogue as the young Edna. Jason Donovan as Norm when young.'

'You are quite left wing.'

'Yes, I am,' says Dame Edna, fingering the cluster of diamonds on her hand. 'You find a lot of extreme left-wing people are rich. I mean Vanessa's got a shilling or two.'

'Does mortality frighten you?'

'No, it doesn't. I'm pretty sure we're once around, and then we reappear in various forms.'

'Would you like to come back as an animal?'

'No, no. I've never cared for animals. There are a few things I don't see the point of. Animals. And south London.'

'How long does it take you to meet your public?'

'Do you know, someone said to me, I think it was Claudia, "Oh, you must think of things to say,"' says Dame Edna. 'I said, "No, I won't. I'm a person." When the phone rings, I don't think, "I won't answer, I must think of something to say." When I wake up in the morning – in the days when Norm was still at home – it's not, "He's still asleep I must think of something to say before he wakes up." Do we live our lives like this? I am a living organism, a person. I don't have a speech to make, a point of view that I have to put across. (I might have a couple of things to *flog*!) So all I have to do is mention them, hold them up, hope they get a little mention. If they don't, no hard feelings. Even if this doesn't even make page seven on the left-hand side.'

'Are you worried about repeating yourself?'

'Yes, I am. Occasionally I say the same thing that I've said before, particularly if it's funny. Particularly if people have missed the point the first time. And you know a number of people have said, "Oh, she's said that before," but a lot of people say, "I wish she'd say it more often." I was very worried that a lot of people in the last show met with horrible accidents. People asked, "Is your show jinxed? Charlton Heston crashed down the stairs and has never been the same since. Survived the chariot race but really didn't survive an appearance on your show."

'Also, of course, you've to have guests who aren't going to die before it's transmitted. There's nothing worse, is there? You know I almost interviewed Salvador Dali last year. Just as well I didn't because, you know . . . people would have gone a bit hushed. "Oh, this is in bad taste." Above all, I like my shows to be in good taste. Taste is the name of the game. People used to look at Australian women . . .' Dame Edna turns to the Australian radio reporter, 'You know, your country of adoption – they used to look and say, "You know, Australia is just sort of yobbos." I think I have made people realise that sharp intellects can emanate from Australia. That there is room for the highly intelligent, the sensitive, the lyrical, the Proustian, *and* Rolf Harris.'

And on that big laugh, Dame Edna's concentration shifts to the table of finger foods in the far corner. 'Is there any food?' she says. 'There's food and drink. For heaven's sake, let's have something . . .'

Dame Edna heads for the table and for Lizzie Spender, who in 1990 would become the fourth Mrs Humphries. After a brief private moment ('Where are we going to eat?' says Humphries, 'I'm starved'), Dame Edna picks up a tray of canapés and passes among the guests offering them food. She brushes past the female Australian broadcaster who threw her the curve ball during the Audience. 'Polish the chip on your shoulder,' says Dame Edna, smiling.

'You churn it up when you go home, you know,' says the woman.

'Don't they need it,' says Dame Edna.

Another female reporter approaches Dame Edna. She is petite, with mousey hair, and a thin clear voice. 'Dame Edna,' she says, 'I wondered what you thought of Barry Humphries and his new life?'

'His new life?' says Dame Edna, her voice bright with bile.

'With his glamorous new lady.'

237

'I've lost touch with that. I think it's some kind of front. Some publicity stunt. Has he been seeking publicity, has he?'

The woman doesn't hear the irony in Dame Edna's voice and ploughs dumbly on. 'I think he's been keeping quite a low profile.'

'I think he sought all that. Sought it. I think he's into publicity in a big way,' says Dame Edna.

'Were you sad when he split up with his wife?'

'Well, I didn't see the newspaper item about that. Is that definite, is it?'

'I heard it was definite,' says the reporter, 'which made me sad because he had those two boys. I felt he had a really nice family.'

'Barry Humphries must be a heartless person,' says Dame Edna. 'I think so. Really, I think, if you put your head above the parapet as he has done, he deserves as much media coverage as possible in that respect. And so do those children. I think you're very wise to publicise it to the hilt. And I would get journalist friends of yours to go to those kiddies' school and perhaps point at them. And say, "These are the victims of Barry Humphries." Or perhaps have T-shirts made for them. I think that would be finally something that society needs.'

'T-shirts saying what?' says the woman.

' "Barry Humphries Is a Disgrace to Australia . . ." perhaps. ". . . And to the Institution of Marriage." Don't you think that'd be a good idea?'

'Yes, I think it would be.'

'And I think you'd probably find that Oscar and Rupert would help knit those T-shirts. And I'll be very interested to know if you publish that.'

'Thank you.'

'What would it be in?' says Dame Edna.

'The ACP.'

'What's the ACP?'

'Australian Consolidated Press.'

'Oh yes, they'd print that,' says Dame Edna. 'Of course they would. Particularly embittered and unfunny old columnists like

238

Ron Sewell. And Trevor Kennedy would publish it. He would. Ring him. If he's not in the office, he'll be in the massage parlour. Publish that!'

With a smile and a flourish of the canapé tray, Dame Edna hard-shoulders the reporter and continues working the room. In the withering exchange – the angriest I've ever seen Humphries – Dame Edna has remained completely in character, never once losing control. On stage and off it, this is what the public wants from a great comedian: never to be at a loss. And Dame Edna never is. She turns denial of feeling into delight. Her glory is her invulnerability. Life is loss; but the rebellion of the capering funny man is not to show it, turning every failure into the triumph of laughter. 'If you experience loss,' Humphries joked to me, 'your lawyer's done a bad job.' It's a kind of heroic detachment for which the clown pays dearly behind closed doors where there is no absolution of applause.

Dame Edna passes round the food. As Dame Edna, Humphries, who never felt himself 'taken in' by his parents or his childhood community, can be absorbed. The public want what he has and will take as much as he'll give. But, like Edna, Humphries must always control the nourishment to ensure getting what he needs. 'Barry only really makes himself laugh,' Claudia Rosenkrantz told me. 'In the talk show, the guests are there to amuse him.' Dame Edna calls her shows 'sharings'; and the word is mischievously chosen for the public. 'I'm really doing it purely for pleasure – that being mine, not theirs,' Humphries says.

Dame Edna stoops to offer a reporter a choice of canapés. He asks Dame Edna if she enjoyed the BAFTA Awards. 'I'm jealous of Victoria Wood,' says Dame Edna. 'Try the shrimpy thing . . . I never thought I'd say that, but I am. I thought if she gets one more award I'll scratch her eyes out. Mind you, she's a gorgeous person, don't you think? I loved it when she got the BAFTA Award for doing *An Audience with Victoria Wood*, didn't you? I did. Because I hadn't heard that material for months.' People listen and laugh, even the waitress who is following around her commandeered tray is transfixed. Dame Edna hands it back to her. 'Goodbye, possums,' she says.

'Goodbye, Dame Edna,' reply the remaining reporters.

Tomorrow, Dame Edna will arrive at Harrods in a horse-drawn carriage. Today, she has done her job. She has taken us on that giddy journey only a great clown can make with the public – to the frontiers of the marvellous.

Acknowledgements

'We'd been there to dinner,' Peter Nichols told me, 'and Barry said to me, "Edna's got a song in the new show, and I'm not sure whether it's really right yet. I wonder if you'd like to listen to it and tell me what you think." So he went into the other room and put on the accompaniment record and stayed in there and sang it as Edna. He didn't emerge because he wasn't in drag. He sang it off stage, so to speak. And then he came in and said, "What do you think?" '

In this book there are also many people on whom I've tried out the material and many off-stage influences. I honour them and thank them most gratefully for their contributions to my little labour of love.

Victoria Chance, my superb Australian connection.

The on-stage voices: the incomparable and elusive Barry Humphries, Stephen Adnitt, Bruce Beresford, Harriet Bowdler, Zoe Caldwell, Peter Cook, Ian Davidson, Nicholas Day, Ian Donaldson, Nick Garland, Katie Harris, Jack Hylton, Clive James, Lynne Kirwin, Peter Nichols, John Perry, Claudia Rosenkrantz, Dennis Smith, Lizzie Spender, and John Wells.

The off-stage voices: my beloved agents Georges Borchardt, Vivien Green, and Richard Simon, whose enthusiasm for the manuscript and my approach cheered me on until it was finished; Liz Bailey, David Finkle, John Fortune, Nick Hern, London Weekend Television, Lewis Morley, BBC Southeast News, and John Timbers for various services rendered; Don Campbell, Richard Dorment, John Fisher, Sylvia Hutchinson, Martha Orrick, and Priscilla Roth for invaluable conversations about an extraordinarily complex performer; also the editorial acumen of Liz Cowen, Mary Tomlinson, Eve MacSweeney of *Vogue*, and Matthew Reisz. My special thanks to Bob Gottlieb of *The New Yorker*, who commissioned the idea as a profile and to Liz Calder of Bloomsbury for her faith not only in the book but in me.

In his many guises Humphries generates an enormous amount of publicity. I have tried to be scrupulous in all quotations; but, in an attempt to keep footnotes from clogging the narrative, I have not always acknowledged the myriad newspaper sources in Australia, England, and America from where some of the Humphries' comments are gleaned. Other than the thirty-four hours of taped interviews with Humphries, the most valuable sources for quotation were Humphries' interviews with John Allen, *Meanjin* (April 1986); Phillip Crookes, *Vogue (Australia)* (November 1976); the 'Penthouse Interview', *Australian Penthouse* (October 1980); Colin Riess and Rob Hardy, *Lot's Wife* (September 1974); and John Wells, *Vogue (UK)* (1976). I have also drawn on Humphries' own chronicle of his life and work in his articles for the *Bulletin* (1965, 1967), *Australian Weekend Magazine* (February 1984), and the prefatory remarks to some of his books, especially *Bizarre* (Elek, 1965), *A Nice Night's Entertainment* (Granada, 1981) and *The Life and Death of Sandy Stone* (Macmillan, 1990). Charles Baudelaire's *The Painter of Modern Life and Other Essays* (Phaidon, 1964), Jules Barbey d'Aurevilly's *Dandyism* (PAJ Pubications, New York, 1988), and Geoffrey Galt Harpham's *On the Grotesque* (Princeton University Press, 1981) have been stimulating companions in what, for me, has been an exciting intellectual adventure.

A NOTE ON THE AUTHOR

John Lahr is the author of fourteen books including the highly acclaimed *Notes on a Cowardly Lion, Hot to Trot, Prick Up Your Ears*, and *The Orton Diaries* which he edited. His short film, *Sticky My Fingers, Fleet My Feet,* was nominated for an Academy Award, and he has written four stage adaptations. He writes a monthly theatre column for *Vogue*.